# CHINA

## 100 YEARS

### OF

## REVOLUTION

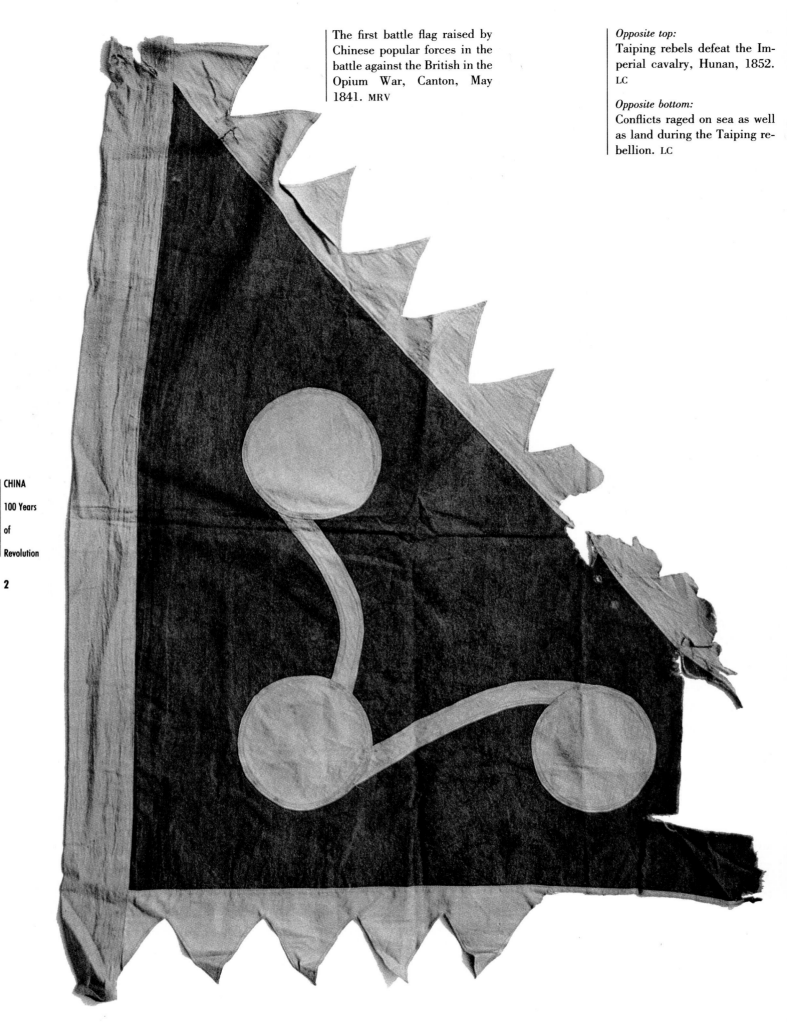

The first battle flag raised by Chinese popular forces in the battle against the British in the Opium War, Canton, May 1841. MRV

*Opposite top:*
Taiping rebels defeat the Imperial cavalry, Hunan, 1852. LC

*Opposite bottom:*
Conflicts raged on sea as well as land during the Taiping rebellion. LC

CHINA
100 Years
of
Revolution

2

The photographs on the preceding two pages, this page, and the page opposite are all from an album of rare hand-tinted photographs from the 1880s. LC

*Overleaf:*
A Chinese scholar (left) and a Chinese lady of quality (right).

*Above:*
A Chinese mandarin.

*Above right:*
A Chinese prisoner in stocks.

*Right:*
Outdoor tonsorial care.

*Opposite:*
A young Chinese nobleman being transported in a traditional sedan.

*Overleaf:*
Japanese and Chinese forces in combat outside Chinchow in 1894. A contemporary drawing. LC

The Japanese accept the Chinese surrender, ending the Sino-Japanese War, 1895. A contemporary drawing. LC

LIFE
LIBERTY
AND THE
PURSUIT
OF HAPPINESS
UNDER
TREATY
RIGHTS.
W. A. Rogers.

*Opposite:*
Japanese troops attack the Peking gates during the Sino-Japanese War of 1894. A contemporary drawing. LC

*Above:*
Uncle Sam and President McKinley lead attack on the Chinese Boxers, 1900. Cartoon by W. A. Rogers. GRA

*Overleaf:*
Foreign troops assault the Imperial City in 1900, relieving the siege of the diplomatic corps. From a contemporary print. LC

# ★HARRISON E. SALISBURY★

# CHINA

## 100 YEARS OF REVOLUTION

## DESIGNED BY JEAN-CLAUDE SUARÈS

HOLT, RINEHART AND WINSTON

NEW YORK

*In memory of Premier Chou En-lai*

Library of Congress Cataloging in Publication Data
Salisbury, Harrison Evans, 1908–
    China: 100 years of revolution.
    Includes index.
    1. China—History—19th century.   2. China—History—
20th century.   I. Title.
DS755.S24 1983      951      83-264

ISBN: 0-03-056073-X
First Edition
Printed in the United States of America
10 9 8 7 6 5 4 3 2 1

*Illustration Acknowledgments*

The photo research was done by Michelle Trudeau (Peking) and by
Don Hamerman and Judith Linn (New York). The author and publishers
would also like to thank those listed below for their kind permission
to reproduce illustrations. The sources and the code letters by which
they are referred to in the captions are:

| | |
|---|---|
| BET | The Bettman Archive |
| BN | Bibliothèque Nationale, Paris |
| CB/M | Henri Cartier-Bresson/Magnum |
| CPS | China Photo Service |
| CUL | Culver Pictures, Inc. |
| DEL | © Michel Delaborde |
| EAS | Eastfoto |
| LEX | L'Express, Paris |
| FRE | The Freer Gallery of Art, Smithsonian Institution |
| GRA | Granger Collection |
| LC | Library of Congress |
| LU | Lu Hsun Museum |

| | |
|---|---|
| MIL | Military Museum of the Chinese People's Revolution |
| MRV | Museum of the Revolution |
| NYL | New York Public Library |
| PIC | Roger Pic |
| ROT | Arthur Rothstein |
| SYS | Sun Yat-sen Museum |
| UPI | United Press International Photo |
| WW | Wide World Photos |

Where no code letters appear, the source for that illustration is unknown.

*A Note on Spelling*

With a few rare exceptions, this book follows the old Wade-Giles Chinese
transliteration system in use since the mid-nineteenth century rather
than the more modern Pinyin system that is the standard now adopted
by the People's Republic of China, the U.S. Library of Congress and
many American publications. The Wade-Giles system has been chosen
since, generally speaking, readers are more familiar with Mao Tse-
tung than Mao Zedong and Peking rather than Beijing, and since much
of the text deals with China before 1949.

*Also by Harrison E. Salisbury*

American in Russia
Moscow Journal—The End of Stalin
Behind the Lines—Hanoi
War Between Russia and China
The 900 Days: The Siege of Leningrad
To Peking—And Beyond
Russia in Revolution: 1900–1930 (with Jean-Claude Suarès)
Without Fear or Favor: An Uncompromising Look at *The New York
Times*
A Journey for Our Times: A Memoir

*Overleaf:*
Mao Tse-tung rallies People's
Liberation Army troops at a
pause during the Long March.
A contemporary drawing. LC

ISBN 0-03-056073-X

# ★ CONTENTS ★

# ★ 1 ★

## CHINA'S SORROW

IN THE SUMMER OF 1929 THE WINDS blew hot and steady off A-la Shan, off Ordos and the Gobi, the great deserts of China's northwest. They had been blowing since winter and all through the spring, and it seemed that they would never cease, day and night, no rain, heating the "ovens" of China, the cities of the plain, beyond endurance, winds that picked up the sand and propelled it horizontally through the air. It cut a man's face to ribbons and buried the straggling millet in a blanket of dun.

At noon the sky was dark as dusk, so filled with dust you could hardly breathe through your nose mask. The rivers had begun to run dry, all except, of course, the mighty Hwang Ho, the Yellow River, China's "sorrow," the continental watercourse that sometimes surged out of its silt banks and cut a new path to the sea hundreds of miles from the old, a river that in spring rose inexorably until its waters lapped across a region as vast as Germany, drowning people like ants in a saucer, wiping ancient cities off the map, changing China's geography with a careless thrust. So it had always been on this rich loess plain where the Han people and China had been born.

As far as the eye could see and farther, the umber soil lay dead, no green, trees gray, stripped of leaves and bark by dying people. The peasants inched themselves on swollen bellies into the cities from the towns, into the towns from the villages, and died in the dust, skin thin as glove leather, bones brittle, skulls crushed like eggshells.

A young man from Kansas City, twenty-four years old, was traveling in North China that summer. He had never seen a famine. The word was hardly known in the Midwestern America from which he sprang. Now he saw cattle cars carrying half-naked starving girls of eleven or twelve to the cities for sale to the brothels and sweatshops (price range $1.50 to $75.00), he saw children with arms like twigs, young women, naked, brown and withered as ducks in a Chinese poultry shop, dead piled in roadside ditches by men who themselves collapsed, adding their bodies to the thousands already heaped up. Fleshy corpses that vanished before they could be buried. Human meat sold openly in the mud-walled bazaars.

The shocked witness of China's recurring catastrophe was Edgar Snow, later to make his name as chronicler of revolution. He had not believed a world like this existed. In that landscape so dry, so dusty, so unearthly that it might have been the moon, he met another improbable traveler, Rewi Alley, a New Zealander who worked in Shanghai as a factory inspector, now spending his vacation trying with a handful of foreigners to save a few Chinese lives.

The scenes described by these two young Westerners would indelibly mark their lives but their words left hardly a trace on Western minds. An occasional item appeared in the newspapers of London and New York: "Famine in China." But this was not news. China *was* famine. China *was* flood. Death in China was not worth reporting. In these years the municipal disposal workers of Shanghai often picked up 20,000 Chinese bodies, dead in the streets and creeks. In the morning there might be a hundred bodies in the streets, possibly two hundred, "normal" deaths, of starvation, of disease, of exhaustion, hardly worth the bother to count. *The New York Times* published twenty-three stories about China's famine in 1929, most of them pleas by missionaries for contributions. On January 14, 1930, *The Times* carried a headline: "2,000,000 Dead and 2,000,000 Starving in Shensi." The dispatch related that one-third of the population of Shensi and Shansi had died of starvation and that two million were doomed to death. Six million in Kansu Province were destitute and faced starvation. Another brief story reported that thousands had frozen to death in the valley of the River Wei. The reports occupied about half a column on page 6. This was the most prominent report in America's leading newspaper of an event that took six million Chinese lives in 1929–1930.

★

In the summer of 1929 China was a civilization in crisis. For nearly a century China had been trying to break out of the endless nightmare into which it had fallen, a kingdom enthralled, enslaved, powerless, it seemed, to shake off the bonds that robbed it of strength and of resolve, drifting closer and closer toward total dissolution. Soon there might be no China. If there were those who did not accept this fate (and, as it transpired, there were some), men and women who still believed in China, in China's future, in a new China, purged and cleansed of ills and evil, strong once again, a nation once again, a proud and patriotic people, few knew their names, not in the world, not in China itself. The pangs of revolution had, erratic as an earthquake, shaken the country for nearly a century. Would change come in time to save China?

Not that disaster was new. In the two thousand years before the summer of 1929 the Yellow River had overflowed its banks, spreading devastation across the countryside, fifteen hundred times, each occasion painstakingly recorded by the scholars. They did not record the hundreds of millions of lives lost, the human sufferings beyond measure in the wars, the oppression, the tragedies.

All of this went on in China's heartland, the North China plain, the lands watered by the changing course of the Yellow River. There had been twenty-six major changes since the records began, the river shifting its entry into the sea from north to south of the Shantung peninsula and back again. Since 1855 it had been entering from the north.

This was the core of the Middle Kingdom and here its ancient capital, Chang-an, now Sian, stood. Here, just outside Sian's walls, the six thousand clay figures of the army of Emperor Chin Shih Huang-ti were later unearthed. Also uncovered was a Chinese village of the year 5000 B.C., a close duplicate of the Chinese villages of today—the same baked-clay huts, the same baked-clay kitchens and stoves, the same hard-earth floors, the same pots, the same artifacts, the same village plan, the same animals, the same people—a monument to the oldest continuous society we know, unchanged at its roots, the village, for seven thousand years.

In 1929 China was a society of peasant villages, living a life so constant that a peasant of that day in his blue cotton jacket and trousers could be dropped into the village of 5000 B.C. and carry on with hardly a change, threshing his grain, sowing his seed, weaving his garments, cooking his meals as he always had. And the peasant of the year 5000 B.C. could go to work in the village of 1929 without asking a question, ignorant that seven thousand years had silently brushed past his threshold.

Keeper of the oldest traditions on earth, a world unto itself, the Middle Kingdom, as the Chinese had called their land for thousands of years and still called it, was in the middle between heaven and earth, above all others, the most cohesive society ever seen, the essence, the Chinese felt, of civilization. Indeed, China, in the eyes of the Chinese, was civilization itself, surrounded by darkness, by a rude and uncultured netherworld of lesser beings.

A lady from Boston visiting China explained to a Chinese, "Boston is the hub of the universe." Replied the Chinese, "And China *is* the universe."

The birthplace of Han China had been this great nurturing bend of the Yellow River, the North China plain, the richest soil known to man, heart of the heartland, source of the Han people, who now as always made up the body of the nation (say, 95 or 96 percent today), the world within the world, the most ethnocentric people we know. By 1929 this land seemed to many devoid of hope, fragmented, submerged by vastly powerful enemies, ravaged by jackal nations which stole its riches, poisoned its culture and enslaved its populace.

Just as the starving peoples of North China enslaved their sons and debased their daughters in a vain effort to survive, so China's putative rulers prostituted themselves and their peoples to the barbarians in desperation and despair. The heritage of China had been bartered, rented, leased, sold, pawned, mortgaged, enfeoffed to the foreigners. China was a land in torment. On every side the portents were black.

**D**isaster had cast a long shadow ahead. China had not come to the brink of dissolution suddenly. It had been, in effect, a study in slow motion.

In the summer of 1650 on the River of the Black Dragon (now called the Amur) a Russian adventurer named Yerefei Khabarov appeared with a small force of musketeers. He fought a battle at a village called Albasin and proudly reported he had killed 661 "Dauriens," captured 243 women and 115 children, seized 237 horses and 113 head of cattle.

This was the first military clash between a Chinese force (actually a Manchu force: the Manchus had just seized the Peking throne) and a European command. Neither side knew this; neither knew whom it was fighting. The Russians didn't know they were battling an outpost of the Chinese Empire; the Manchu warriors had never heard of the Russian Empire.

China's frontiers were seldom quiet and the fighting along the Amur attracted little attention. By 1689 the Chinese inflicted a sharp defeat on the Russians, and the two parties signed the Treaty of Nerchinsk. Russia abandoned pretensions to the Amur and turned to the north and the east, to the Bering Straits, Alaska and northern California.

Almost all memory of the Battle of Albasin was lost at the court of the Manchu Ching dynasty in Peking. Albasin was only one of countless collisions on distant borders. The Empire rolled ahead in glory, and a hundred fifty years would pass before the question of the northern barbarians rose again.

But other barbarians, Western barbarians, the "red-haired ones," appeared and at the turn of the eighteenth century had been permitted to establish themselves, under strict regulation, at Canton, China's southern port and traditional trading city.

The first to come were the Portuguese, followed by the Spaniards, the Dutch, the English, the French and eventually the Americans. Steadily the trade grew and widened; steadily intercourse between the great isolationist Empire and what it perceived as small, distant, barbarian states, tribute-bearers, denizens of a world beyond the realm of civilization, ex-

CHINA

100 Years

of

Revolution

23

panded. Peking had no concept that what had appeared at Canton was, in effect, the leading edge of a European society vastly superior in technology, organization and military means. Because the Chinese believed in the utter supremacy of the Chinese way it was impossible for a clear vision of Canton's significance to penetrate their minds.

For generations trade flourished. At its heart was the traffic in tea, Europe's great addiction, tens of thousands of chests, until in 1808 the English were bringing twenty-six million pounds of China tea into their country. Nearly everyone was drinking it. Tea was accounted a benign addiction, even a civilizing addiction, replacing the curse of gin in the English working class. It became a national tradition.

The money, the silver dollars, flowed into China. Fortune after fortune was made by the Chinese. The Emperor benefited from enormous assessments levied on the Hong merchants, that small monopoly of Canton traders who dealt with the foreigners. The British East India Company monopolized the transport of tea to England and its princes and merchant captains benefited handsomely, but profits to the company, contrary to legend, were small. Trade was a one-way street. The Chinese sold tea (and silk and spices and speciality products) but they bought little. They didn't need or care for British woolens. They bought cotton and cotton goods but never enough to balance the books. As Emperor Chien Lung had informed George III: "We possess all things. I set no value on objects strange or ingenious and have no use for your country's manufactures." The principal export to China was gold and silver, especially silver.

Finally, the East India Company thought of opium.

★

It is wrong to say that opium destroyed the Chinese Empire, that it brought to ruin an edifice which had survived for thousands of years and which had served to rule and unify the Han peoples, no matter what alien conqueror chanced to seize the Dragon throne. There had been many of these aliens, and always China's higher civilizations, her civil service, her exquisite culture, her technical advancement, the sheer mass and momentum of Han society had kept China on the track. Perhaps a pause of some years was required to absorb the alien rulers into China's complex melting pot. But the country went ahead, invigorated by the new blood of the conquerors.

This had been the case with the Ching dynasty, the Manchu warriors who overthrew the Ming and took control of China in the mid-seventeenth century. For a hundred years the Ching were strong and vigorous. The incidents on the River of the Black Dragon were fleabites; the Canton trade and the traders little more than a curiosity and a source of unexpected revenues, a kind of cultural anomaly within the broad boundaries of the Empire. The Canton trade was something that could be turned on or off; the regulations changed and changed again. What was not perceived was that the world was shrinking: a voyage from England to Canton in the mid-eighteenth century required eight months; by 1800 the time had been cut to a little more than three months; by the fourth decade of the century it was halved again. But in China time had not changed. It still took a month for an Imperial rescript to reach Canton from Peking. The world was moving. China was not. The virility of the Manchus was short-lived. The system that had carried China through millennia was breaking down. As Lord Macartney reported after leading the first English mission to Peking in 1793: "The Empire of China is an old, crazy, first-rate Man of War which a succession of able and vigilant officers have continued to keep afloat for these 150 years. But whenever an insufficient man happens to have the command on deck adieu to the discipline and safety of the ship. She may perhaps not sink outright; she may drift some time as a wreck and will then be dashed to pieces on the shores; but she can never be rebuilt on the old bottom."

Opium. It had been known in China and grown in China and as early as the 1700s had become a minor fad of the leisure classes, and in response the Emperor prohibited its smoking and growing in 1796. At that time possibly fifteen hundred chests of opium a year were coming in. By 1820 the figure neared five thousand; by 1830, ten thousand chests; by 1838–1839, forty thousand. British revenues from opium now surpassed 18 million dollars (about 3.5 million pounds) a year, a staggering gain. In a few years opium had become more important than tea. A map of the drug's use looked like a chart of a man's circulatory system, the addiction spreading along river routes, fanning out from Canton, Swatow, Amoy, Foochow, Ning-po, Shanghai, coursing through the veins of China. No one knew how many addicts there were, possibly two to four million, heavily concentrated in the bureaucracy, the upper class, the higher levels of the middle class. One out of five officials in Peking was said to smoke opium, as well as nearly one-third of the provincial officials.

England drank tea; China smoked opium. England waxed rich; China took the path to degradation. It was almost as simple as that. Of course Marxist scholars would later say that the decay of China's system was inevitable, that it was dictated by the laws of history, the inevitable collapse of feudalism and the rise of industrialism, the dialectic. Perhaps. But in the 1830s China's feudal structure stood intact, unbreached, with not even the beginnings of an industrial age to be seen, not a whisper of a bourgeois society emerging. The system, true, was rotting from within, but this was not new in China's history; only the perceived cause was new: opium and the money opium represented.

Opium. The problem was visible and terrifying. It saturated all levels of Chinese society and the extraordinary profits of its trade first corrupted the Canton system, and then, through Canton, infected the increasingly decadent Ching establishment. But Emperor Tao Kuang was neither stupid nor ignorant. To be certain, his vision of the world beyond China was imperfect. He did not even possess the terminology with which to construct a concept of the outer world. He knew little more about it than he might have culled from this description of Europe written by one of his courtiers soon after he came to power in 1820:

"The big island located on the sea of great cliffs northwest of France is England. . . . Europe's people are all tall and white. Only those who live in the northwest, where it is very cold, are short and dwarfish. They have big noses and deep eyes. . . . Whether young or old all have beards. . . ."

In the year in which Tao Kuang took the throne five thousand chests of opium entered China. From the beginning the Emperor strove to find some means of dealing with the evil. Opium was being sold openly in Peking, smuggling went forward on a grand scale and cultivation of the poppy spread through Shansi Province. By the 1830s the Emperor was encouraging a grand debate over what could be done.

Some officials boldly proposed legalizing the trade. They doubted the ability of any system to prohibit its import and cultivation, because of the corrupting power of the money it generated. Be realistic, they argued; permit its sale, control its use and let the throne profit from the trade. These arguments were opposed by the Moralists, who felt there could be no compromise with evil. If opium were legalized, soon the whole country would be lighting up pipes.

The Emperor heard the arguments and came down on the side of prohibition. At his order an effective campaign was waged by a hard-working and incorruptible Canton governor general named Teng Ting-chen, who by 1838 had paralyzed the Canton drug traffic, destroying the network of "fast crabs"—the boats the smugglers used—and had arrested, imprisoned or executed more than two thousand Chinese dealers and addicts. Since Canton was the entry point for all supplies, opium traffic stagnated. Not a chest was being sold. The British traders faced bankruptcy.

Now Emperor Tao Kuang increased the pressure. In the long debate in Peking about opium, an exemplary official, Lin Tse-hsu, governor general of Hopeh and Hunan, had emerged. He argued that unless the opium problem was solved China would soon possess no army, simply because she would not be able to find any soldiers fit to serve. Lin's moral zeal converted the Emperor. Lin recognized that cutting off the supply of opium was not sufficient to wipe out addiction. He was prepared to threaten with death addicts who persisted in smoking, but he also believed addicts must be helped to rid themselves of the habit: they were, in effect, the victims of an illness and must, like China itself, be restored to normal health.

No longer, said Lin, could China limit its action to measures against her own people. The foreign traders played a critical role. It was they who had brought the drug into the country and they must be dealt with. The Emperor agreed. He invested full confidence in this man whose reputation was so pure he was called "Lin Blue Sky," and after repeated meetings, the Emperor dispatched Lin to Canton on January 8, 1839.

Lin sent an appeal to Queen Victoria, who was twenty years old and had been on the English throne for only two years. "I have heard that the smoking of opium is very strictly forbidden by your country. Why do you let it be passed on, to the harm of other countries? Suppose there were people from another country who carried opium for sale to England and seduced your people into buying and smoking it? Certainly your honorable ruler would deeply hate it and be bitterly aroused. May you, O Queen, check your wicked men and sift your vicious people before they come to China, in order to guarantee the peace of your nation, to show further the sincerity of your politeness and submissiveness."

There is no evidence that the young queen ever saw Lin's letter, which was taken to London on his behalf by a friendly English trader. Nor did the government of England respond.

Lin compelled the English to close down the opium trade (it had already been virtually suspended by Governor General Teng). The Canton trade press reported in January 1839 that "there is absolutely nothing doing and we therefore withdraw our quotation [for opium]." Lin ordered the British and other foreign traders to surrender their opium stocks, 21,603 chests. He had three trenches dug, a hundred fifty feet long, seventy-five feet wide, seven feet deep, at Hu-men on the Pearl River delta. There, beginning June 5, 1839, as he was later to write, "I had water diverted into the trenches. Then I had salt sprinkled into the pools. Finally I had the opium thrown into the pools and added lime."

The mixture was flushed into the sea before the unbelieving eyes of high Chinese officials and foreign merchants. They were impressed. The whole operation took twenty-three days, and when it was done not a chest of opium remained in Canton.

★

For the moment there was hope. China was free of opium. Lin was showered with honors by the Emperor and offered high posts. He refused and went forward with what he perceived as the second stage of his job—to prevent foreigners from resuming the traffic. To this end he demanded that all traders, in return for permission to trade, sign a bond to abide by China's prohibition of opium traffic.

The British refused, and on September 4, 1839, a small British naval force attacked a fleet of Chinese war junks at Kowloon (the British traders had fled Canton and were running low on water and provisions at their anchorage at Hong Kong) and sank them. What would go down in history as the Opium War had started but neither the British nor the Chinese were aware that they had gone to war; months would pass before it would become plain that the world's oldest empire and the nineteenth century's most aggressive new empire had embarked on a collision course, which the young Tory leader William Gladstone would describe thus: "A war more unjust in its origin, a war more calculated to cover this country with permanent disgrace, I do not know. . . . The flag is hoisted to protect an infamous contraband traffic; and if it were never hoisted except as it is now hoisted on the coast of China, we should recoil from its sight with horror."

Despite Gladstone's words, the war was quickly and efficiently won, although Emperor Tao Kuang still was not clear about what happened. How could he have been? Just before the outbreak of hostilities, he had received a memorial from a court official giving him an estimate of English military power: "The English barbarians are an insignificant and detestable race, trusting entirely to their strong ships and large guns. . . . Though waterproof, the ships are not fireproof. . . . When once on fire we may open our batteries upon them, display the celestial terror and extermine them without the loss of a single life. . . . Without therefore despising the enemy we have no reason to fear him."

But if the Emperor was still confused, Lin Blue Sky was able to look the truth squarely in the eye. He had purchased foreign cannon to try to oppose the English guns. He had bought a foreign ship to experiment in the tactics of Western war. He knew the answer to the tragedy: English firepower, English weapons, English technology. Against them Chinese bravery, even the fanatic dedication of the Manchu bannermen, was no match. They could not stand up to the English shot and shell, the fast-firing guns, the heavy artillery. The West was stronger, far stronger than Lin had known, far stronger than the Emperor could imagine. Lin was not a man given to self-deceit. It was, of course, his probity, his moral rectitude which had played so great a role in bringing about the confrontation, unexpected by either side, which led to the war and to the quick and total defeat from which the Ching dynasty never was to recover.

Inevitably, Lin paid the price. The Emperor who had so highly complimented him now heaped blame for the disaster on this honest man. Lin was denounced to the English as the source of all the trouble and sent in exile to distant Ili in Sinkiang. As he made his arduous way to the western desert he set down his thoughts in a private letter to a friend, forbidding its publication lest it further offend the Emperor. He offered his *post facto* analysis and then added: "What was to be done, what was to be done?"

In 1929 the question still had no answer, but there were, in the distant and remote areas of the River Hsiang, in mountainous areas of central and western China, and in obscure hideaways in the French Concession of Shanghai and other urban centers, growing numbers of dedicated, daring and sometimes suicidal young people who called themselves Communists and thought they had found the answer.

# THE HEAVENLY KINGDOM

IN THE SPRING OF 1836 A TWENTY-two-year-old schoolteacher named Hung Hsiu-chuan went to Canton from his village of Hun-hsian, about twenty miles distant, to take the civil-service examinations. He had failed them in 1828 and now, after years of study, with the support of his well-to-do peasant family and the village elders, he was making a second try. Again he failed.

Walking down a crowded Canton street one day, he encountered two Protestant missionaries, an elderly American named Edwin Stevens, and another, possibly a Chinese convert named Liang A-fa, an associate of Dr. Robert Morrison of the London Missionary Society who was in Canton translating the Bible into Chinese.

Stevens was wearing a long robe and possessed a full beard. The second man was middle-aged. He handed Hung a set of nine slim Gospel tracts written by Liang A-fa and entitled *Good Words for Exhorting the Age*—a mixture of Chinese Biblical translations and Gospel preachments, Epistles of the Disciples, Old Testament Prophets and the Book of Genesis, presenting a fundamentalist Christian doctrine which stressed the Ten Commandments, the omnipotence of God, the awfulness of sin and the uncompromising choice between salvation and damnation, between heaven and hell.

Hung, concerned about his failure in the examinations, went back home, as he recalled, with no more than a glance at the tracts. He spent the next year in study and in 1837 took the tests for a third time. Again he failed. Now he had a seizure, suffered from delusions and had to be carried back home in a sedan chair. He sang loudly and wildly. His father found a slip of paper on which Hung had written "Hung the Heavenly King and Emperor of the Great Way." He told his sister he was "the Emperor of Great Peace, with the sun in my left hand and the moon in my right." The village decided he had lost his mind.

After forty days Hung emerged a calmer, quieter, seemingly a more sober and solemn man. He possessed a vivid recall of his visions. He had been visited by a kindly old woman, the Heavenly Mother, who had said: "Son of mine, you are filthy after your descent to earth. Let me wash you in the river before you are permitted to see your father." He was taken into the presence of the Father, a golden-bearded, venerable figure in a black robe, attended by a middle-aged man, Hung's Elder Brother. The Father gave him a sword and ordered him to exterminate all evil demons.

Hung resumed his career as a teacher and his study for the Imperial examinations. After six years he tried again, and for the fourth and last time he failed.

One day a cousin named Hung Jen-kan was browsing through Hung's bookshelf and came upon the tracts, read them and urged Hung to do likewise. At this, the first time (as he later remembered) he examined the pamphlets, he leaped to the conclusion that he was the Son of God and Christ's younger brother. He fused in his mind the message of the tracts, his visions, and his meeting with the two missionaries in Canton; the older man with the beard became God, the middle-aged man became Jesus. He interpreted his hallucinations as a visit to heaven in which he met God, saw his Brother Jesus and was commanded by God to carry out the mission of freeing the world from evil and demons, and bringing back the people to the worship of the Lord.

★

Thus was spawned, in the mind of an obscure Kwangtung peasant's son, the religious-political movement that became known as the Taiping rebellion, a movement without parallel in China, or indeed in the world, which came within an ace of toppling the Ching dynasty before 1850. It would have put China into the hands of a neo-Christian militarized theocracy, American missionary-inspired, egalitarian, infused with primitive Communism (a mixture of early Christian and Chinese practices), highly moralistic, puritanical, totally opposed to opium, tobacco, drink and sexual licentiousness, though believing in equality of men and women. Hung and his followers were nationalistic, anti-Manchu, an extraordinary amalgam of Chinese and Western Christian philosophy. Their society broke radically with Confucianism and most Chinese traditions; it was a society of Brothers and Sisters, united in the "Heavenly Kingdom of Great Peace," Taiping tien-kuo, a kind of mid-nineteenth-century Moral Majority, now seen by the Chinese Communists as their spiritual ancestor, and viewed by almost all Chinese as their first revolutionary attempt to cope with China's decline and the rise of the Western challenge.

Hung Hsiu-chuan was a Hakka, his parents were Hakkas, he came from a village of Hakkas. The Hakkas had moved south from central China in the thirteenth century under military threat from the north. They were called "the Guest People" by their neighbors. The Hakkas were Han Chinese, but they had distinctive costumes, customs and dialect and lived an uneasy existence amid often hostile neighbors. They had long been trained in cooperation, collaboration and military self-sufficiency in order to survive in alien and dangerous surroundings.

In this milieu Hung, aided at first only by his cousin Hung Jen-kan, his family and a few friends, set out to do God's will and bring about heaven on earth. He and his friends went into the countryside and preached the evangelical doctrine Hung had hammered together from the Gospel tracts, Chinese ethics and anti-Manchu nationalism. Hung and his associates ranged the Hakka areas, making converts, smashing idols, denouncing opium and gambling. There was in Hung a strong populist strain, as well as one of Han chauvinism.

"Each year," Hung preached, "the Manchus transform tens of millions of China's silver and gold into opium and extract several millions from the fat and marrow of the Chinese people and turn it into rouge and powder. How could the rich not become poor? How could the poor abide by the law?"

Hung called for the exorcism of the "Manchu demons" and the destruction of the "tartar dog, Hsien-feng" (the Emperor), whom he described as ravaging Chinese women and imposing vulgar Manchu customs.

"Can the Chinese still call themselves men?" he asked.

He set the Ten Commandments into Chinese poetry and made them the code by which his followers lived. Violators were beheaded. His followers were Brothers and Sisters and were adjured to live in total continence until the heavenly order was established. Hung needed no elaborate chapel in which to celebrate his faith. He and his followers simply wrote the name Jehovah on a piece of paper, knelt before it and offered their prayers, partaking of the sacrament of Christ, bread and wine.

The movement quickly assumed a military-evangelical-patriotic character and roared through central China like prairie fire. Hung had too psychotic a personality to provide consistent leadership, but several associates (each of them a "King" in the Taiping terminology: King of the East, King of the West, King of the South, King of the North) demonstrated remarkable military competence. Their followers became exemplary soldiers, fighting with total bravery, certain that if they died in battle they would go straight to heaven.

For a time there was a women's corps of a hundred thousand, organized in female regiments with all-women's barracks, completely segregated from the all-men's barracks. It resembled the segregation later practiced in the "blue ant" period of the Chinese Communist Revolution, when similar injunctions against sexual relations were ordained, this time on the grounds of population control.

The Taipings cut off their pigtails, a style imposed by the Manchus, to wear their hair in what would today be regarded as hippie-style, and so were called "The Long-Haired Ones" by the Manchu authorities.

**B**eginning in July 1850 the Taipings swept through city after city. Before the movement was crushed fifteen years later, they had operated in sixteen of China's eighteen provinces, had captured and held, at least for a time, more than six hundred walled cities, and for years controlled much of the valley of the Yangtze, establishing their capital in Nanking, China's traditional southern capital, in 1853. They now christened Nanking the "Heavenly Capital." They boasted a treasury six times larger than that of Imperial Peking (mostly silver and gold seized in Nanking); they had two to four million supporters and the fiercest, best-disciplined, best-led troops China had ever seen, a "band of Brothers" with a mandate from heaven. They instigated a land distribution program not unlike that which would later be pursued by the Communists. All land belonged to God, but parcels were given to the individual peasant for his use in a complex cooperative system.

The movement picked up support from other restive elements: bandits, secret societies, local private armies, dissidents. All were sworn to the Taiping principles. If they could not lead a life of austerity and discipline they were executed. Or, more often, they simply melted away. Some, in the lower ranks, still sang the bandit songs:

> *The upper classes owe us money*
> *The middle classes ought to wake up*
> *Lower classes, follow me,*
> *It beats renting an ox and plowing barren land.*

On his thirty-seventh birthday, January 11, 1851, Hung proclaimed his Heavenly Kingdom. The Imperial throne tottered, unable to find a way of coping with this remarkable crusade burning with fiery hatred for the Manchus and casting aside so much of China's traditional way of life. Foreigners were impressed with the Taiping movement, as they visited the capital at Nanking, praised its order and cleanliness, entered into provisional relations with the rebels.

But all was not well. Hung was too unstable to rule. His principal "Kings" quarreled. Puritanism broke down. The leaders established huge harems and lived in luxury. This began to debase the Cromwellian discipline of their forces. An expedition to capture Peking failed. The Manchu court developed better commanders. Taiping's control of the Yangtze slipped away. Götterdamerung struck on the night of September 1–2, 1856. At Hung's behest his lieutenant kings, Wei Chang-hui (the North King) and Shih Ta-kai (the Assistant King), hastened back to Nanking. Wei assassinated Yang Hsiu-ching (the East King), who had usurped Hung's role as God's "Second Son." Wei slaughtered twenty thousand men that night and in the next few days. It seemed that the killing would never end. Finally Hung turned on Wei and killed the North King, along with two hundred of his followers. It was not unlike Hitler's *Kristallnacht* or the Great Purges of Stalin.

Foreigners turned away from the Taipings. The Reverend Isaachar J. Roberts, an American Southern Baptist missionary, had played an unwitting role in the early movement. Hung and his cousin Hung Jen-kan, an extremely able man, had spent three weeks of Bible study with Roberts in Canton in 1847. Hung was evolving his neo-Christian philosophy at the time and proved an apt pupil. Now, in 1861, Hung invited Roberts to Nanking; the Baptist minister spent fifteen months in the Heavenly Capital.

Roberts finally left in disgust. He said that he believed Hung's opinions were "in the main abominable in the sight of God." He added: "In fact, I believe he is crazy, especially in religious matters, nor do I believe him soundly rational about anything."

He concluded that Hung had invited him to Nanking in the hope that Roberts would undertake a mission to convert foreigners to Hung's gospel. "I would as lief convert them to Mormonism or to any other 'ism' which I believe unscriptural, and so far, from the devil," he said.

When, in 1860, Taiping forces threatened to take Shanghai, a Yankee adventurer named Frederick T. Ward from Salem, Massachusetts, organized a mercenary force consisting of a few Europeans, two hundred Filipinos and five or six thousand Chinese. Although they were far from victorious in all their engagements, they gained the designation "Ever Victorious" from the Emperor. When Ward was killed, an English adventurer, Major Charles George Gordon (later known as "Chinese" Gordon), took command. Gordon had more success, got into a fearsome row with his Imperial allies when they executed a group of Taiping commanders who had surrendered on his promise of safe conduct, but, after being richly appeased (a gift of seventy thousand taels), resumed his command.

The downfall of the Taiping movement was not far off. A first-class military leader, Tseng Kuo-fan, had emerged among the Manchus, and he rapidly closed in on Nanking. There Hung died on June 1, 1864, after an illness of twenty days probably arising from a suicide attempt. The Imperial troops broke into Nanking with little difficulty.

The slaughter went on for three days. "The Chin-huai Creek was filled with bodies," Tseng reported to the Emperor. "The fire raged for three days and nights. Not one of the hundred thousand rebels in Nanking surrendered himself when the city was taken, but in many cases they gathered together and burned themselves and passed away without repentance. Such a formidable band of rebels had rarely been known from ancient times to the present."

The Taiping rebellion was crushed. It seemed that not a spark remained. The Imperial throne was saved. The foreign traders were coming to realize that their interests were better served by a weak Chinese ruler whom they could twist and manipulate (a conclusion that strikingly foreshadowed Stalin's policy of favoring the weak Nationalist Chiang Kai-shek over the vigorous Chinese Communists). In fact, China was entering a kind of dynastic interregnum in which the foreign powers, with their unequal treaties, their imposition of extraterritoriality, their leases and concessions, their overriding of China's national rights, were becoming a substitute for Chinese national sovereignty.

The Taipings had vanished, the heads of all the leaders and tens of thousands of followers chopped off and spiked on poles, carried about the country, sent in triumph to Peking. They were gone. The trouble was over. But, of course, it was not. China and the Manchus staggered on, deeper and deeper into what was to be a century of humiliation. The spirit of the Taipings smoldered on in the ashes of the vanished "Heavenly Kingdom."

The Taipings had, in fact, offered China an alternate system, a new kind of relationship between governors and governed, a communal approach to property, an egalitarianism of men and women, a break with the ancient tradition of family and patriarchal clans. The Taiping rebellion augured the end of the China of Confucius, proved a cryptic portent of the future on which China was embarking, the painful revolutionary task of adjustment to the culture and technology of the West.

Dr. Sun Yat-sen, who was to become the father of China's revolution, was born just as the Taiping rebellion was being drowned in blood, and he would draw liberally on that experience in formulating his principles of nationalism, democracy and socialism, the famous "Three People's Principles," the San Min Chu I. His notions about land, its redistribution and common holding for the benefit of the people, stemmed from Taiping ideas, as did his concept of the regulation of capital. Like the Taipings, he found support from secret societies and brotherhoods. He saw Hung's chief error as his failure to understand democracy, his reliance on Chinese and neo-religious notions of divine dictatorship. Dr. Sun was a Christian, a Christian of understanding and principle. He did not mix elements of Chinese superstition into his Methodism.

Nor was Dr. Sun alone in his appreciation of the Taiping movement.

Karl Marx, his hopes of European revolution shattered by the failure of the uprisings of 1848, turned his eyes eastward and was heartened by the Taiping movement. "It is to be rejoiced at," he wrote in 1850, "that the most ancient and stable empire in the world is on the eve of a social upheaval which, in any case, must have extremely important results for civilization."

To be sure, Marx knew little of what was really happening in China; he had a need to find a revolutionary spark somewhere in the gloomy international atmosphere. His mood was not unlike that of Lenin in 1919 when, losing faith in the revolutionary upsurge in Germany on which he had counted to sustain the precarious Bolshevik Revolution, he looked to the East and saw hope in the revolutionary forces of Dr. Sun Yat-sen. At least in numbers, Lenin observed, they weighed extraordinarily on the world's scale.

In the long run, Marx and Lenin proved right. Not only did the Taiping uprising furnish inspiration, slogans, goals and philosophy for Dr. Sun Yat-sen and his Nationalist Kuomintang, they also provided models and tactical examples for the Chinese Communist movement—especially for Mao Tse-tung, a peasant from a fairly well-to-do background, not unlike that of Hung Hsiu-chuan, rooted in the countryside, a strongly egalitarian, puritanistic, charismatic man. Mao did not, of course, present himself as a Heavenly King or his movement as a Heavenly Kingdom. But, stripped of the Taiping cant, life as it was to evolve in Mao's Red Army stronghold of Yenan had its resemblances to that of the Taipings in their idealist phase. And the trouble that would emerge in the Communist "heaven"—that is, the internal divisions, strife, aberrations and traumatic delusions of the Cultural Revolution—resembled in frightening ways the malaise that finally brought down the Heavenly Kingdom of Taiping.

## 3

## AT LAST, REVOLUTION

HUNG HSIU-CHUAN WAS DEAD, HIS Taiping rebellion smashed, the Taipings scattered to the winds, but neither their memory nor the social and political forces that set them in motion had passed away.

In the village of Hiang-shan, not far from Canton or from Hun-hsian, where Hung Hsiu-chuan, the Taiping founder, had been born, the legend lingered, the tales were told as people lounged in the courtyards of a breathless summer night or huddled indoors during the endless monsoon rains.

In this village a boy named Sun Wen was born to a peasant family in 1866, two years after the Taiping fires had been extinguished. He was one of six children, four of whom were to survive. The village was poor, and like many families in Kwangtung Province the Suns had a tradition of going abroad to seek their fortune. At fifteen, Sun's elder brother, Sun Mei, went to Honolulu, where he would become a prosperous businessman. Sun Wen attended school, studied the Confucian Four Books and Five Classics and dreamed of becoming another Hung Hsiu-chuan. At the age of thirteen he went with his mother to join the brother in Honolulu. Later Sun Wen returned to China, studied medicine in Hong Kong, went into practice, became a Methodist, got married, offered free services to the poor of Canton, and determined to dedicate his life to bringing about a revolution in China. Around the world he would become known as Dr. Sun Yat-sen.

It was hardly surprising that Dr. Sun took the path of a professional revolutionary. In truth, it was difficult for young Chinese not to become revolutionaries. Their country was crumbling about them, and the Empress Dowager Tzu Hsi—a woman whose intrigues would make those of a later "empress," Chiang Ching, the wife of Mao Tse-tung, seem like a children's game— had grabbed the reins of China in her knotted hands in 1861 and would not relinquish them until her death in 1908. Hers was a reign of unparalleled length, profligacy, corruption, ignorance, superstition, stupidity and evil.

The Empress Dowager possessed no redeeming quality. There was no crime she did not commission or commit. Poison and murder were everyday weapons. Her mind was choked with superstitions. Her ignorance had no limit; in cunning she was supreme. She spent funds that had been appropriated for a modern navy on a marble boat in West Lake. She cut short the "Hundred Days of Reform" in 1898 of the Emperor Kwang Hsu, which might—just might— have given China a chance to enter the path of renovation, renewal and restoration. She beheaded the chief reformers, "the six Gentlemen, the six Martyrs," as they came to be called, and imprisoned the Emperor, who was never again to emerge from his golden cage. She presided over the partition of China into territories and ports ruled by and exploited by the great foreign powers. She witnessed the loss of the Ryukyu Islands to Japan in 1879; the loss of Ili and Sinkiang to Russia in 1880 (the territory was later returned, then taken back, still later returned again); the loss of Annam and Cochin China (Indochina) to France in 1884–1885;

the loss of the Pescadores and Taiwan to Japan in 1895; the loss of most of Manchuria, first to Russia then to Japan.

In plain fact, China was being devoured by the European powers and Japan while the Empress played at court games. The chief restraints on the great powers were their own rivalries. Only the United States appeared to China to be less voracious, in part because it claimed no special privileges (although benefiting from those that others gained), and in part because of its Open Door policy, which committed it to the preservation of China's territorial integrity.

Nothing seemed capable of halting China's dissolution. Within the numberless villages, behind the shrouded walls of the hutungs, the alleys of Peking and Canton and Shanghai, the blood of the Chinese boiled with anger, humiliation and desire for national revenge, for some act that would restore China's glory. The mood of chauvinism, of hatred for the foreigners who were carving China's flesh and roasting it on their imperialist spits, mounted to *luan*, to an almost insane rage. *Luan* is a Chinese term for madness, mass madness, mindless violence, the chaos that sweeps people who have been agonized beyond human control. No people was more passive, more orderly, more regulated by custom, ritual and tradition than the Chinese, but when the bonds burst no people exploded with such vehemence. The emotion was shared by the Imperial court, by humble scholars in ancient libraries, by coolies on the streets, poor peasants in Hupeh and Shensi. As frustration mounted, the passion more and more became anti-foreign and anti-Christian, a bent encouraged by the court to divert hostility from the Manchu rulers and the Empress Dowager. Christianity, the missionaries and their Chinese converts came to be seen as a spoke on the iron wheel of Western imperialism.

China's internal tensions mounted. Her economy began to fall apart under the blows of the new Western industrialists. They built railroads, which put the Grand Canal, linking Peking and central China, almost out of business. Hundreds of thousands of Chinese lost their jobs and starved. Small business was ruined. The treaty ports under foreign control—Shanghai, Hong Kong and the rest—disrupted traditional trading patterns. Western goods replaced China's ancient hand manufactures. Inevitably, the Yangtze and the Yellow River rose in flood. Famine and death spread misery over China. Again and again blame was heaped on the "long noses."

★

In these black hours a secret society called the I-he Chuan, "The Righteous and Harmonious Fists," rose like a thundercloud, moving from province to province and into the great cities. The Righteous and Harmonious Fists swore a secret oath to kill all foreigners and all Chinese collaborators. They believed they possessed a magic which rendered them immune to bullets. If their belief was strong enough they could take wing and fly through the heavens. The spirits of millions of dead Chinese warriors fought at their side. They wore frightening dress and armed themselves with swords and spears, rejecting the weapons of the West, guns and cannon. They vowed to kill one dragon (the Emperor, whom they believed, correctly, to be pro-foreign), two tigers (the Emperor's European-inclined advisers) and three hundred lambs (Chinese Westernizers).

These were the Boxers, as the foreigners called them, and they etched a fiery pattern on China's descent into *luan*. The Empress Tzu Hsi and her entourage courted the Boxers, diverted them from their anti-Manchu goals, harnessed them to the service of the regime and aimed them against the "foreign devils." The Boxers ravaged the land, killing Christian Chinese where they found them, spiking their heads on sticks, beating women and children to death, burning huts and houses, tearing Western missionaries limb from limb, sacking churches, destroying missions.

In Peking the Empress Dowager encouraged the Boxers to attack her enemies, the pro-Western intellectuals, the great families that had come to understand that China must change, that she could save herself only by adopting the technology and achievements of the West. When General Cheng Wen-ping lined up fifty Boxers of the Golden Belt Society and shot them to prove that the Boxers did not possess immunity from death, the Empress rejoined: "If we cannot rely upon the supernatural formulas, can we not rely upon the hearts of our people?" She plunged forward into one more disaster, one more step down the slippery slope.

*Luan* swept Peking like a typhoon; everything flew before it. Half the Imperial troops joined the Boxers. The court and the courtiers joined as well. They took part in the frenzy of Boxer rituals, they burned the magic incense, they lighted the magic papers, they frothed at the mouth in the rites that the Boxers believed made them immune to foreign bullets. Nervously the foreign embassies, behind the walls of the Legation Quarter, brought in more troops and prepared against attack. The wise among China's statesmen warned of disaster, but Jung-lu, the Imperial commander who had no use for the Boxers, threw up his hands: "Heaven wills it, what can we do?"

Officially (but secretly) the Empress gave the order for the Boxers to attack and for the Imperial troops to fight by their side. Within the embassy fortifications were 450 troops of half a dozen nations, 475 diplomats and other foreigners, including 50 servants, and 2,300 Chinese Christians. The Boxers attacked like dervishes, screaming like banshees, garbed like monsters. The Imperial troops were promised fifty taels for each live male European captive, forty for a female, thirty for a child. Methodically the Westerners manned their guns, mowing down the crazed Boxers, turning their "immunity to death" into heaps of Chinese bodies.

Within Peking *luan* reigned. Chinese raged through the streets, destroying the courtyards and homes of anyone believed to have an association with the West. Thousands of Chinese died. In the Legation Quarter foreigners stood to their guns, their task made easier because regular Chinese Army commanders, not touched by *luan*, feared a day of reckoning and did not press their attack. They declared a truce so that the foreigners could replenish supplies of food and water. On August 14, 1900, a column of eighteen thousand Western troops fought its way into Peking from Tientsin, to ransack the capital anew. When it was over Peking lay in ruins, some of the great houses burned by the Boxers, some by the foreign devils. No one was more bloodthirsty than the Germans. The Russians posed as friends of the Chinese but one Russian general shipped home ten trunks of confiscated jewels and gold.

In all, 231 foreigners, mostly missionaries and their families, were killed. The Peking casualties included the chancellor of the Japanese embassy and the German minister, Baron von Ketteler. Chinese casualties ran to thousands, among them many of the most advanced, most progressive men and women in China. The Empress Dowager fled to Sian, compelling her prisoner, the Emperor, to accompany her. The foreign powers imposed a staggering indemnity of 67 million pounds (about 350 million dollars) and wholesale new indignities against Chinese sovereignty. The United States provided one bright spot. It directed that its indemnity, 33 million taels, be spent for Chinese education.

Looking back, Marxist scholars came to regard the Boxer Rebellion as a "primitive form of patriotic peasant uprising." The peasants, the Marxists said, had the right motive but the wrong methods. That seems unrealistic. Almost all of China had been swept up by the *luan*, a madness so irrational, so uncontrolled that its roots seemed better explored by the theories of Freud than those of Marx.

Gradually *luan* ebbed and again China groveled. Foreign mud (opium), foreign devils (troops) had brought China to the point of no return. The question now was not *how* would China survive, but *could* she?

★

In agony, young China and many of the older generation turned to foreign models, to foreign thought, to European study, to find a source of strength with which to halt China's destruction. They began to examine the example of Peter the Great in Russia and his remarkable reforms during the eighteenth century, which turned Russia into a great power. They studied the Meiji Restoration in Japan, which had moved a still-medieval society onto modern rails in the mid-nineteenth century. Western missionaries increasingly identified themselves with China's cause, and young Chinese sought from them knowledge of Western science, Western medicine, Western education, Western thought, Western philosophy and Western culture.

No more typical product of China's soul-searching would appear than the Canton doctor of the free clinics, Sun Yat-sen, a man of brisk intelligence, keen conscience, unbounded energy and unusual exposure to foreign ideas through his life in Hong Kong and Hawaii. Like many Chinese, he had been astounded by the cleanliness and order of Hong Kong. Only fifty miles separated Hong Kong and Canton, but the two cities were centuries apart—Canton crowded, filthy, diseased, buried in muck; Hong Kong clean, comfortable, healthy, an oasis in the pestilent swamp of China. For thousands of years China had considered herself the epitome of civilization, but she lived amid garbage and excrement, clouds of flies, every kind of epidemic disease. Her people died untended on the streets of her cities. In Hong Kong the British colonists had created a spic-and-span town in thirty years.

Dr. Sun vowed to end China's disgrace if it cost his life. He would overthrow the Manchu regime and launch a new, democratic order. Night after night he and three friends argued revolution, talking so much they became known as "the four great and inseparable scoundrels." Dr. Sun decided to base himself on the support of overseas Chinese (much more advanced than most of his mainland countrymen), on the secret societies that had provided strength for the Taipings, on the Christian converts, already imbued with Western ideals, and on those missionaries who hoped to modernize China. He founded the Revive China Society on November 24, 1894. A month or two later he raised the flag of "blue sky, white sun" in revolt in Canton. But his plot was exposed, forty-six comrades were executed and Dr. Sun fled to Japan, cut off his queue, adopted Western dress, then went on to Honolulu and America, following the familiar trail of the exiled revolutionary seeking funds and support among his countrymen abroad. He was a good money-raiser and, it was said, one secret of his success was to promise his supporters roles for their sons and relatives in the Chinese revolutionary regime-to-be.

On to London Dr. Sun went, arriving on October 1, 1896. He fortuitously met his old Hong Kong medical mentor, Dr. James Cantlie, and at Cantlie's suggestion, he took up lodgings on Gray's Inn Road. Ten days later, on Sunday, October 11, as Dr. Sun was on his way to church, he was kidnapped by three men who lured him into the Chinese Imperial embassy and held him prisoner in a bare third-floor room. From there they proposed to ship him to China, execution and death.

Sun tossed messages from his window, weighted with English pennies and ha'pennies, hoping someone would pick them up. No one did. He made friends with one of his warders, a man named George Coyle who agreed to take a message to Dr. Cantlie saying, "Your friend since Sunday has been held here in the Chinese embassy; they want to send him to China where, undoubtedly, he will be hanged. The situation of this unfortunate is very sad and unless something is done quickly he will be taken away and no one will know about it."

Dr. Cantlie lived almost next door to the Chinese embassy. He got Sun's message late on the night of October 17. He and his friend and fellow physician from China, Dr. Patrick Manson, rushed to the local police station. The police sent them to Scotland Yard. Scotland Yard thought they were drunk or demented; diplomats did not engage in kidnapping and conspiracy. Not in London. The doctors tackled the Foreign Office. No response. They went to *The Times*, but the editors wanted to consult the Foreign Office before printing anything. They went to the Chinese embassy and met polite denials. Fearing Dr. Sun might be spirited out of the embassy at any moment, Dr. Cantlie hired private detectives to mount a twenty-four-hour watch. Later the Chinese embassy hired the same detective agency to watch the detectives who were watching the embassy. On October 19, Dr. Manson met with Lord Salisbury, the Prime Minister, who promised to take action. Nothing happened. Finally, the doctors went to court. They brought a *habeas corpus* action in Old Bailey. It was thrown out.

The situation seemed hopeless until a liberal newspaper, the *Globe*, learned of the proceedings at Old Bailey and sought out Dr. Cantlie, who confirmed the details. On October 24 screaming headlines in the *Globe* told the world of the kidnapping of an innocent Chinese (believed to be a subject of British Hong Kong) being held in the Chinese embassy under the nose of Scotland Yard. Every newspaper in London picked up the story. *The Times* published its long-withheld dispatch. Crowds gathered outside the Chinese embassy. The next day, Sun was freed. The headlines had carried around the world. At a stroke Dr. Sun became the most famous of Chinese revolutionaries, the most famous revolutionary in the world.

★

**N**ow, like his predecessor, Karl Marx of Germany, and his contemporary-to-be, Vladimir Lenin, Sun made his way to the great circular reading room of the British Museum, a neat, fine-looking Chinese in Western dress. There he sat, perusing Henry George and the single-taxers, reading the French philosophers Jean Jacques Rousseau, Saint-Simon and Fourier, the economists Ricardo and Malthus, the English thinkers Charles Darwin and John Stuart Mill. Did he read Karl Marx? So the Marxists were to say, but there is hardly a trace of Marxism in Sun Yat-sen's thought or practice. At the British Museum, Sun hammered out the principles of his revolution. It was to be social as well as national, based on his Three People's Principles: nationalism, democracy and socialism. In what would become a familiar practice for the Chinese revolutionaries, he drew strongly on American parallels. His first hero was George Washington and he worshipped Abraham Lincoln, believing that the Three People's Principles constituted a Chinese equivalent of Lincoln's declaration of a government "of the people, by the people, for the people."

Sun embraced socialism but in a rather generalized form, emphasizing the regulation of capitalism, not its abolition—he had too many businessmen supporters to promise anything like that. On the question of land he was more radical and yet more traditionally Chinese. He stood for the old Chinese utopian ideal of "all land to the toilers" and he backed his convictions with arguments drawn from Henry George and John Stuart Mill.

After nearly two years of study Dr. Sun was ready for a new attempt at revolution. He returned to Japan, where he had won strong support from an active Chinese colony and from the Japanese Liberal Party, which saw him as China's man of destiny, the man who would lead China's regeneration.

The chaos generated by the Boxer uprising gave Dr. Sun's movement new momentum, turning foreign and Chinese attention toward the cause of revolution. Then came Russia's defeat by Japan in the war of 1904–1905. Not only did Russia erupt in revolution—the dress rehearsal, as it came to be called, for 1917—but the event also provided a powerful impetus for China's revolutionaries. Chinese morale was lifted by the realization that a new Asian power could inflict so shattering a defeat upon a great European power. And 1905 in Russia showed the Chinese they were not alone in their aspirations for revolution.

A revolutionary surge swept China. Dr. Sun acquired a new voice for his movement, first in a magazine called *Twentieth Century China* published in Tokyo, and then in the *People's Tribune*. Year after year Dr. Sun's organization, the United League (or the Revolutionary League, as it was later openly called), carried out uprisings—six in Kwantung, others in Kwangsi and Yunnan. Dr. Sun's tenth attempt came in Canton in the spring of 1911, a powerful revolt by his supporters that almost captured power, failing at the last moment with the loss of Dr. Sun's famous "seventy-two martyrs" (actually the total was eighty-five, including six Chinese students who had come from Japan to take part in the battle).

Sun Yat-sen was in America, raising funds and enrolling supporters, in these exciting 1911 days. Early in October 1911, he received a coded message from his colleagues in China which he could not decipher because he had sent his codebook ahead in his baggage to Denver, where he was scheduled to lecture at the university. When he got to Denver on October 10, he deciphered the message. It told of a forthcoming uprising in Wuhan, the great central complex of Chinese cities on the Yangtze. The next morning he rose late and went out at about eleven o'clock to take his breakfast, buying a copy of the *Denver Post* on the way. It carried big headlines. The rebels had captured Wuhan, capital of Hupeh Province—their greatest victory so far. Wuhan had been taken by a revolutionary army of two thousand. New victories followed quickly: Chang-sha on October 22, Yunnan on October 21, Shanghai three days later, Chekiang, Fukien, Canton on November 9. In six weeks the rebels had swept to success in nearly two-thirds of China. Nanking fell on December 4. The end was near.

Dr. Sun did not rush directly back to China, but took a bit of time (not unlike Lenin, who was in Switzerland when Russia's 1905 and 1917 revolutions broke out and did not hurry home). Dr. Sun decided first to go to London to get British support for his cause. In London Dr. Sun always stayed with his old friends the Cantlies. Even before his arrival a messenger from the Chinese embassy two doors away had brought a telegram addressed simply to "Dr. Sun, London." When the smiling doctor appeared, Mrs. Cantlie handed the message to him. He read it and thrust it into his pocket without comment. The next day she asked him what it was. "Oh," he said, "didn't I tell you? They've asked me to become President of the Chinese Republic."

And so they had. After winning the backing of the English and accepting congratulations from Premier Clemenceau in France, he returned to Shanghai on December 25, Christmas Day, and a few days later was elected provisional president of the new republic by a vote of sixteen of the seventeen electors.

It was thought in Shanghai that Dr. Sun had arrived with suitcases full of money and pledges of funds from the European powers. He had not, as he later said, brought a single farthing.

The only thing he brought in his baggage was the spirit of revolution. It would not survive long. He took office as provisional president at Nanking on January 1, 1912. He served until February 16, 1912, forty-seven days. Even before his election he had promised to make way for the northern warlord, the former War Minister of the Ching regime, Yuan Shih-kai, who now presented himself as the angel of republicanism.

The Revolution became a travesty. Dr. Sun and his forces had driven the Manchus from the throne but they had failed in almost everything else. Yuan Shih-kai made Dr. Sun Director of Railroads and embarked on a campaign to have himself crowned Emperor. The Republic was a republic in name only. Dr. Sun's followers won a sweeping victory in the new parliament, but as the historian C. P. Fitzgerald has noted, they spent most of their time appropriating money for their own use. "Truly 'a monkey dressed up in the robes of the Duke of Chou,' " said Fitzgerald, citing from the Chinese classic *The Monkey King*. Yuan soon sent parliament packing. Sun's first triumph had turned to ashes. China had not yet escaped from the blind alley. As Dr. Sun said bitterly, "Without revolutionary reconstruction what's the use of a revolutionary presidency?" Among the great powers, only the United States seemed interested in the new Chinese Republic. The British helped Yuan to sabotage it.

Dr. Sun fled to Japan. There was nothing for it: he would have to launch his battle for a new China all over again. Soong Ai-ling, the eldest daughter of one of Sun's staunchest supporters, Charles Jones ("Charlie") Soong, had been serving Dr. Sun as his secretary. Now she was about to marry H. H. Kung, an emerging figure in Chinese finance. She suggested that her sister Soong Ching-ling might take her place as secretary. Ching-ling had been studying in America and graduated from Wesleyan College in Georgia. Dr. Sun agreed, and in 1914 the brilliant and beautiful young English-speaking Chinese woman arrived in Tokyo. On October 25, 1915, Dr. Sun, long separated and newly divorced from his first wife, married Soong Ching-ling. He was forty-nine. She was twenty-three. Tongues never ceased to wag among Methodist Chinese.

# ★ 4 ★

## THE STUDENTS RISE

**J**UST BEFORE NOON ON SUNDAY, May 4, 1919, detachments of Chinese students in neat formations, each from one of thirteen colleges in Peking, began to march into the large square in front of the Tien an Men to the Forbidden City. The last to arrive was the detachment from Peking University, which had organized the demonstration. It had been delayed because government officials were trying to persuade the students not to come out.

By 1:30 P.M. the delegations, three thousand students in all, mostly in Chinese traditional robes but some in Western dress, were standing quietly in place. They listened patiently while General Li Chang-tai, the Peking commander, spoke, urging them to go back to their schools; then they went ahead with their meeting.

They carried five huge blue-and-white national flags and scores of placards, scrolls, posters and white flags with inscriptions denouncing officials who had yielded to the infamous Japanese Twenty-one Demands and to the action of the Versailles Peace Conference that had confirmed Japan's occupation of the Shantung peninsula, formerly a German concession.

The slogans heralded:

Refuse to sign the peace treaty.

China belongs to the Chinese.

Down with the traitors.

The names of Tsao Ju-lin, Lu Tsung-yu and Chang Tsung-hsiang [officials associated with the concessions to the Japanese] will stink a thousand years.

Boycott Japanese goods.

The students adopted a resolution:

"Today we swear two solemn oaths with our fellow countrymen: One, China's territory may be conquered but it cannot be given away; two, the Chinese people may be massacred but they will not surrender.

"Our country is about to be annihilated. Up, brothers!"

The students marched through the streets of Peking, quiet and orderly. Spectators stood silently, weeping. Westerners cheered. Some waved their hats. The students distributed leaflets as they passed. Police did not interfere. The demonstrators marched to the Legation Quarter; they were not admitted, but four were permitted to go to the American legation, where they hoped to meet with the American minister, Paul Reinsch. He was absent but he later reported: "Their patriotic fervour had been brought to the boiling point by the first inkling of the Paris decision on Shantung. The first impulse of the students was to see the American minister. . . ."

The march continued through the heart of Peking until it reached the house of Tsao Ju-lin, Minister of Communications, who was regarded as the worst of the "traitors." The students broke into the house, smashed the furniture and set fire to it. They found Chang Tsung-hsiang, the Chinese minister to Japan, in the house and beat him badly. Tsao was not present, having escaped in disguise.

John Dewey arrived in Peking just in time to see the May Fourth demonstration. His first impression was that it was "a college boys' roughhouse." A few weeks later, in a letter home, he admitted he had been mistaken. "To think of kids in our country from fourteen on, taking the lead in starting a big cleanup reform political movement and shaming merchants and professional men into joining them—this is sure some country!"

Dewey stayed in China for nearly two years, lecturing at Peking University. His pragmatic reformist thought was to play an important role in the evolution of China's politics.

★

**N**ever in the history of China had an event like May Fourth occurred. Its impact was enormous. Agitation spread from city to city. The Chinese took special pride in their young people. They had galvanized the nation in patriotic fervor directed against the government, against Japan, against the Allies (in particular against President Wilson, whose Fourteen Points and talk of establishing democracy in the world had persuaded many Chinese to believe that Versailles would right the wrongs the great powers had inflicted on China).

At a stroke China was transformed. Many Chinese came to consider May Fourth the most important single event in their century of shame, the period from the 1840s to the 1940s, the catalytic act that set China on the painful upward climb from the abyss of humiliation into the new nationhood of the People's Republic and Mao Tse-tung which would occur thirty years later, on October 1, 1949.

Everything that happened after May 4, 1919, was different from everything that happened before. So the Chinese felt; so many still feel.

Of course it was not so simple as that. The decisions of the students in their excited meetings in the first days of May, their united action, their slogans, the response of the authorities who made only *pro forma* efforts to halt them, the total sympathy of Chinese and foreign onlookers, the lightning spread of the movement to every corner of China, the swift action of the government to reject the Treaty of Versailles and dismiss the officials blamed for the submission to Japan's demands, the abandonment of naïve hopes based on the idealistic words of Woodrow Wilson, the fierce determination of young China to take the fate of the country into their hands—all this could not have been the product of a few hours of talk or a few days of organization, or even a response to one single action such as Japan's Twenty-one Demands or Wilson's repudiation of his Fourteen Points.

The mood of China was epitomized on the evening of May 3 by a student who told his comrades that if they did not agree to march on the morrow he would, then and there, kill himself in their presence.

Nor had May Fourth much connection with the earlier generations of rebels, the Taipings, the misguided and misused Boxers, or even with Dr. Sun Yat-sen, his Three People's Principles and his concentration on rather crude and ineffective military plots.

May Fourth was different in dimension, in depth and in impact.

If it was true, as most historians conceded, that from 1911 onward China steadily descended into anarchy, an era of warlords and spreading chaos, it was also true that the downfall of the Manchus in 1911 had, in effect, ushered in a period of extraordinary revolutionary gestation. No longer was it a matter of Dr. Sun and a handful of émigré Chinese agitating overseas

Chinese communities and plotting with small contingents of quasi-Westernized Chinese, largely centered around Canton, to overthrow the Empress Dowager. Now it was young China bursting every bond, striving to find a philosophical and ideological basis on which to reestablish their country.

Frenziedly, the young people of China studied foreign languages—English, German, French, Japanese—hunting for the key to the new way. They plunged into Ibsen, Tolstoy, Dickens, Shaw, Kropotkin, Tagore, Maupassant, John Dewey, the Russian Narodniks, the Anarchists, Bakunin, Bertrand Russell, Marx, Engels and, with the dramatic events of the Bolshevik Revolution in Russia, Lenin and Trotsky.

They did not care where they found their ideas. They grasped the newly printed, newly translated books and journals before the ink was dry on the pages.

It was, as many came to realize, China's renaissance. The country had never seen anything like it. For ten centuries the bound feet of China's women had been symbolic of unchanging moral and aesthetic values. Now, in a few years, the feet of the women and the minds of everyone were being unbound.

The renaissance brought into being a whole new language. Under the leadership of the brilliant poet and philosopher Hu Shih the classical language, which had been the medium of China's art and literature for two millennia or three, was abandoned for the vulgate, the simple language of the streets and the peasants. Hu Shih returned to China from study in the United States at Cornell and Columbia and proclaimed death to the classical language. Henceforth he would write his poems only in the vulgar tongue. He placed himself at the head of the New Culture Movement, identifying a revolution in art with the revolution in China's politics. New forms, new shapes, new images, new concepts, new words. It was, in a sense, not unlike the revolution in art and culture that burst forth in Russia in the decades preceding 1917. The magazine *La Jeunesse* became spokesman for the new world, the most exciting journal ever published on Chinese soil. Young Chinese could not wait to read it, issue by issue. They lined up at the print shop to receive copies fresh from the press. Students at Peking University—Peita, as they called it—founded a magazine called *Renaissance*, published solely in the vernacular. It was, as Hu Shih said, as though all culture in the West had until 1916 been written in Latin; then, at a single turn, writers began to employ English, French, German, Italian, the spoken word of the people.

Overnight there were new gods, new leaders. Hu Shih, an anti-Confucian pragmatist, a liberal, the prophet of change but of controlled change, rational change, was one. Ultimately he would put his skills and his philosophy to work in the government of Chiang Kai-shek, notably as China's ambassador to the United States. Another leader was Chen Tu-hsiu, editor of *La Jeunesse*. He offered young China the slogan "Democracy and Science," and backed representative and democratic government, a government of constitutional law. He opposed the use of force to impose a doctrine on the people. He believed in freedom of speech, freedom of political choice, freedom of opinion, individuality, equal rights for men and women, and an end to Confucianism, which he said was based on submission and a rigid allocation of roles in society. His views were almost indistinguishable from those of contemporary liberal Americans, dedicated to the Bill of Rights, social justice and the democratic process. Within two years Chen Tu-hsiu was to become a founding member of the Chinese Communist Party. As he once said, as a child he had been very stubborn. He had been whipped by his father and flogged by his teachers, but "no matter how hard I was whipped I never uttered a single cry."

Li Ta-chao was the son of poor peasants in Hopeh Province. He was the man who introduced Marx and Engels to China's youth. Li managed to make his way to Japan shortly before World War I and studied at Waseda University. He came back to China in 1916 and plunged into the New Culture Movement, often writing for *La Jeunesse*. In 1918 he was appointed librarian and professor of history at Peking University. Immediately his radical thought attracted the students. He formed a Marxist Research Society and edited a special issue of *La Jeunesse* on Marxism which appeared, coincidentally, in May 1919, the month of the extraordinary May Fourth events. Li's approach to Marxism was eclectic. He put enormous emphasis on the role of the young, supported the democratic process, opposed the forcible imposition of doctrine from above, favored a concept of government that drew on the principles of Woodrow Wilson and John Stuart Mill. He felt that the ideas of Marx must be revised to meet the reality of contemporary conditions and saw the peasantry which constituted 90 percent (or more) of China's population as the major element in China's revolution. He urged young Chinese intellectuals to "go to the people," in the spirit of Russia's nineteenth-century Narodniks. His views had a profound influence on his assistant at Peking University, a young man of well-to-do peasant origin named Mao Tse-tung. Li became a founding member of the Chinese Communist Party. On April 28, 1927, he was strangled to death by Chang Tso-lin, the North Chinese warlord.

Lu Hsun was the laureate of the May Fourth Movement and of the Chinese literary revolution. He was thirty-eight at the time of May Fourth, son of a prosperous Yangtze family. He had gone to Japan in 1902 to study medicine. There he became a writer and a strong supporter of the common language, which he adopted as the language of his satires. His "Diary of a Madman" provided a metaphor of the Chinese nation. His "True Story of Ah Q," the tragic tale of a country bumpkin, is the most famous story of contemporary Chinese literature. Lu Hsun was a democrat and a radical driven to the left by the banality of his country, a passionate opponent of Confucianism, a pessimist in many ways but a fervent believer in change and in the necessity for radical intellectuals to bond themselves with the Chinese masses. No one was more aroused than Lu Hsun by May Fourth, by the stunning example of the Russian Revolution. Although the Chinese had only a peripheral contact with Russia, they learned, said Lu, "that there were two classes in the world. At the time it was a discovery no less momentous than the discovery of fire."

The question that Lu Hsun posed to young China was simple: "Vast territory, abundant resources, and a great population—with such excellent material are we able only to go round and round in circles?"

One man of the future was not present for May Fourth. This was Mao Tse-tung. He had given up his post as assistant to the librarian Li Ta-chao and had abandoned Peking. He started out on a lazy, wandering journey which took him to the traditional shrines of Confucius, the philosopher's grave in Shantung Province, the heights of the sacred mount Tai, the birthplace of Mencius, Suchow, which is the scene of the classic *Romance of the Three Kingdoms*, and China's ancient southern capital, Nanking. Eventually he arrived in Shanghai in time to see a group of friends off for Europe, a work-study group going to France. He had been a member of the group himself, but changed his mind, perhaps because he had trouble learning French. (At about the same time, Chou En-lai, whose name later would be so intimately associated with that of Mao, took off from Tientsin on a similar educational mission to Europe.) After Mao's friends sailed, he borrowed some money and pushed on back to Chang-sha in his native Hunan, where he arrived as the great May Fourth demonstration occurred in Peking.

Mao Tse-tung was twenty-six years old. His name was unknown outside a small circle of students and educators in Chang-sha and an even smaller group in Peking. It was not the first and would not be the last time that Mao would be found striking out in one direction while the other leaders of China in revolution were confidently moving in another.

The May Fourth movement more or less passed Dr. Sun by. After the sudden and unexpected death of Yuan Shih-kai in 1916, Dr. Sun had made a comeback, participating in the establishment of a revolutionary South Chinese government at Canton. But the experiment had been brief, and he had been compelled to flee to Shanghai. There he busied himself reconstructing the rules of his party, giving it stricter discipline and more central control, renaming it the Kuomintang, the Nationalist Party, plotting and seeking allies in hopes of winning his way back to Canton. Although his position in Shanghai was precarious, Dr. Sun had sent a telegram of congratulations to Lenin on the October 1917 Revolution on behalf of the "South Chinese Parliament." He sent it via Chinese overseas residents in Canada, and it did not reach Moscow until the late spring of 1918. Lenin replied to Dr. Sun with a cordial response through Foreign Minister Chicherin on August 1, 1918; neither Lenin nor Dr. Sun held a very secure position at the time.

About a year after May Fourth, in April or May 1920, Grigorii Naumovich Voitinsky and an overseas Chinese named Yang Wing-chai arrived in China. They had been directed by the Third Communist International in Moscow, the Comintern, to make contact with Communists in China. They had no idea whether there were, in fact, any Communists in China, or of where to find them. They went first to Peking and then to Shanghai. These meetings bore no immediate fruit, but in July 1921 the Communist Party of China was founded at a series of meetings held first in the Boai girls' school in the French Concession of Shanghai and then on an excursion boat on South Lake, halfway between Shanghai and Hangchow. There were thirteen party members present, representing a total membership of fifty-seven in China (there were more members in Europe, particularly in France and Germany, and in Paris in 1924 a founding meeting was held of overseas Chinese at which Chou En-lai and Chu Teh joined the movement).

The founding meeting at Boai girls' school was not an auspicious one. Neither of the two men who had emerged as the pillars of the tiny movement, Li Ta-chao, the Peking University librarian, and Chen Tu-hsiu, the Peking University literature professor, was able to be present. However, Hendricus Sneevliet, who called himself Maring, a Dutch representative of the Comintern, was on hand to guide the proceedings.

Of the thirteen young men who gathered in the girls' school and then on the excursion boat (the site was changed because secret-police agents had been seen in the vicinity of the school) only one bore a name that would later be known beyond the borders of his own country. This was Mao Tse-tung, who, at twenty-seven, was a bit older than most of his comrades. Not one of the founders was a worker or a proletarian. All, like Mao, were intellectuals, mostly students from middle-class families. Mao was from the countryside but he was no ordinary peasant. His father had been an aggressive, upwardly mobile farm owner, a grasping, tight-fisted man of the type the Russians called a *kulak*—the word literally means "fist." Mao's father had pulled himself up by hard work, sharp practice and good luck. He had steadily increased his landholdings, had moved into the buying and selling of grain, lending money to poor peasants at usurious rates and taking advantage of his neighbor's bad luck to acquire land. Mao was as stiff-necked as his father. From early childhood he was at odds with his parent, and when he had a chance he broke away from home, borrowing money from neighbors to get himself into school, the Tungshun primary school. Mao paid his father twelve dollars a year for the loss of his labor.

The Tungshun primary school was fifteen miles up the road from the sprawling, almost luxurious (in country terms) house where Mao grew up at Shao Shan. There he borrowed a book from a schoolmate called *Heroes and Great Men of the World* and for the first time heard of world figures like George Washington, Benjamin Franklin, Napoleon, Peter the Great, Gladstone, Garibaldi, Montesquieu and Lincoln. His favorites were Washington and Lincoln, because they had freed their country from foreign domination and built it to united nationhood.

"I read a biography of Franklin," Mao once told his party associates. "He came from a poor family, afterward he became a writer, and also conducted experiments on electricity. He talked about man being a tool-using animal."

"We need men like these," Emi Siao, a classmate and neighbor of Mao's, recalled him saying.

Years later Mao told Edgar Snow: "I first heard of America in an article which told of the American Revolution and contained a sentence like this: 'After eight years of difficult war Washington won a victory and built up a nation.' "

That declaration could serve as a metaphor of Mao's life.

After a year's study—a gawky scarecrow of an eighteen-year-old, head-and-shoulders taller than his classmates, garbed in hand-me-downs, compelled to go back to his farm for a pair of homemade leather shoes when his sandals wore out, chronically short of money—Mao was ready to go on to Chang-sha, the provincial capital. Mao's head was always in a book, usually classic Chinese tales of adventure, the famous *Shui Hu Chuan* ("Water Margin"), the tale of the 108 bandits known in the West as *All Men Are Brothers; The Romance of the Three Kingdoms;* and *Hsi Yu Chi* ("Travels to the West"). He read and reread Chinese stories of adventure, war and fighting until he could repeat the tales word for word. To the end of his life he would delight in Chinese legends, reading the books by the hour and adorning his speeches with homilies from the narratives; indeed, he culled his strategy and tactics in battle from the legendary heroes of China's feudal ages. He was, it may be said, far more familiar with these stories than with the works of Marx and Engels, a fact not infrequently cast up at him by Soviet polemicists after the breach between the Communist regimes of Russia and China.

In Chang-sha, forty miles distant from his birthplace, Mao was to see his first newspaper, a Sun Yat-sen organ called *Strength of the People,* and there he would fall under the influence of a progressive professor, Yang Chang-chi, who was to play a role in Mao's life and in the revolutionary movement. It was 1911, the year of China's revolution, the downfall of the Manchus, the Canton uprising and the "Seventy-two Martyrs." Mao wrote a declaration and posted it on the school bulletin board, calling for Dr. Sun to return to China and become president of a coalition government. Mao later was to describe his philosophy as a mixture of liberalism, democracy, reformism and utopian socialism. "I had somewhat vague passions about nineteenth-century democracy, utopianism and old-fashioned liberalism," he recalled, "and I was definitely anti-militarist and anti-imperialist." He wrote a twelve-thousand-word essay on the obscure neo-Kantian philosopher F. Paulsen and became an ardent physical culturist, following the precepts of Professor Yang Chang-chi, who possessed a stern passion for cold baths, no breakfast and long hikes. Mao climbed hills, plunged into icy streams and slept in unheated rooms or corridors. He took "rain" showers and "wind" baths. He shouted poems into the wind to improve his lungs and speaking ability. Mao's ardor for body training, as he called it, resembled, detail for detail, the fitness program followed by Lenin in his adolescent years in Russia three decades earlier. Whether aware of it or not, Mao and Lenin were conditioned by the Victorian ethic of puritanistic English gentry.

"To struggle against heaven," wrote Mao at this period, "what infinite joy! To struggle against earth, what infinite joy! To struggle against man what infinite joy!" Later Mao recalled thinking that if he only kept himself fit he could live for two hundred years.

Perhaps it was natural that Mao's first published work would be entitled "A Study of Physical Culture." It was signed with the *nom de plume* "Mr. 28 Strokes." Twenty-eight brush strokes were required to write the name Mao Tse-tung. It was a signature Mao would employ not infrequently in his life.

When revolution came to Chang-sha in 1911, Mao was confused. He wanted to participate in the new order but he didn't quite know what to do. He was still very much a backcountry boy. He wound up enlisting in the army for a few months, thinking the army would have a role in the Revolution. Since it didn't, he got out. His army pay of seven dollars a month was spent entirely on newspapers and books. When he got out of the army he was still uncertain what to do. He applied for admission to half a dozen schools, including a police academy, one where they taught soap-making, and a business school for which his father advanced tuition money, thinking Mao might make a good bookkeeper on the farm. But Mao soon dropped out and began spending his time in the Chang-sha library reading Adam Smith's *Wealth of Nations*, Darwin's *Origin of Species*, John Stuart Mill on ethics, Rousseau, Montesquieu, Spencer and Huxley and studying the geography of Europe and America.

By chance he was admitted to Chang-sha's First Normal School, one of the best, most progressive educational institutions in China. It was here that he fell under the influence of Professor Yang, and met Professor Yang's serious, pale, brilliant daughter, who would become his wife. He also met the Siao brothers, Emi Siao (Emi made up his first name after going to Moscow to study) and Siao Yu, who was to be Mao's closest school friend and political associate for several years.

From books written by the Siao brothers—Emi became a Soviet Communist, and Yu became a staunch anti-Communist—an extraordinary, intimate picture of Mao's early life can be drawn. The Siao brothers came from Siangsiang, less than twenty miles from Mao's home at Shao Shan.

★

**P**rofessor Yang had a formidable reputation. He was called the "Confucius of Chang-sha" and in 1918 he was appointed to the Peking University, a great honor. By this time Mao had become a favored student—one of his best, Yang believed. Once Mao wrote a paper called "A Discourse on the Force of the Mind." Professor Yang liked it so much he gave Mao a grade of "100 plus 5." Evenings Mao and two or three other students spent at Professor Yang's house, listening to him talk and engaging in discussions on the future of China. Siao Yu recalled that Professor Yang rated Siao number one among his students and Mao number three.

Siao was a class or two ahead of Mao, but the two quickly became close comrades, spending night after night in discussions, sometimes about brushing teeth (Mao never brushed his teeth; in later life they would be black and diseased but even then he was reluctant to see a dentist);

sometimes about neatness (Mao was very disorderly; Siao was a model of order); sometimes about cleanliness (Mao took lots of cold plunges but didn't bother to wash, and often, Siao recorded, his body and clothes were so dirty Siao was reluctant to sleep on the same *kang*, or brick-heated bed, with him). Mao chided Siao for spending so much time taking baths. Siao rejoined that Mao "smelled awfully sweaty." Siao recalled asking Mao, "If a great hero does not clean and sweep out his own room how can he possibly think he is capable of cleaning up the universe?"

"A great hero," Mao rejoined, "who thinks about cleaning up the universe has no time to think about sweeping rooms."

They talked of more important matters, of course. They spoke of their teachers, of discipline, of the school curriculum (Mao was much interested in military training; Siao was not); about foreign countries, such as Germany and the United States; classical Chinese literature; calligraphy (Siao claimed to be far more proficient than Mao). When Siao graduated he went to work as a teacher and Mao displayed enormous interest in what it was like to teach—a foreshadowing of his own career.

In the summer of 1917 Siao and Mao embarked on an adventure—a begging trip which was to take them through five counties. This experience, which remained bright in the memory of each man through his whole life, gave Mao his first deep insight into the life of ordinary people and peasants; it also provided a pattern for later and more serious inquiries into peasant life that he undertook at a time when his comrades in the Communist Party had fixed their attention on the urban proletariat.

The begging trip was Siao's idea. He had tried begging twice before, once for a day and once for three days, wandering into the countryside without money, living by his wits and by the charity of the people. Begging, as Siao noted, has traditionally been considered an honorable profession in China rather than a mark of poverty or disrepute, as in the West.

Mao could not believe Siao was serious until he told of his earlier begging expeditions. Then Mao decided to accompany him. Years later he recalled his trip with warmth, telling Edgar Snow that everywhere they went they had been kindly treated by the peasants and that they spent not a single copper.

Mao wore old white shorts and tunic and carried a shabby umbrella and a bundle, wrapped in cotton cloth, consisting of a change of clothes, a towel, a notebook, writing brush and ink box. Siao carried the same kind of bundle but included a rhyming dictionary and some paper. Neither took a cent. They spent six weeks in the countryside, walking three hundred miles, begging their meals from peasants—sometimes good meals, sometimes poor—spending nights where they might, having long conversations with peasants, occasionally looking up friends, or being given money to eat in wayside taverns. Once they encountered a tiger at night (Mao slept right through the episode) and once they met a beautiful young woman who told their fortunes. She predicted that Mao might become a great officer, a prime minister or a great bandit chief. He was, she said, very audacious and had great ambition but no sentiment.

"You could kill ten thousand or even a hundred thousand people without turning a single hair," Siao remembered her saying. "But you are very patient. If you have not been killed by your enemies when you are thirty-five you can consider yourself safe by the time you reach fifty and you will be luckier day by day. Around fifty-five you will be still more fortunate. You will have at least six wives but not many children. I see that you and your family do not get along well together."

*(Text continues on page 65.)*

林文忠公像

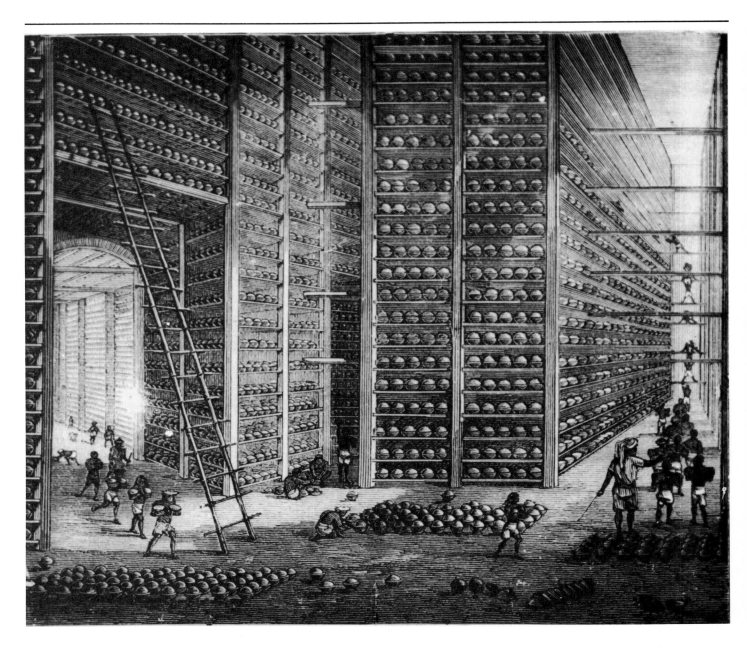

*Overleaf:*
Lin-Tse-hsu was called "Lin Blue Sky" for his honesty and incorruptibility. Lin sought unsuccessfully to halt the British opium trade through Canton in 1839, touching off the so-called Opium War. MRV

An Indian opium factory catering to the China trade in the mid-nineteenth century. The balls of opium await packing for shipment to China. NYL

Upper-class opium den, Canton, turn of the century. LC

English boats smuggling opium in Canton harbor, 1839. MIL

Daumier's comment on China after the Perry expedition to Japan: "Chinese admire a quadruped from France and a biped from the same country" (May 13, 1854). LC

Chinese scholars, late Ching dynasty, turn of the century. LC

An American cartoon warns Chinese Boxers that Uncle Sam will teach them a lesson. BET

*Opposite:*
A Japanese cruiser sinks Russian warships, 1904. The Japanese victory encouraged China's revolutionaries by demonstrating the ability of an Asian state to defeat a European power. LC

The British, French, Russians and Germans carve up China— a turn-of-the-century French cartoon. BN

U.S. and other foreign troops witnessing executions of Boxers in Peking, 1900. MIL

Boxers, captured during the outbreak of 1900, awaiting execution. MRV

American and Japanese troops occupying the Taku forts, which protected approaches to Peking, 1900. MRV

Imperial Russian troops take over China's Liaotung area after the czarist treaties of the mid-1890s. MRV

Tzu Hsi (Empress Dowager from 1861 to her death in 1908) in a sedan chair, surrounded by eunuchs. FRE

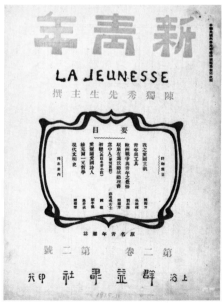

*La Jeunesse*, edited by Chen Tu-hsiu, was the organ of China's radical and revolutionary youth after World War I. MIL

Teng En-ming, a founding member of the Communist Party from Sian. MIL

Li Ta-chao, Peking University librarian, early patron of Mao Tse-tung and a founder of Chinese Communist Party. MIL

Tsai Ho-sen, Communist Party leader in Chang-sha, close friend of Mao, killed by the Kuomintang. MIL

Ho Shu-heng, a founding member of the Chinese Communist Party. MIL

Chen Tu-hsiu, editor of *La Jeunesse* and a founding member of the Chinese Communist Party. MIL

A workers' group at the An-yang coal mines, near Chang-sha, led by Li Li-san (second row, second from right), an early Communist Party leader. Mao Tse-tung and Liu Shao-chi also aided in organizing the An-yang mines. MRV

*Opposite:*
Lu Hsun, famous Chinese writer, idol of the young students of the May Fourth Movement. LU

鲁迅　一九三〇年九月
二十五日五十岁于上海

Marshal Vasily Blyukher, chief Russian military adviser to Dr. Sun Yat-sen and Chiang Kai-shek.

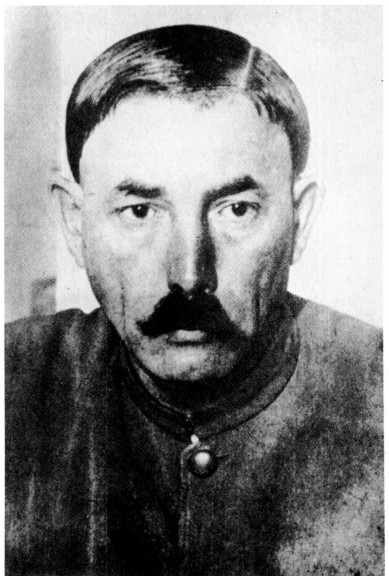

Mikhail Borodin, Soviet adviser to Dr. Sun Yat-sen in Canton. He was compelled to flee for his life when Chiang Kai-shek turned on his Communist supporters in 1927.

Workers' heads, chopped off in executions ordered by Chiang Kai-shek, displayed in baskets on the main Shanghai thoroughfares, April 1927. MRV

Mao thought his fortune was a big joke. So did Siao.

A flood on the Yangtze brought the adventure to an end. They came back to Chang-sha by boat. Neither Siao nor Mao could swim. Not until 1954 would Mao learn to swim—going every evening to a pool at Tsinghua University with his bag, changing his clothes. In three months he became a good swimmer. In 1966 he plunged into the Yangtze at Wuhan and took a swim that shook the world that was China.

Both Siao and Mao kept diaries of their begging trip. Neither diary has survived, apparently. They had a sidewalk photographer take their picture when they got back to Chang-sha. Siao left his in his family's house in Hunan. Years later, when the house was confiscated by the Communists, the photograph vanished, presumably unrecognized by Mao's adherents.

Young China was struggling in every way to break the tentacles of the Great Powers, which were crushing the life from their country, and at the same time they had excitedly begun to ransack the trove of Western knowledge and experience. Almost every boat leaving China carried in the steerage a party of students bound for France or Germany or Belgium, anywhere that Western knowledge might be available.

In July 1918 a Chang-sha group headed by Siao and Mao made their way to Peking to seek the assistance of Professor Yang Chang-chi in getting to Europe. A student work program had gotten under way in which Chinese students shipped to Europe at the lowest fares (thirty dollars for "fourth" class), then divided their time between working, often as common laborers, and studying in the universities. Many men whose names were later famous in the Chinese Revolution—Chou En-lai, Chen Yi, Li Li-san and others—entered this program.

For a while Professor Yang permitted Mao, Siao and two other friends to live in a shed at the back of his house. A bit later they rented rooms in the Three Eyes Well hutung near the university. There were eight students, with a single *kang* to sleep on and one overcoat among the group. They wore it successively when they went out in winter cold. When Mao wanted to turn over in bed, as he recalled later, he had to warn the students on either side of him.

Peking was not all politics. Mao liked to wander in the old city, strolling through the grounds of the old Imperial Palace. "I saw the early northern spring," he told Edgar Snow. "I saw the white plum blossoms flower while the ice was still solid over the North Sea." He watched the ice crystals on the willows and formed poems in his mind, recalling the words of a Tung-dynasty poet, Tsen Tsan, who had spoken of ice-covered trees that looked like ten thousand peach trees blooming.

The job Mao got in the Peking University library was a menial position checking out newspapers and dusting books. It paid eight dollars a month, and later Mao felt that no one had noticed him, not even Li Ta-chao, though this seems doubtful. He had the highest recommendations from Professor Yang and was one of a lively and increasingly prominent Hunan student group. Mao joined the Philosophical Society and the Journalism Society, was introduced to leading young radicals by Professor Yang and began to fall in love with Yang Kai-hui, Yang's daughter, a very quiet, serious-minded, pale girl with an excellent education, a fine mind and as strong an interest in China's future and revolution as Mao was developing. Mao had been married at the age of fourteen by his parents, to a young woman of twenty, a marriage designed to join the two family economies, but the marriage was never consummated,

CHINA
100 Years
of
Revolution

65

nor did the pair ever live together. Mao's interest in Kai-hui was another thing. She was eight years younger than he. They talked and walked together.

When Mao returned to Peking in the winter of 1919–1920, having missed the May Fourth excitement, Professor Yang was dead. Mao and Kai-hui ignored the old funeral rituals. They went for pony rides in the Western hills, and less than a month after Professor Yang's death they embarked on a trial marriage, a very radical act. Within a year their first child was born. The formal marriage occurred sometime in 1920 in Chang-sha. Fifteen years later, in talking to Edgar Snow, Mao was unable to recall the date.

The marriage was a symbol of the times: not an arranged marriage, but a love match, a deliberate and open defiance of the old customs of China by two young people who represented the spirit of new China, the tall lanky middle-peasant boy who had become a tough, determined intellectual, and the slight, brilliant, totally dedicated young woman, with unbound feet and unbound mind, whose life would be sacrificed to the movement ten years later when she was captured in Chang-sha in 1930 and brutally slaughtered by an execution squad of Chiang Kai-shek's Nationalist Army.

Now, like many young Chinese radicals, Mao for the first time was reading Karl Marx, the *Communist Manifesto*; as he later recalled, "Three books especially deeply carved my mind and built up in me a faith in Marxism." These were the *Manifesto*, a book by Karl Kautsky whose name he had forgotten, and a cheap potboiler by a man named Thomas Kirkup called *A History of Socialism*. From this time forward Mao called himself a Marxist, although he had only a vague notion of what Marxism was. He was not unlike the young Americans of the 1960s who proclaimed themselves "Maoists," then added that they had not read Mao but were "emotional" Maoists. Mao now had, as Ross Terrill remarked, "the faith."

Up to this point his ideas had been a mixture of anarchism, democracy and idealism. He continued to be a strong supporter of America, the Monroe Doctrine and the Open Door policy even after he had begun to call himself a Marxist, even after he had gone to Shanghai and talked with Chen Tu-hsiu, founder-to-be of the Communist Party.

And although Mao now considered himself a Marxist, present-day Marxists would have considered his ideas very far from any "Communist Party line." Of course, at this point there was still no Communist Party in China. Anarchism was and would be for a considerable time a powerful and attractive idea for young Chinese, and at least as strong an influence among them as Marxism. In fact, few of them drew a distinction. Hard and fast lines were slow to emerge. There was too little knowledge in China of Marxism. Supposedly, it was being put into practice in the Soviet Union, but even there Lenin's ideas were not entirely clear, and he was far from being the only spokesman in the new revolutionary Russian government.

Chinese students were beginning to return from Europe. Some of the two hundred thousand or more Chinese who had been enlisted as a labor corps for work behind the front in France had begun to come back, many of them indoctrinated with new ideas for change stemming from Marxist and anarchist propaganda.

A pool of activists and potential activists—with ideas that ranged far beyond mere opposition to the old regime, to international predatory powers, to warlordism, to simple nationalist solutions—was beginning to form in Peking, in Shanghai, in Hong Kong and Canton and other Chinese centers.

★

**D**r. Sun Yat-sen no longer seemed at the heart of the Chinese revolutionary movement. He was spending most of his time in Shanghai and it was far from clear whether he would be able to regain power in Canton, which was beginning to be called China's "southern capital," reflecting the dissolution of the country into spheres dominated by warlords.

Then, late in 1920, the moment for which Sun Yat-sen had hoped arrived—the militarists in Canton fell out and Sun Yat-sen's supporters were victorious. Once again Dr. Sun returned to Canton. On December 8, 1920, he was able to form a new government with himself at its head. His forces took over Szechwan Province, and put Chungking under their rule, and with the reconvening of the 1913 parliament in Canton at the beginning of April Dr. Sun was formally named again President of China.

CHINA

100 Years

of

Revolution

## MOSCOW TAKES A HAND

**T**HE CHINESE COMMUNIST PARTY evolved on the narrowest possible basis. When Grigorii Voitinsky and his associate Yang Wing-chai arrived in China in 1920, they found less than a handful of Marxists or would-be Marxists including Li Ta-chao, the Peking University librarian whose philosophy contained liberal and democratic elements which would increasingly prove anathema to Moscow, and Professor Chen Tu-hsiu. Chen felt that Marxism must be adapted and revised to meet Chinese conditions which he saw as differing not only from those in Western Europe, upon which Marx founded his social outlook, but also from those on which Lenin and Trotsky based the Russian Revolution.

Chen moved to Shanghai about this time and thus became the key to Communist liaison there. For practical purposes, there were two small coves of Communism identified by Voitinsky, one in Peking and one in Shanghai, on which he urged the Comintern to rely in developing a Chinese Communist Party.

In fact, Voitinsky and the Comintern were engaged in a scouting expedition. Lenin had by no means decided what his China policy should be. He gave the Comintern mission sanction to form a Chinese Communist Party. But at the same time he was exchanging cordial greetings with Dr. Sun Yat-sen and seeking to establish diplomatic relations with the northern warlord government in Peking. In other words, Lenin was covering all his bets. He did not know much about China; he felt China could be important to Russia; a relationship with China would be helpful to his young and feeble Soviet state and he had no intention of foreclosing any prospects.

Lenin had another interest in China. The Bolsheviks had taken power in full expectation that they were part of a wave of revolution sweeping Europe. They felt it was accidental that the Revolution triumphed in Russia. According to the theories of Marx it should have occurred first in Germany, France or England. The Bolshevik hold on Russia was tenuous. They were engaged in a life-and-death fight against the Germans, the savage anti-Communist Whites and Russia's erstwhile allies, the English, the French, the Americans and the Japanese, who were fighting the Communists in a dozen places—the Far North, the Ukraine, the Volga, the Caucasus, Central Asia and Siberia. By 1921 it was evident to Lenin that his hopes for revolution in Europe, especially in Germany, had gone glimmering. The will-o'-the-wisp of revolution in distant China was thus psychologically appealing if of little practical significance. Lenin devoted great attention to propaganda about Asian revolution and was delighted with whatever he could find—whether it be Dr. Sun Yat-sen's Kuomintang or the Communist embryo nourished by Voitinsky.

No better sample of the material from which the Communist Party of China would be forged could be found than Mao Tse-tung, now living back in Chang-sha. There he devoted his time to setting up an educational society, writing newspaper articles (many of them favoring an independent Hunan and many favoring release of Chinese women from their traditional bondage) and, most important, to establishing a bookshop. He got the three rooms for his bookstore at a nominal rent from Yale-in-China, which was happy to assist a young Chinese who was working to eliminate illiteracy—as they thought. The store sold radical books, and soon Mao had branches in seven other towns. He sold Kirkup's *History of Socialism,* a pamphlet about Marx's *Das Kapital,* and left-liberal magazines like *La Jeunesse.* He taught in, and quickly became director of, the First Normal School, which he turned into a forcing bed for radical youth. Now that his father was dead—of typhoid fever in 1920—he enlisted his family in his endeavors. His brother Mao Tse-min enrolled in the normal school. His brother Mao Tse-tan went to a local high school and Mao Tse-hung, Mao's adopted sister, went to a normal school in Heng-yang.

Mao may have called himself a Marxist, but his program for an independent Hunan and, in general, for independence for each of China's provinces had no Marxist overtones. It expressed pure local chauvinism. He thought that independence of the provinces would be followed by national unification, "just like the road from division to unity followed by America and Germany."

★

In the spring of 1921 Siao Yu came back to Chang-sha. He and Mao embarked on a series of protracted conversations in which they sought to clarify and possibly unify their thought. To Siao it was clear that Mao had moved sharply in the direction of Marxism. His attention, Siao thought, was more and more centered on the Communist youth movement rather than the student study society in which both had collaborated earlier. Siao thought Mao had acquired a much stronger interest in the Russian Revolution and the example of the Russians—certainly a stronger attraction than he, Siao, possessed.

Siao had favored reform and gradualism. Mao disagreed. "If we want to bring reforms we must have a revolution. If we want the revolution to be successful the best thing we can do is to learn from Russia."

Mao felt this was the only path China could follow and strongly urged Siao to join with him. But Siao was antagonistic to the pressures that he felt Communism applied to people.

Mao rejoined: "In the final analysis political influence is quite simply the constant maintenance of pressure."

This took them into discussions of freedom and personal liberty. Mao denied that Communism would remove freedom of choice, but he conceded there would have to be laws, possibly even arbitrary laws. The individual, he said, must obey the state and must make sacrifices for the good of all.

Their philosophical disagreement widened but their discussions went on. Each had the same ultimate goal in mind—a unified China in which the rule of justice and humanity would be applied. Mao said that to change China it was necessary "to be hard on one's self and victimize part of the people." Siao disagreed with making part of the people pay the price for the betterment of the whole.

"Communism, in theory," Siao said, "is an excellent principle and it should certainly be put into practice. But this must take time."

To which Mao replied that he admired Siao's patience, "but I cannot wait even two years. I want us to achieve our goals tomorrow."

The discussions went on and on and finally Mao exclaimed, as Siao recalled, "What a pity that you disagree with the theory of Karl Marx."

Of course, neither Siao nor Mao had any idea of what Marx had actually believed about China. There were few areas about which Marx was more ignorant or more in the thrall of Mitteleuropa's bourgeois prejudice. In an analysis of China written in 1853 he said the Chinese were characterized "by overbearing prejudice, stupidity, learned ignorance and pedantic barbarism."

His principal interest in China was linked to an idea that disruption of the China market for European trade would touch off a general European economic crisis, which would promptly be followed by political revolutions on the Continent. As for revolution in China, he didn't give it a thought.

★

The talks between Mao and Siao were still in progress when Mao got an invitation to come to Shanghai for the founding meeting of the Chinese Communist Party. It was the spring of 1921 and Mao told Siao in confidence that he had been named a delegate from Chang-sha. He wanted Siao to join in the meetings. Siao agreed to go to Shanghai but not to attend the party conference.

"I'm not prepared to have any part in the formation of the Communist Party," Siao said. To which Mao replied: "If we work hard, in about thirty to fifty years the Communist Party may be able to rule China." (In fact, it would come to power in twenty-eight years.)

The two left Chang-sha and took the steamer up the river. They traveled together to Hankow, still arguing about Communism. Then they went separately to Shanghai, where they met again in mid-July in a house on Valon Street, in the French Concession. The party meetings were already under way. Each day Mao attended them; each night he and Siao continued their arguments. After a few days, the delegates, with Siao tagging along, moved to nearby South Lake. Mao and Siao took a room, again Mao urged Siao to join the talks, again Siao refused. The night after the final meeting, Siao and Mao argued under the mosquito net until almost dawn about the decision to form a Communist Party on the Russian model and "fight to the end." Siao urged Mao again not to follow the Russian path, to form a "free Communist Party," but Mao said, "Let's talk about that again in a thousand years."

The pair slept fitfully, got up early and took a train for Hangchow and the famous West Lake, one of China's most beautiful scenes, a favorite tourist spot. On the way they went on talking about Communism and spent most of their time, as Siao recalled, criticizing Chen Tu-hsiu. Both Siao and Mao thought he was too much of a scholar, too much of a bourgeois to lead a proper Communist Party. They favored Li Ta-chao, perhaps because they knew him better. But the Russians, it seemed, preferred Chen Tu-hsiu.

Mao became party secretary for Chang-sha but nothing much changed. He went on with his school, went on with his writing, used the school to train and bend students to the Communist movement, recruiting them for his organization. He was hardly strong in theory. His writings still leaned toward anarchism. He began to take an interest in the labor movement, particularly in the big coal mines in An-yang in eastern Hunan. He got some help in bringing revolutionary ideas to the An-yang workers—he was joined by Li Li-san and Liu Shao-chi, both important figures-to-be in the Communist Party but then, like Mao, young radicals just testing their wings. There were twelve thousand miners in An-yang. They worked a fifteen-hour day. Mao began to experiment in appealing to workers. He had never done this before. He used simple devices to gain their interest. On a blackboard he scrawled the character "I," part of the ideogram for "work." The top line was, he said, the heavens. The bottom was the earth. The worker was the pillar that held up the heavens. In Chang-sha Mao led a strike of six thousand construction workers and helped unionize typographers and textile workers. He conferred with Sneevliet in November 1921, probably over tactics in organizing the urban proletariat. Lenin was still playing the field, encouraging and following up whatever possibilities seemed to be open in China.

There was a continued whimsicality in Mao's relationship to Communism. He worked very much on his own and along lines he himself initiated. The party held its Second Congress in Shanghai in 1922. Mao was in Shanghai when the congress met but he did not attend. Years later he explained that he had forgotten the address of the meeting place. Not much of an excuse. Mao was militant but he was not disciplined. Nor would he ever be.

**D**r. Sun and the Soviet Union approached each other slowly and with considerable caution. Lenin had laid down as a foundation for Soviet policy toward China the abrogation of Russia's "unequal treaties," those imposed over the past century by the czarist government upon a weak Imperial China. The policy was enunciated first in a declaration by Lev Karakhan, Assistant Commissar of Foreign Affairs, on July 25, 1919, when he proclaimed that "All secret treaties made before the revolution with China, Japan or the allies are hereby abrogated," adding that "The Soviet government has renounced the conquests made by the czarist government which deprived China of Manchuria and other areas. . . . The Soviet government abolishes all special privileges and gives up all factories owned by Russian merchants on Chinese soil."

Karakhan renounced Soviet ownership of the Chinese Eastern Railroad (which was in the hands of the White Russians) and renounced Russia's share of the Boxer indemnity (also in the hands of the White Russians). He suggested negotiations with Peking regarding the annulment of the Treaty of 1896, which had granted Russia special rights in Manchuria, of the Peking protocol of 1901 on the same subject and of all agreements with Japan from 1907 through 1916 relative to China; that is, Russia would not only see that China got back rights that Moscow held but would also renounce its acquiescence in anything the Japanese had obtained.

The Karakhan declaration had a profound effect in China. It was seen by Dr. Sun and most Chinese as evidence of a genuine desire by Communist Russia (in contrast with the European Allies and the United States) to right the age-old wrongs done by the West to China.

Nevertheless, as the years went by, the Russians did not void *any* of their treaties with China. They did their best to hang on to the Chinese Eastern Railroad. At the end of World War II they reasserted the privileges they once possessed in Manchuria and took over many that had belonged to the Japanese. Even after the establishment of Communist rule under Mao Tse-tung in 1949, they hung on to most of their concessions and added new ones in China's northwest Sinkiang Province. All of these treaties and concessions finally became central to the blazing conflict between Soviet Russia and Communist China after 1960—all this lay in

CHINA
100 Years
of
Revolution
71

the future. The fact was that after the Karakhan declaration the Soviet Union appeared to most Chinese, and particularly to Dr. Sun, as an extraordinarily benevolent power, with a deep interest in promoting China's welfare and in warm, close relations.

The first direct conversations between Dr. Sun and a Soviet representative occurred in the autumn of 1920. The Comintern agent Voitinsky, after meeting with Li Ta-chao and Chen Tu-hsiu in search of Communist roots (or seedlings), met Dr. Sun, who was then in Shanghai, having been ousted from Canton. The Sun-Voitinsky meeting was exploratory on both sides, but it was followed by a letter from Soviet Foreign Minister Chicherin, which Sun received in June 1921, after having been elected President of South China at Canton.

Chicherin expressed confidence that close relations would be established between China and Russia and added: "Your country is now firmly advancing forward, your people are consciously carrying on the struggle against the oppressive regime of international imperialists. Trade relations between our countries should be quickly established. We hope that China will take the path of friendly relations with us."

Dr. Sun expressed to Chicherin the wish that he might personally maintain contact with him and his other friends in Russia. He wanted to learn from the Soviet Union, particularly about the organization of the Communist Soviets, or Councils, about the Red Army and about popular education.

He pointed out that Chicherin's letter took nine months to reach him and inquired whether any other letters might be en route. Mail service wasn't very good. He sent his reply by way of London, where he understood the Russians had a trade mission. Dr. Sun sent a delegate to an Eastern Peoples' Congress held in Moscow and Petrograd in January 1922, possibly as a result of a meeting with the Comintern representative Sneevliet in the summer of 1921 in Kweilin. Dr. Sun had been in that city preparing a military expedition to the north.

After the Congress finished its work, a young English-speaking Russian named S. A. Dalin, of the Far Eastern section of the Comintern, was directed to go to Canton and hold conversations with Dr. Sun. This was no easy matter. The Soviet Union had not yet been able to establish diplomatic relations with any of the Great Powers (this was one reason Lenin was eager to set up a connection with China), and making the trip from Moscow to Canton was difficult. Dalin took the Trans-Siberian across Russia, a journey of two weeks. He reached the border at Manchuria Station and from there went by the Chinese Eastern Railroad, still held by White Russians, to Harbin, where he took the South Manchurian Railroad, run by the Japanese, to Mukden. He went from Mukden to Peking by a railroad nominally Chinese but run by the English. Then he went by Chinese railroad to Shanghai. He took a boat from Shanghai to Swatow and went by foot into Kwangtung Province, where, on April 27, 1922, he caught the train for Canton. There he and Dr. Sun engaged in an extraordinary series of conversations that laid the basis for the ultimate collaboration of China and the Russians.

The two men met at least twice a week, speaking in English, with Chang Tai-lei (a Communist youth leader who was to be slaughtered at his post as Canton Commune commissar by Chiang Kai-shek's forces in 1927) as occasional translator. The talks went on until mid-June 1922, when a sudden uprising in Canton caused Dr. Sun to flee to Shanghai (Soong Ching-ling escaped to Amoy, then made her way to Shameen Island and later to Shanghai).

The conversations, in Dalin's memory, covered a panorama of subjects. Dr. Sun gave him a lengthy account of his revolutionary efforts and policies and questioned him on Soviet life and policy, particularly organizational and military issues.

When the Canton uprising of mid-June occurred, Dr. Sun took command of a gunboat and continued to fight for several days, carrying on a naval bombardment of his foes' headquarters. Through his Foreign Minister and close associate, Eugene Chen, he sent a series of messages to Dalin. He assured the young Russian that he was not giving up the fight, that if he lost hope of regaining power he would go to the Soviet Union but was confident he would come out on top. He described himself as "disillusioned with almost all that I had earlier believed." Now, he said, he was confident "that the one real and genuine friend of the Chinese Revolution is Soviet Russia."

So, said Dalin, Dr. Sun made the great turn in his thinking that opened the way for collaboration with Soviet Russia. Sun's final act before leaving Canton for Shanghai was to send through Eugene Chen a message scribbled on a piece of paper torn from a school notebook; in this message, he swore he would not give up the battle and asked that his friendly regards be given to Lenin. Dalin returned to Moscow and delivered the message.

Slowly the Russian position on China was beginning to take shape. Not all the activity, by any means, was centered in Canton. Since 1920 the Far Eastern Republic, a satellite of Moscow's which held an uncertain sway over eastern Siberia and the Maritime Province, had maintained a diplomatic mission in Peking, a foot in the door, as it were, for Moscow. The Far Eastern mission was held at arm's length by the northern warlord regime but finally, on September 20, 1920, Peking disaccredited the czarist embassy, opening the way for establishment of relations with the Communists. First Peking acknowledged the representatives of the Far Eastern Republic. The next step, obviously, was a tie with Moscow. This turned out to be difficult. The Russians sent a mission to Peking headed by the experienced diplomat Adolf Abramovich Joffe. Joffe arrived in Peking in August 1922. He had been one of the Bolshevik negotiators of the 1918 Brest Litovsk Treaty and in 1927 would commit suicide, leaving behind a bitter attack on Stalin as his political testament. But now, in 1922, he was on the full crest of his reputation as a top negotiator of the new "Red" diplomatic corps.

Joffe had important issues to discuss in Peking: the question of Mongolia, then as now effectively a Russian protectorate but then as now claimed by China as within her sphere of influence; the questions of Manchuria, the Japanese influence, control of ports and railroads and, not least of all, the "unequal treaties." There is no question but that Joffe was prepared to make great concessions in return for close Chinese friendship or an alliance directed against Japan.

But he was stonewalled by Wellington Koo, Peking's American-educated Foreign Minister. Koo insisted on settlement of all these issues before, not after, diplomatic recognition.

The talks came to nothing and sixty years later the unequal treaties that Lenin and Chicherin had grandiosely declared void are still in force, still on the agenda between Russia and China, the issue still unresolved, but now Moscow supports their legality like a rock and China denounces them as the scandal of the ages.

Balked in Peking, Joffe turned his eyes south to Shanghai. There Sun Yat-sen had never been busier. Sneevliet had again appeared on the scene and was meeting often with him. Sun was meeting equally often with fledgling members of the Communist Party, trying to nudge them toward negotiation and consolidation with the Kuomintang. Indeed, the question in generalized form had come up at the vaguely recollected Second Congress of the Chinese Communist Party which had been held, so it was said, in July 1922 (Soviet sources claim it was held in May), the one Mao did not attend because he had lost the address. The handful of Chinese Communists were left-oriented. They had little use for Dr. Sun. They did not see why hardly a year after the party's birth it had to be subordinated to a nationalist movement that they considered weak, corrupt and hardly revolutionary.

Nonetheless Sun had meetings with Li Ta-chao and Chen Tu-hsiu. Li criticized the Kuomintang, saying it was poorly organized and had no clear programs. Sun replied that it had 150,000 members and the Communists had only a handful. Li responded that most Kuomintang members were not revolutionaries, that the party was filled with old intelligentsia, officeholders, military men and ordinary politicians. Yet Li said he wished to enter the Kuomintang and, in due course, he was received by Dr. Sun as the first of the Communist enrollment.

Throughout the autumn, contacts between Sun and the Communists grew, constantly pushed by Sneevliet. In mid-November Joffe came to Shanghai and engaged Sun in lengthy discussions. The Soviet position in the Far East had been strengthened by Marshal Blyukher's defeat of the White Russian irregulars in eastern Siberia, and on October 25 Chicherin issued a new proclamation on the importance of friendship between Russia and China, stressing Russia's support of China's full economic and political independence. He pointed out that Russia was the only important power to support full independence for China and offered Russia's "genuine sympathy in the aim of the Chinese people to create a unified democratic China."

A joint communiqué was issued by Sun and Joffe on January 26, 1923, proclaiming Russia's support and sympathy in China's struggle for independence. In a private exchange Sun made clear he hoped and expected that Moscow would send him a political adviser accompanied by a military mission. "I hope he comes soon," Sun added. Joffe indicated that this would be done.

The communiqué had hardly been published when Dr. Sun regained control in Canton. The path was now open for an unprecedented collaboration of Chinese Nationalists, Chinese Communists and Russian advisers in the cause of the Chinese Revolution.

Unknown to Dr. Sun, to the Chinese Communists, to the Comintern representatives, a critical situation was developing in Moscow that would affect them all profoundly. Indeed, few outsiders in Moscow had much notion of it, and even within the intimate circle of Vladimir Lenin there was more ignorance than knowledge.

This event was an internal party split that deeply disturbed Lenin, himself semi-paralyzed by a series of strokes. A struggle for power had begun, pitting Leon Trotsky, then as widely known as Lenin, against Josef Stalin, a Georgian party member, almost unknown outside the inner Bolshevik circle.

Trotsky had come late to the Bolsheviks—not until after the February 1917 Revolution—but he had won Lenin's respect and admiration, and had played a leading role in the Revolution, particularly in organizing the Red Army. Everyone knew that Trotsky was the logical man to succeed Lenin. But this did not sit well with other ambitious and able Bolsheviks, men like Kamenev and Zinoviev, leaders of Moscow and Petrograd; Bukharin, the party's number-one intellectual and theorist; and particularly with Stalin, who had no great name but had been building a machine loyal and obedient to himself.

Even before becoming ill Lenin had worried about this rivalry, particularly the quarrel between Stalin and Trotsky. Lenin was increasingly concerned about Stalin's tactics and the danger of splitting the party.

It would never be entirely documentable, but already Stalin was beginning to look across the international horizon for a sphere in which to demonstrate his ability. Whether by the late autumn of 1922 or the early winter of 1923 he had decided that China would be this special field cannot be determined. But events were speeding his decision. In March 1923, at the moment that the Sun-Joffe agreement began to take shape, Lenin suffered another stroke which deprived him of the power of speech and effectively removed him from the leadership of the Soviet party and the Soviet Union. Although he lived on until January 21, 1924, he played no role in the opening to the East that he had initiated.

Stalin, not Lenin, would be the mover of Soviet policy in China; and his decisions would be made with an eye firmly on China as a demonstration of Stalinist skill and success in the field of international revolution, and of Stalinist wisdom in shaping a foreign policy favorable to the national interests of the Soviet state. At first this difference would be too subtle to measure; in the end it would be decisive.

In June 1923 the Third Congress of the Chinese Communist Party met to confirm the incorporation of the party into the Kuomintang. Chen Tu-hsiu favored the move, because he did not think China was yet ready for a Marxist revolution. Also because the Comintern and the Russians favored it. Many Chinese Communists, including Mao Tse-tung's fellow Hunan comrade and later rival, Chang Kuo-tao, strongly opposed joining forces with Dr. Sun. On this occasion Mao came to the meeting. He had the address and this time he was all for the Russian party line. "There must be a great revolutionary union," he said. He wanted a broad national union of Dr. Sun's Kuomintang and the Communists against the Japanese and other foreign imperialists. And that was what the Third Congress approved.

The Congress, with Mao voting in the majority, endorsed union with Dr. Sun and elected Mao to the fourteen-member Central Committee. Mao took over the party's organizational department, replacing Chang Kuo-tao, and transferred his activities from Chang-sha to Shanghai, the first act in a long, uneasy relationship between Mao and Chang.

In August 1923, Dr. Sun sent his brilliant young chief of staff, Chiang Kai-shek, to Moscow at the head of a small delegation that included the Communist youth leader Chang Tai-lei. There they would spend three months studying the organization of the Red Army and of the Communist Party, meeting with Trotsky, President Kalinin, Foreign Minister Chicherin, A. V. Lunacharsky, Ya. E. Rudzutak, S. S. Kamenev, Stalin and other leading Bolsheviks, inspecting Soviet warships at the Kronstadt naval base, participating in a session of the Moscow City Soviet and spending time in the Soviet military academies. Chiang Kai-shek was regarded as a radical, far-left, Communist-leaning Chinese military figure.

On October 6, 1923, Mikhail Markovich Borodin, attended by two young military aides— one named Vladimir Polyak and the other, Yukov—arrived in Canton, to serve as Dr. Sun's Soviet political adviser. For three years and eight months Borodin would stand at the very center of the Chinese Revolution, a dominating, wise, romantic, doomed figure.

# ★ 6 ★

## B O R O D I N

**M**IKHAIL BORODIN'S REAL NAME
was Mikhail Markovich Grusenberg. He was born in Vitebsk, Russia, on July 9, 1884, and apparently grew up in Riga, the capital of Latvia, then as now a part of the Russian Empire. He was thirty-nine years old when he arrived in Canton, English-speaking, clever, audacious, an old revolutionary, a man of personal attraction and a gift for taking what he called "the long view," a tactician, a natural psychologist, a leader. He charmed almost everyone he met. He was a skilled secret operative of the Soviets and of the Comintern. He could slip around dangerous corners and move in and out of countries, leaving little or no trace. He spoke slowly and walked on the balls of his feet. Vincent Sheean thought he resembled a lion or a panther.

Not a great deal ever became known about Borodin's early life. As he said, "What good are facts?" He was born in what the czarist regime called the Pale of Settlement, that is, the region where Jews were permitted to reside. But by the time he was a young man he had turned his back on his Jewishness, the Jewish religion, the Yiddish language and *shtetl* life. He called himself a Russian, he spoke Russian and he attended a Russian university. But he began his political life as a member of the Jewish Bund, the Jewish socialist group then powerful in Poland, in the White Russian Pale and in the ghettos of the Baltic. However, he left the Bund at nineteen and joined Lenin's faction of the Social Democratic Party in 1903, early enough to establish close personal ties with Lenin. He participated in the 1905 Revolution and attended several Bolshevik congresses, notably one at Tammerfors in Finland in December 1905 and the important unity congress of the Social Democrats in Stockholm in 1906. There, possibly by chance, he had a seat next to a young delegate from Georgia, Iosif Dzhugashvili, later better known as Stalin. The two became well acquainted and cast identical votes on most issues. It would prove a fateful encounter. Borodin was moving up in revolutionary circles but suddenly he dropped out, went to London and tried to get a job teaching Russian. He put a classified ad in the *Daily Telegraph* using the name Richter. Possibly that had a significance: it was the same *nom de guerre* Lenin had used a few years earlier in London. Harassed by British police, Borodin took a boat for Boston, worked there for a while at Harvard (so he said later) and went on to Chicago, where he soon made his mark in business and married Fanya Orluk, a girl from Vilna, who would be his companion and comrade on many a party mission.

Borodin armed himself with some business courses at Valparaiso College in Indiana—shorthand, typing, rhetoric, civil government—and, coincident with the birth of his first son, Frederick, started a night school in Chicago, teaching English to Russian emigrants at two dollars per student per term. He had forty students at the start and the number grew rapidly. Soon he bought out another school and was running what he called the Berg Progressive Preparatory School with several hundred students.

Borodin was active in émigré Russian circles, participated in Hull House, Jane Addams's famous institution on Chicago's West Side, joined the Socialist Party (American) and seemed to draw away from his attachment to Vladimir Lenin.

Like most émigré Russians Borodin hailed the February 1917 Revolution. He supported the provisional government and attended meetings sponsored by it in Chicago. He showed no wish to return to Russia. He had a growing business, two big and prosperous night schools, a good many other activities, a wife, two sons. He was enthusiastic about the Revolution, but Chicago had become his turf. November 7, 1917, changed that. When Lenin and his Bolsheviks came to power the pull to return became irresistible, and in July 1918 Borodin packed up, leaving his family behind, boarded the Norwegian steamer *Bergensfjord* and within a month was in Moscow.

Borodin was thirty-three. He had become accustomed to using a good many different names (but never his own, Grusenberg). He had seldom been Borodin in the United States. He was known as Berg (the name of a man from whom he had bought one night school), M. Grosenberg, M. G. Grosenberg and Michael Altshuler. He was, according to police records, five feet ten inches tall, but he gave the impression of being taller: almost everyone felt that he was over six feet. He had a solid build (later on he would appear slim, strained and almost skeletal), with rather high cheekbones, an aquiline nose, a broad forehead and bushy brown hair. He looked like a businessman (as he always described himself abroad) but also a scholar (which he liked to appear). He wore a four-in-hand tie and sometimes a high winged collar. He smoked a pipe and, like many pipe-smokers, used it to accent his conversation, puffing contemplatively, lighting and relighting it, tamping it down and ruminating as he went through the pipe-smoker's ritual. He was smooth-shaven in Chicago and for a considerable period thereafter, but in China he favored a thick, Stalinesque mustache. There he tended to wear the white linen suits favored by Europeans in the hot cities of South China like Canton.

From the day of his arrival in Canton, Borodin got on well with Dr. Sun. He concealed from Sun his deep concern about the ramshackle political situation and devoted his talents to trying to shore up Sun and strengthen his position and that of the Kuomintang.

A shaky situation was hardly a novel experience for Borodin. Immediately on arrival in Moscow in 1918, he had been assigned by Lenin to undercover work. Borodin smuggled agents into the United States, enlisted, improbably, Carl Sandburg, not yet a well-known poet, as a courier for bringing Soviet funds to the United States. (Sandburg was immediately detected in the enterprise.) Borodin attended the first meeting of the Comintern in 1919 and secretly conveyed funds abroad for revolutionary purposes. He traveled on a Mexican diplomatic passport and managed to pass money to underground representatives in Germany and Switzerland, where he may have enlisted his old friend Jane Addams to take money back to Chicago. According to M. N. Roy, an Indian Comintern official whom Borodin brought into the party, Borodin carted five hundred thousand dollars' worth of Romanov jewels to the West Indies, hoping to get them into the United States.

What happened to the jewels (diamonds, according to one version) has been a subject of controversy for more than fifty years. Fearful they would be seized by U.S. Customs, Borodin apparently gave them to a fellow traveler. The traveler then disappeared. To this day it has not been established whether Borodin had the jewels in the first place and lost them, or whether the whole scenario was a cover story.

What is known is that Borodin did visit his family in Chicago, meet with fellow radicals there and then went to Mexico, where he participated in the founding of the Mexican Communist Party. From there he made his way to Spain to lay the foundation for a Spanish Communist Party and then sneaked into Holland for the first and only meeting of the West European Bureau of the Comintern. Under a wagonload of hay he was smuggled across the frontier to Germany, and slipped back into Moscow in the spring of 1920, having spent nearly two years on conspiratorial missions.

Borodin put his skills to work in helping to stage and stage-manage the Second Comintern Congress in 1920, moving in and out of Russia along smugglers' routes, utilizing false passports and false identities, to get to Berlin (then headquarters for Soviet operations in the West). He tried to convert Enver Pasha, the Turkish leader, to Communism but failed; he lent a hand to looking after Clare Sheridan, a vivacious early Communist sympathizer who almost moved into the Kremlin with Kamenev and escorted Isadora Duncan around Moscow. He undertook a dangerous Comintern assignment in England, was caught by Scotland Yard and returned to Petrograd only in March 1923, after a six-month prison sentence.

This, then, was the man who was to play the key role in the Chinese Revolution until mid-1927.

Within two months of arriving in Canton in October 1923, Borodin had an opportunity to show his mettle. He had had many meetings with Dr. Sun, enough so that he was able to inform Lev Karakhan, who was in Peking as a Soviet special envoy to negotiate with the warlords, that Sun might fall at any moment. The local warlord Chen Chiung-ming, who had previously thrown Sun out of Canton, returned to the attack. Sun's defeat was imminent. Borodin had been soft-spoken with Sun up to this moment; now he felt he had nothing to lose. He proposed (and began to carry out) practical steps, organizing volunteers from the young Communists and workers of Canton. He urged Sun to appeal to the masses, to offer the eight-hour day to labor and offer land to the peasants. Sun found excuses for not meeting Borodin. Finally, on December 18, Borodin had a showdown. All Sun wanted to talk about was fleeing Canton. He wanted to go to Japan. Borodin said if he had to go to Japan he could continue to Russia via Vladivostok, and Sun seemed pleased, but Borodin was not ready to give up. He told Dr. Sun, "So long as the enemy has not broken into Canton there is hope. We must continue the party work with the masses."

Sun remained dubious and went to pack his bags, but word that reforms were being discussed had reached the people. The defense stiffened. That night Chen Chiung-ming began to withdraw his army. Canton was saved and Borodin's position was strengthened. Dr. Sun gave him full credit for the victory and went to work to put Borodin's proposals into effect, assuring him they were identical with those that he himself had long had in mind. Borodin didn't care who got the credit as long as the deed was done. Preparations were rushed for a national congress, the first for the Kuomintang. A group of Americans meeting with Dr. Sun told him that Borodin was a pseudonym and asked whether he knew the Russian's real name (Grusenberg).

"I do," said Sun.

"What is it?" Sun was asked.

"It is Lafayette."

★

Borodin's ascendancy and Dr. Sun's commitment to work with the Soviet Union and the Communists were sealed at the Kuomintang Congress. But not without remarkable battles. Neither the Communists nor the Nationalists wanted to agree. Borodin was compelled to invoke Moscow's authority to whip the Communists into line. Then he had to turn his talents to Dr.

Sun, who had wilted under the opposition of his right-wing supporters. After days of talk and maneuver, Borodin finally achieved victory.

The next day was January 25, 1924. Word arrived of Lenin's death in Moscow on the 21st. Arriving in Canton on the same day as the news were the first members of the Soviet military mission, Aleksandr I. Cherepanov and Nikolai Tereshatov. They witnessed one last battle over the new program of Dr. Sun. The right wing of the Kuomintang utilized the three days of official mourning for Lenin to organize a final attack on Nationalist-Communist collaboration. But they went down in defeat and the question quickly turned to that of Soviet military collaboration and Dr. Sun's long, long delayed plans for an expedition to the north, to unite China under his leadership.

The year 1924 was a year of preparations—preparations for the great march north and the completion, it was hoped, of the Chinese Revolution. Dr. Sun was eager to move. Now that he had at last, largely thanks to Borodin and the Russians, created a reliable base in South China he wanted to get on with the task, to move north, cross the Yangtze, take over Shanghai, Wuhan and the great Yangtze valley and finally oust the corrupt military regimes in Peking.

Borodin was more cautious. He wanted to build a foundation, strengthen popular support, develop trade unions, carry propaganda to the peasants and, paramount, construct a reliable military force.

The first step in the military program was the creation of the Whampoa Military Academy, of which Chiang Kai-shek, back from Russia, became commandant. Later Chiang would try to paint this period of his life as anti-Communist. It was not. He had picked up valuable knowledge in Russia and Whampoa had a staff of Russian military advisers, as well as bright students. Chou En-lai, just at the beginning of a career that would take him to the highest levels of the People's Republic, was deputy director of the political department and worked intimately and smoothly with Chiang Kai-shek, who seemed very close to the Communists. Ho Chi Minh, an obscure Vietnamese nationalist who had already successively been a member of three Communist parties—the French, the Russian and the Chinese—and who would found a fourth, the Vietnamese, was a student at Whampoa. The Whampoa cadres would play leading roles in the next twenty years of warfare within China.

Borodin and Dr. Sun became inseparable—Borodin cultivating Sun, educating him in how the Russian Revolution had been accomplished, flattering him, wooing him, persuading him sometimes reluctantly to take step after step along the radical path. Borodin had his most difficult time with Dr. Sun on the question of land reform. This had been one of Sun's original planks but, after all, he felt dependent on the landlord class for support and funds and he was reluctant to turn his words into action. But some progress was achieved. The Kuomintang set up a Peasant Bureau and a Peasant Institute, and soon thousands and tens of thousands began to follow in Sun's train.

Mao Tse-tung was based in Shanghai now, working closely, sometimes it seemed almost exclusively, with the Nationalists. No Communist was stronger in his support of the Kuomintang than he, and when the Nationalists formed their Peasant Bureau Mao was instantly attracted. He had never lost his strong attachment to the land. A friend of his was running the Kuomintang Peasant Institute. Mao was one of the first speakers invited to address it. He spoke at the Third and Fourth Communist Party congresses about the peasant question but his collaboration with the Nationalists cost him the confidence of his Communist comrades. He lost his Central Committee seat at the Fourth Congress, in January 1925.

Mao played no active role in the events of 1924. He did meet a few times with Dr. Sun and talked at least once with Borodin, who remembered Mao as being "excessively self-assured." Mao was disappointed in Dr. Sun—he did not seem the imposing figure of Mao's youth—but Mao was not in tune with the times. After he lost his post on the Communist Party Central Committee he went back to his father's farm in Shao Shan, still owned and run by the Mao family. He was somewhat estranged from his wife, Yang Kai-hui, but there was a big family reunion on the Chinese New Year in late January. Kai-hui and the boys came. Then Mao plunged into another intensive tour of the countryside, meeting with peasants, organizing them, testing their mettle, seeking their opinions, assisting in the formation of peasant unions, sinking his roots deep in the Chinese soil, once again convincing himself that the key to China lay in the countryside and that if revolution was to come it must come from the land, on which 95 percent of the Chinese lived and worked.

Sometime toward the end of October 1924 (the precise date seems to have escaped history) a tall, handsome, dark-haired, dark-mustached, broad-shouldered Russian military man arrived in Canton and was introduced to Dr. Sun Yat-sen as Zoe Vsevolodovich Galin. There was, in fact, no such person and to any Russian even the name seemed improbable.

Galin was actually Vasily Konstantinovich Blyukher, one of the ablest young Soviet commanders. He was thirty-four years old, had served with distinction in the Czar's army during World War I, joined the Revolution and was sent to the Urals during turbulent 1918, where he led a famous cavalry raid on the rear guard of the enemy White Russian and Czech forces. He became architect of the victory of the Red Army over the coalition of White and interventionist forces in Siberia and the Far East, engaging in some of the bloodiest fighting of the Civil War. It had been Blyukher's mop-up victory against a vicious band of outlaws, criminals and conscripts on the territory of the Far Eastern Republic that had cleared the way for Moscow's big casino, the effort to propel Dr. Sun's Chinese Revolution into success.

The peculiar name "Galin" had come about, one of his young aides recalled years later, because Blyukher was far too well known to enter China under his own name. He would have been arrested or assassinated by the Japanese or the northern warlords. He had to have a *klichka*, a pseudonym. His wife was named Galina, so he took Galin as his family name. He had two children, a girl named Zoya and a boy named Vsevolod, so he utilized the girl's name for his given name, "Zoe," a masculine name that had no existence in Russian, and turned his son's name into his patronymic, Vsevolodovich. He invented the name in Vladivostok just before taking off for his Chinese assignment. There would come a time when the name Galin would be better known than Blyukher, after his great days in China and, again, during the Spanish Civil War. The reputation of Galin as a military leader was to become as great as that of Borodin as a revolutionary.

There were sharp differences between Borodin and Blyukher in temperament and style. A young military specialist who accompanied Blyukher said that, to the Chinese, Borodin represented the unforgettable embodiment of the Soviet Union, the wisdom and will of the Bolshevik Party.

"Even if Borodin was not the author of policy but merely a man who carried out the tactics rather than a strategist," he said, "everything that he did he did with generosity, with inspiration, with sensitive tact, with a knowledge of people and, if I may say so, with resourcefulness, talent and taste."

When Borodin came into the office where the young officer worked it was an event; each of his words seemed to be chosen with care and each gesture had a significance. No one was in any doubt that Borodin *was* the Soviet political mission.

Blyukher, said the young man, differed from Borodin. He had a contradictory personality. He was at his best when faced with a major task or danger. Everyone knew he was the marshal of revolution, a wise strategist and commander.

"If Borodin had great political talent," said the officer, "then Blyukher had great military talent. We were witnesses of a remarkable legend: though he began as an errand boy in a shop and a simple factory worker, Blyukher's military gifts had been released by the Revolution and at the head of a popular army he had liberated half the Czar's empire."

It was not easy for these two men to collaborate. Only their dedication to China's cause, and the exercise of patience, enabled them to work together.

They gave their best for China and, in the end, suffered a common fate. Each in his time was to perish under Stalin's heel, Blyukher in 1938 and Borodin in one of the northern prison camps in 1952.

**B**lyukher arrived in Canton only days after another warlord effort to topple Sun. This was put down with efficiency, dispatch and strength (despite some waffling by Sun) with the aid of the new military forces of the Whampoa Academy, decisive advice by Borodin and new artillery just arrived from the Soviet Union aboard the ship *Voronsky*.

Dr. Sun's health had been failing, and on November 13, 1924, after a great victory rally, he sailed for Hong Kong, Shanghai and Tokyo, intending to go on to Peking for political consultations before launching a northern expedition. This was not to be. His illness rapidly deepened and he collapsed at Tientsin. He was rushed to Peking and operated on at the Rockefeller Union Medical College, where on January 5, 1925, it was discovered he had advanced cancer of the liver. He died March 12, breathing the words, it was said, "Peace . . . battle . . . save China." He left behind a message dated March 11 directed to the Central Committee of the Soviet Union which concluded with these words:

"I have ordered the party [the Kuomintang] to be in constant contact with you. I firmly believe in the unchanging support which you have shown to this moment for my country. In bidding you farewell, my dear comrades, I want to express the hope that soon will come the day when the U.S.S.R. will greet a great, free China as a friend and ally and that in the great battle for liberating the enslaved peoples of the world both allies will advance to victory hand in hand."

Borodin stood by in Peking during the last days, as did Lev Karakhan, Moscow's special envoy in Peking. What influence Borodin or Karakhan may have had on the shaping of Sun's last statement has never been established. Whatever the circumstances, the words made clear that Borodin's ideas were being projected into the future of the relationship between Russia and China, which would now move forward in the absence of its original authors, Vladimir Lenin in Russia and Dr. Sun Yat-sen in China.

Nonetheless, the death of Dr. Sun would prove a blow to Soviet-Chinese collaboration. Even before Dr. Sun had died Blyukher, moving swiftly and with confidence, had taken over direction of the Whampoa Military Academy, had begun to whip into shape the divisive and inefficient Canton troops and drafted plans for another and, he hoped, decisive blow against the durable Chen Chiung-ming. Blyukher was a man who drew up a precise plan, assigned each unit a specific objective and double-checked each move. He did so in this case and then got approval from General Hsu, the commander of the Kuomintang troops, and members of the government.

As the core of his force for what came to be known as the First Eastern Campaign, Blyukher utilized two regiments of Whampoa cadets and some Canton troops under General Hsu. Again and again Blyukher's forces, only one-quarter or less the size of the opposition, drove Chen off the battlefield.

These successes convinced Blyukher of what he probably already believed—that small, well-led, well-disciplined, well-indoctrinated troops could defeat large bodies of poorly trained, poorly motivated, poorly led opponents. The warlord troops that Blyukher would encounter on the drive north were composed of men forced into service at gunpoint, untrained, poorly fed, poorly paid and with no political motivation. Many of the commanders had no military skills.

"The chief role," Blyukher said, "should be played not by quantity but by quality. Three or four divisions of three regiments each should be fully sufficient [for the northern expedition]."

He thought these could be augmented by local and provincial forces as the drive went forward and as individual commanders became aware of the fighting ability of trained and motivated troops. "Of course," he added, "not all the commanders of the old formations will accept these reforms."

Before 1925 was out Blyukher launched another expedition, the Second Eastern Campaign, which was even more successful than the first. The soundness of his military judgment, the wisdom of his training patterns, tactics and strategy was confirmed. No one then, or later, was to offer serious challenge to him as a military leader in China, neither the Communists nor the warlords, whether Nationalist or anti-Nationalist. Blyukher knew his business and was better at it than anyone in the field. But the problem of the Revolution was not military strategy. It was politics.

★

Canton was a strange city, a city of contradictions. It had seen more insurrections, more revolutionary plotting, more coups d'état than any other place in China. There was always some political conspiracy being put together in the dimly lighted restaurants along the riverbanks or in the quiet classic gardens of the walled compounds. The streets along the Bund were lined with opium dens, houses of prostitution and gambling halls. Bookstores abounded, some choked with revolutionary literature, others filled with classics, others with pornography. Foreigners jostled traditionally gowned Chinese. Automobiles were rare. Most belonged to the military and usually there was a guard or two, armed with rifles or sawed-off shotguns. Streets were bedecked with banners; often the most violent revolutionary slogans appeared in gold letters on red paper or were painted in red on white cloth. Canton was the kind of place where anything could happen and usually did. Everything there was politics and almost everyone was involved in politics.

Normal caution would have dictated a considerable pause for reassessment by the Russians after the death of Dr. Sun. Soviet-Chinese collaboration was Sun's policy. Borodin worked for and with Sun. Borodin's and Russia's influence was almost totally dependent on Dr. Sun. Russia's writ ran as far as Dr. Sun's. No further. With Sun's death the position of Russia and Borodin was thrust into uncertainty. There was no successor to Dr. Sun. If Borodin was to be criticized (as later he was) it should have been for basing himself so narrowly on Dr. Sun. With Sun gone Borodin had no ally to turn to.

A struggle for the succession broke out. One contender was Dr. Sun's son by his first wife, Sun Fo. Another was the brilliant young brother of Dr. Sun's second wife, T. V. Soong. Among Dr. Sun's older associates only one, Liao Chung-kai, was close to Borodin, and he lost his life to assassins on August 20, 1925.

The only figure who seemed able to find his footing in the political confusion was Borodin. More and more he took it upon himself personally to direct the Revolution. It was a risky role for a non-Chinese but there seemed no alternative. Borodin's Chinese Communist colleagues found him confident and self-assured. The Trotsky-Stalin quarrel in Moscow was raging but Borodin got straight through to Stalin. He did not have to refer matters to anyone else. There was no doubt in the minds of the informed that he was Stalin's man and that it was Stalin's cards he was playing. He had little use for the Comintern. He tended to override the Chinese Communist Party and the formal apparatus of both the Soviet party and the Soviet state. He did not have to communicate through Karakhan. Blyukher's channels to Moscow were by no means so direct, and this caused friction between Borodin and Blyukher. Borodin was not an ambassador, not a member of the Kuomintang, he did not speak for the Comintern, yet as Chang Kuo-tao, the Hunan Communist leader and rival of Mao Tse-tung, pointed out, Borodin was Russia's voice in China. Borodin reminded Chang of the legendary Chinese *ssu-pu-hsiang*, a creature with the horns of a stag, the neck of a camel, the hoofs of an ox and the tail of a horse.

Helped by Blyukher's reliable work at the Whampoa Academy, Borodin kept his head above water and the Revolution alive. By late autumn the success of the Second Eastern Campaign and some remarkable juggling of the shaky Communist-Kuomintang alignment gave Borodin a triumph. He was hailed at a victory banquet December 11, 1925, in Swatow by both Wang Ching-wei and Chiang Kai-shek, the strongest (and rival) military figures of the Kuomintang. Chiang was lavish in his praise, calling Borodin the "Marshal Foch" of China, the true successor and disciple of Dr. Sun, the man on whom the Revolution depended.

It was, it seemed, a moment of triumph for the Comintern's secret agent, the onetime Chicago language-school proprietor. Of course Borodin was not Moscow's only hand in China, but in the summer of 1925 both Blyukher and Lev Karakhan had returned to the Soviet Union, where they spent weeks in discussion of Soviet policy. Stalin was pulling out in front in the struggle to succeed Lenin. China was his strongest foreign-policy card. He could not afford defeat there: it would expose him mercilessly to the charge already advanced by his enemies that he was too narrow, too parochial, knew nothing of foreign affairs, lacked Trotsky's brilliance and Bukharin's skill; that, in fact, he was no internationalist, not a real revolutionary. The answer to Stalin's critics was China: the ability of the Soviet operatives there to pull off the biggest of coups, to bring in China on the side of world Communism. There could be no turning back.

Would things have been different if Borodin had gone back to Moscow? Possibly. But would the Soviet position have survived Borodin's absence? Not very likely. Not even if Blyukher had stayed behind. Blyukher was a military man. He did not understand or get on well with Chinese politicians. Nor would Karakhan have constituted an alternative. Karakhan was a skilled diplomat but he could not learn the delicate balance of Kuomintang politics overnight.

The fact is that at this point Borodin had *become* the Chinese Revolution. Rightly or wrongly, it would have gone down the drain if he had removed his guiding hand from Canton.

Which raised the question—if Borodin *was* the Chinese Revolution, was it not doomed to failure? Could it be expected that any foreigner could bring to success a revolution in a nation like China? This was the question that Moscow should have asked. There is no evidence that it did, and by this time Borodin could not have answered it objectively. He was too committed and events were moving too fast in Canton. It took all of his attention to cope with them— and to cope with critics in the Chinese Communist Party and their fellows in Moscow, men like Karl Radek, who now headed Moscow's Sun Yat-sen University, all of them certain that the Revolution should move more swiftly, that the Communists should end their Kuomintang alliance and that bloody repressions of workers in Shanghai, Hong Kong and Canton were opening the way to a direct Communist takeover.

★

Such thoughts bothered both Borodin and Moscow. In late January 1926 an important commission from Moscow arrived in Peking. Its task was to decide what Russia should do next. Or perhaps its task was to lay the foundations for what Stalin had already decided to do.

At its head was Andrei S. Bubnov, an Old Bolshevik who, like Borodin, had attended the 1906 Congress in Stockholm. Bubnov had been a member of the Politburo at the time of the 1917 Revolution and had been a strong supporter of Stalin since the critical years of Lenin's illness. Now he was serving as Stalin's political chief in the Red Army, methodically weeding out commanders thought to be loyal to Trotsky. His presence was a guarantee that the commission would do Stalin's bidding. A. I. Yegorov, military attaché of the Soviet embassy in Peking, later to become a great Red Army commander and shot in 1938 along with Blyukher, participated in the sessions.* Karakhan, acting Foreign Minister and a specialist on China, came back from Moscow for the meeting. So did Voitinsky, the Comintern man who had been in at the creation. The proceedings were top-secret. Borodin left Canton on February 4, 1926, to participate. If all went well he hoped to go on to Moscow later. His personal conducting of the Chinese Revolution was on the line and he was nervous. Most of the decisions of the past year had been his. A lot was at stake.

On February 14, 1926, Aleksandr I. Cherepanov, Borodin's enterprising young Soviet military adviser, emerged from the embassy building in Peking where the commission sessions were being held. He and his fellow adviser Nikolai Tereshatov had just finished reporting on their work with Chinese troops in Canton.

They heard a high-pitched shriek and around the corner came Norman, Borodin's eight-year-old son, holding aloft a bleeding finger and calling for his mother, Fanya, who was standing nearby. Fred, the Borodins' fourteen-year-old, had wounded his brother as they were playing. As soon as Fanya had bandaged the finger and admonished Fred, she invited the officers to Borodin's quarters nearby. They found him waiting, wearing the Chinese gown that he often wore in Canton and which, Cherepanov thought, splendidly fitted his broad shoulders.

---

*Bubnov, Karakhan and most of Stalin's agents in China would eventually be executed.

Borodin was anxious to find out what tack the commission was taking. He encouraged the young officers to tell him about their hearing and then let them read the draft of the report that he was to present. In this report Borodin strongly urged that the Northern Expedition long planned by Dr. Sun to consolidate the Revolution be undertaken—in part because he believed that once the quarrels of the northern generals quieted down, the British would instigate them to attack in the south and bring the Canton Revolution to an end. Everyone, he suggested, was expecting Canton to relax, including many supporters of the new regime. If this spirit was permitted to prevail, he felt, the Northern Expedition would never be undertaken and the Revolution would peter out.

"To remain in Canton and not prepare for the Northern Expedition," he said, "actually means not to take the great road of national revolutionary movement." Sooner or later, he said, the strength of the Revolution would be exhausted.

**B**ubnov, in essence, accepted Borodin's view. Together with the members of his commission he set off for Canton to observe conditions at first hand. They arrived by steamer on March 13, Bubnov traveling under the name of Ivanovsky. All of the Russians used false names: N. V. Kuibyshev, brother of V. V. Kuibyshev, member of the Soviet Politburo, whom Borodin had left in charge in Canton, called himself Kisanko; Tereshatov's real name was Teslenkov; Kuibyshev's deputy I. Ya. Razgon called himself Olgin, etc.

Bubnov expected to make a speech to the Politburo of the Kuomintang—to announce that Russia was going forward with her aid, to promise support of the Northern March. Instead, on March 20, Chiang Kai-shek seized the Whampoa Military Academy, arrested all the Communists in the academy, the commanders of the First Army; in Canton, he suppressed labor-union protests, put the Russian advisers under house arrest, surrounded the villa where Bubnov and his mission were staying and announced himself commander-in-chief of the Kuomintang armies.

The day after his coup, Chiang Kai-shek met with a low-level Soviet delegation. He refused to see Kuibyshev. He said that if Kuibyshev and his aides, Rogachev and Razgon, were ousted and Borodin and Blyukher came back all would be well. He met with Bubnov and the Soviet commission and apologized. He hadn't meant to arrest them and they could all go free now. But Bubnov still didn't get to make his speech. Chiang met with Chou En-lai and Chang Kuo-tao. Chou, as Chiang Kai-shek's political deputy, was in an embarrassing position. He had been relieved of his duties by Chiang. Now Chiang pretended to be friendly. He was all civility and politeness. He created a senior section for the Communist cadres at Whampoa and put Chou in charge (but Chou continued to be blamed by local Communists for not foreseeing Chiang's coup).

Kuibyshev and his assistants were shipped away. Borodin and Blyukher got back as fast as they could. It wasn't easy: Borodin had to go roundabout from Peking via Mongolia and the Trans-Siberian to Vladivostok, where he took a boat for Canton. Borodin and Blyukher conferred in Vladivostok but took separate boats so they would not be lost together if something happened. By the time Borodin got to Canton, on April 29, things had quieted down. Chiang Kai-shek was promising to be good, talking about his dedication to China's revolution, to world revolution. He was full of apologies. He released the Communists and unionists. Borodin kept telling his associates: What do you expect from the Kuomintang? It is a toilet, like all bourgeois parties, and no matter how often you flush it, it still stinks.

Borodin and Bubnov invented elaborate explanations for Moscow. Chiang Kai-shek hadn't really known what he was doing. It was all Kuibyshev's fault. He hadn't understood how to treat Chiang. Now that Borodin and Blyukher were back it would be all right. Chiang was their man. They could handle him. The Revolution would go on. The Northern Expedition would move forward. China would go Red. Chiang was Moscow's man. March 20 was an aberration.

The talk was reassuring. It papered over what had happened, made it seem less important. After all, Bubnov could hardly tell Stalin that the moment he arrived in town Russia's protégé turned against his sponsors. That wasn't what Stalin wanted. He wanted to be reassured, wanted to know that his judgment had been right. He didn't want to hear the kind of stories that were going around from those who had accompanied Chiang to Moscow in 1923, stories about how, when Chiang had been taken to the Military Museum and saw an exhibit on Napoleon's 1812 invasion of Russia, he began to compare himself to Napoleon. That was the last thing that Stalin wanted to be reminded of. Stalin wanted to know that the Chinese Revolution was on track. That it was coming up to speed. That his man in Canton would demonstrate that he, Stalin, knew what was what about international revolution, that Trotsky was just a puffed-up doctrinaire, whereas he, Stalin, had the know-how, had the man, held the key to China.

The hard fact was that neither Stalin nor Borodin had an alternative to Chiang Kai-shek, a reality that Borodin admitted in so many words, as Chang Kuo-tao was to recall many years later. Borodin had no means of influencing events except that, as he said, "In my pocket I still have some green stuff." When Chang asked Borodin how much "green stuff" his pocket held he would not say, but he had a lot. He also had the ability to provide Chiang Kai-shek with Soviet arms and ammunition. Borodin was not impotent.

Chiang certainly understood that Borodin had little choice, and he subtly made Borodin aware that he had it in his power to treat him as he had the other Soviet plenipotentiaries: he could, if he wanted, arrest Borodin and ship him out. Borodin knew this; that he went on dealing with Chiang showed the weakness of the Soviet position.

But there was another side to the coin. Chiang wanted the Northern Expedition and for this he needed the Russians, needed Russian guns, Russian support, Blyukher's advice and counsel. He promised Borodin he would continue to "love and protect" the Communist cadres in the Whampoa Academy, but at the same time he made Borodin give him a list of all Communist members in the Kuomintang. Borodin complied, though he knew what it meant. All he could hope now was that as the game was played out some alternative would turn up to the wiry, calculating Chiang Kai-shek.

★

Whatever Borodin's thoughts, the plain fact was that the next phase of the Revolution was in the hands of this small man with the shaven skull who looked at the world through narrow eyes and who himself, in General Stilwell's unforgettable phrase, looked like a peanut. Chiang Kai-shek was a self-made man. Born in 1887, he had pulled himself up from a lower-middle-class family in Chekiang Province (his father was a salt-seller), propelled in his career by an ambitious mother. Chiang had some training in a Japanese military academy and a fling at minor revolutionary and military activity. A year or two after 1911, he showed up in Shanghai. His Shanghai experience has never been totally explored, and Chiang and his agents have been at pains to blur the evidence. By one means or another, he more or less kept afloat in a city dominated by ruthless underworld gangs, by the notorious Green Circle, which controlled opium and smuggling, extortion and prostitution. Once, according to gossip, Chiang sank below the surface, abandoning himself for months to the life of the singsong houses, drink, drugs and dissipation.

He had a hand in small-scale finance, working for brokers on the fringe of the financial community. He became associated with Chang Ching-chiang—a millionaire stock-exchange man, a dealer in antiques and other value commodities, a cripple who had to be carried about in a chair, whom Chiang was to call "elder brother"—and with Huang Ching-yung, a notorious underworld figure. Chiang had already made connection with Chen Chi-mei, a gangster with revolutionary sympathies, a tough boss whose nephews, Chen Li-fu and Chen Kuo-fu, came to wield extraordinary and vicious power under Chiang, forming what was called the "CC Clique" within Chiang's government, brutal and reactionary. It was in these years that Chiang developed relationships with important Chinese business and banking families and came to the attention of one of the most remarkable of contemporary Chinese entrepreneurs, Charles Jones Soong. Chiang, a traditional Chinese, had gone through an arranged marriage at the age of fourteen with a Miss Mao, who bore him two sons, one of whom, Chiang Ching-kuo, ultimately became Chiang's successor. Chiang had at least one additional marriage and many concubines. Now, in the mid-1920s, he stood on the eve of his last and most important marital alliance, that with the family of Charlie Soong, who had founded a fortune on returning from the United States by selling Bibles door-to-door.

Soong Ching-ling, Charlie Soong's second daughter, was by now the widow of Dr. Sun. Soong Ai-ling, the eldest girl, was the wife of Dr. H. H. Kung, by now one of China's most skillful financial operators, head of the fabulously wealthy Kung family, a direct descendant of Confucius. The third sister, Mei-ling, was almost as American as she was Chinese. Charlie was an Americophile, having spent his youth in the United States. He thought that Americans, particularly those south of the Mason-Dixon line, were more Chinese than many Chinese. He was a Methodist and all his children were brought up to Methodism. Mei-ling attended Wesleyan College for Women in Macon, Georgia (as had Ching-ling), and went on to graduate from Wellesley.

When Mei-ling returned to China, svelte, beautiful and Western, she spent time with her sister Ching-ling and Dr. Sun. It was there Mei-ling met Chiang. After the assassination (in 1916) of Chiang's Shanghai patron, Chen Chi-mei, Dr. Sun had picked up Chiang as a military protégé. Somewhat reluctantly Chiang found himself undertaking more and more of Dr. Sun's assignments. When Dr. Sun died Chiang unsuccessfully bid for the hand of Ching-ling. He then transferred his suit to the twenty-five-year-old Mei-ling. Chiang, who was forty-one, had to undergo a rigorous examination by Charlie's redoubtable widow, whose family had been Christian for three hundred years. She knew a great deal more about Chiang's Shanghai days than history has recorded. The price she imposed for marrying Mei-ling was Chiang's conversion to Methodism, a price he accepted; he pronounced himself dedicated to this faith for the rest of his life.

The couple was married in Shanghai on December 1, 1927, with the director of the local YMCA, Dr. David Yui, officiating. There were fifteen hundred guests. A portrait of Dr. Sun was suspended from the ceiling of the ballroom of the Hotel Majestic on Bubbling Well Road, and a Russian band played "Here Comes the Bride" as Mei-ling appeared on the arm of her Harvard-educated brother, T. V. Soong, who later would serve Chiang Kai-shek as Foreign Minister. A Chinese tenor sang "Oh, Promise Me."

There never was to be a resolution of the question of what, if any, relationship existed between Chiang's Green Gang or Circle, the CC Clique, Dr. Sun and the Soongs. Who was using whom? Did the Soongs pick Chiang Kai-shek, throw their support to him and thus assure his climb to the top? Why did Dr. Sun attach Chiang to himself after the death of Chen Chi-mei? Did the Soongs spot Chiang as a winner and put a bet on him by marrying him to Mei-ling? And what were the enduring relationships between the murky shadows of Shanghai, the CC Clique and Chiang?

There would be no absolute answers to these questions. What is certain is that in 1926 Chiang Kai-shek was forty years old. He had been, for whatever reason, a protégé of Dr. Sun. Up to this point he had held the highest regard for Borodin and the Russians. He had been specially picked to head the first Kuomintang mission to Moscow. In 1925 he had sent his son Chiang Ching-kuo, then fourteen, to Moscow to be educated. There Chiang Ching-kuo was to stay until 1937, when Stalin, as a special favor to Chiang Kai-shek and as a measure of their newly formed United Front, sent him back to his father. In the meantime, Chiang Ching-kuo would attend the Sun Yat-sen University in Moscow, where Chinese Communist cadres were educated, would join the Young Communist League, would quarrel with Stalin's protégé Wang Ming and suffer various kinds of punishment and exile—all as far as ever came to be known, without a word of protest from Chiang Kai-shek. No one was more skillful than Chiang at playing his political shots from every side of the billiard table. Now he had maneuvered his way to the top of the Nationalist hierarchy. It was his turn to try to bring about the Chinese Revolution.

## 7

# CHIANG KAI-SHEK EMERGES

THE SOUND OF A SINGLE BUGLE at 4:00 A.M. on the morning of April 12, 1927, ended the dream of the Chinese Revolution, or, more accurately, the rattle of machine-gun fire a few seconds later tore the fabric of the dream to tatters. It would be decades before it could be woven again, and its pattern would be radically different.

The bugle sounded, as Harold Isaacs, chronicler of China's revolutionary tragedy, reported, in the headquarters that Chiang Kai-shek had established in the old Foreign Ministry bureau on Route Ghisi, just outside the French Concession in Shanghai. Chiang had entered the city in March, riding high on the success of the Northern Expedition.

The expedition had finally been launched July 9, 1926, with a quick drive into Hunan and the capture of Chang-sha. It rolled northward, picking up momentum. Yochow on the Yangtze fell August 22; Han-yang, Hankow and Wuchang—the giant Wuhan complex—in the first week of September. Within a month the Nationalist armies held the middle Yangtze valley. Columns led by Chiang Kai-shek made slower progress but captured Nan-chang in the first days of November and Kiukiang, on the south bank of the Yangtze, November 5. As revolutionary forces moved north, propaganda teams, led by Communists, spread out ahead of the armies, rallying the populace. Hundreds of thousands and soon millions of peasants began to join the movement. The armies were augmented by volunteers from the countryside and by the forces of regional generals struggling to catch a place on the bandwagon. All seemed glorious, all seemed successful, all seemed revolutionary. The posters that went up, the speeches that were made, the banners that were unfurled proclaimed in fiery red the victory of the People's Revolution.

The thunder of the propaganda almost drowned out memory of the March 20 coup in Canton, but it could not quite muffle what was now happening—the suppression of labor unions, the recruitment of gangsters to attack strikers and to pillage leftist headquarters, the instigation of terror, Chiang's deals with local warlords, his use of "silver bullets," bribes to bring generals to his side. Canton provided an example. While Borodin looked on without protest, Chiang's local warlord ally organized riffraff from the slums and waterfront, formed them into a "Central Labor Union" and loosed them on the workers, killing at least fifty in six days of fighting. Labor demonstrations were forbidden and troops sent to patrol the streets. Gambling, prostitution and opium dens sprang back. All the old graft and corruption flourished anew.

The great Canton–Hong Kong strike, which had paralyzed British commerce, was stamped out. Similar outbreaks, similar repressions followed in the wake of Chiang Kai-shek's armies, except at Wuhan, where the strong influence of Communists and left-wing elements in the Kuomintang created the impression of a vibrant revolutionary city. Hundreds of thousands joined the radical regime, workers swarmed into unions, peasants volunteered, the flush of red carmined the great triple-city. But it was the flush that dabs the cheeks in the last stages of consumption.

Although his armies stood at the gates of Shanghai, Chiang Kai-shek stayed in the ancient, feudal, reactionary city of Nan-chang, behind old fortress walls. Shanghai waited. Chiang did not come. Finally Shanghai blew up. It rose in a great revolutionary drama, an event that took its place beside that of Petrograd in 1917 and the storming of the Bastille, a spectacle that would always burn in the minds of those who witnessed it.

Shanghai would inspire countless journalistic accounts, novels, dramas, poems and films, but none so vivid as that of André Malraux, who captured in *Man's Fate* the pathos, the contrast, the heroism, the irony, the horror, the tragedy.

The warning signals had come in October 1926, when poorly organized Communist attacks on police stations were brutally suppressed, possibly with Chiang's connivance. But popular sentiment could not be contained. Enormous demonstrations turned Shanghai into a sea of humanity on November 28, and again on December 12.

The International Settlement and the French Concession, refuge of foreign capital and rich Chinese, trembled behind sandbagged barricades. Thousands of British, French, Japanese and American troops and scores of warships were hastily brought in to defend the oasis.

The streets of Shanghai rattled with revolutionary tremors as Chiang's armies came closer and closer. They entered Chekiang, his home province, and on February 17, 1927, took Hangchow and advanced to Kashing and Sungkiang. They were less than twenty-five miles from Shanghai.

People went into the streets to wait for Chiang Kai-shek. A general strike closed the city down—trams, cabs, post office, factories, businesses, department stores, offices, banks.

But Li Pao-chang, Shanghai's garrison commander, was not intimidated. He sent his execution squads out, bands of huge bullies armed with broadswords. They grabbed demonstrators, students, ordinary citizens, anyone they could lay hands on, forced them to their knees, slashed off their heads with the great swords and paraded through the city displaying the severed heads, dripping with blood on sharpened bamboo poles or great platters.

The police of the International Settlement and of the French Concession arrested scores of radicals, Communists and students and shoved them over the line into Chinese territory for Li Pao-chang's executioners. Later Chiang rewarded Li with command of the Eighth Nationalist Army. No one was more vigorous in the suppression than the chief of detectives of the French Concession, Huang Ching-yung, generally known as Huang Mapi, Pock-marked Huang. The detective chief also headed the Green Gang, which ran Shanghai's underworld. Not a few Chinese believed that Pock-marked Huang personally had inducted Chiang many years earlier into the Green Gang as a member of "Twenty-second Generation" (the gang's inner circle)— one of the events in the blanked-out period of Chiang's life.

Despite Pock-marked Huang's "feast of heads," the workers of Shanghai would not be denied. With Chiang still idling on the city's doorstep, they stormed out at noon on March 21 in a general strike and insurrection. Every worker in Shanghai came out. Some five thousand men organized assault groups, many initially armed only with knives and clubs, and attacked the police stations.

By late afternoon the insurrectionists held the entire city, except for Chapei, the heart of the working-class section. There the police clung on, with the support of White Russian mercenaries who roared through the narrow alleys in armored cars, pouring machine-gun fire into houses and shelling buildings from an armored train near North Station. By afternoon of the next day the battle was over and Shanghai was in the hands of the workers. At dusk Chiang's First Division entered the city. It had been ordered to stay out but the troops insisted on marching in to support the workers.

★

Five days later Chiang Kai-shek himself entered Shanghai, the remarkable city that had given him his start up the ladder. Chiang had not awaited his formal return to renew his old contacts. Pock-marked Huang had gotten in touch with him at Kiukiang in November and already was organizing underworld toughs into "labor unions" in the pattern of those employed by Chiang in Chang-sha, Kiukiang and Nan-chang to smash the workers.

On that Saturday afternoon of March 26, 1927, Chiang went straight from wharfside to the Foreign Ministry bureau. The first man he received there was Pock-marked Huang. The second was T. Patrick Givens of the political branch of the Shanghai police.

The next days were busy. Chiang had only a few troops in Shanghai, and the First Division in Chapei was hardly reliable: it had defied orders and come to the aid of the Shanghai workers. Busy days. Arrangements. Chinese businessmen and bankers to see. Arrangements for "finance." First, a three-million-dollar loan to Chiang Kai-shek. Then another of seven million. Then plans for another fifty million dollars to set up a new capital at Nanking. The problem of the First Division to resolve. The takeover of the city administration. Vicious clashes broke out between Chiang's men and workers carrying posters which read: "Hail the National Revolutionary Army!" "Hail Chiang Kai-shek!"

Chiang was hailed around the world by the Communists. *Pravda*, the German Communist paper *Rote Fahne*, the French Communist paper *L'Humanité*, a delegation of high international Communist leaders—including Earl Browder of the United States,* Jacques Doriot of France and Tom Mann of England, then visiting Canton, Hankow and Shanghai—all praised Chiang Kai-shek. So did Stalin, in speeches in Moscow. It was an hour of sweet triumph for the man who had emerged from the slums of Shanghai to wear the colors of both Dr. Sun Yat-sen and Stalin.

To be sure, there were rumors that Chiang was preparing a coup. Hsueh Yueh, commander of the First Division, came to the Communist Central Committee in Shanghai and warned that Chiang had ordered him and his troops to leave. He offered to arrest Chiang on charges of plotting counterrevolution. The Communists couldn't decide what to do. Hsueh Yueh reluctantly moved out his troops and Chiang moved in a reliable detachment.

So the hour finally came, April 12, 4:00 A.M. The gangs of Pock-marked Huang debouched from the International Settlement and the French Concession, where they had been concealed. They descended on the workers in Chapei, Nantao, Woosoong, Pootung. They shot the Communists where they found them. They broke into the General Labor Union headquarters in the Huchow Guild in Chapei. By luck the trade-union leader, Ku Chen-chung, and his deputy Chou En-lai escaped in the confusion. Most of the leaders perished in resistance or were instantly shot when taken prisoner. The final stand was at the big Commercial Press building on Paoshan Road. By noon it fell. Between four and seven hundred workers were killed on the first day, thousands in the days to come. Shanghai was in the hands of Chiang's bullies.

---

*Browder returned to China in late 1927 as a Comintern operative with the cover of serving as secretary of the Pan-Pacific Trade Union and editor of its paper, *Pan-Pacific Worker*. He remained in Shanghai about two years.

There was one more spark of rebellion in Shanghai—a mass rally on April 13—but this was attacked by Chiang's Second Division. Hundreds more were killed. It took hours to clear the bodies from the streets. For days the killing went on. The heart of revolutionary Shanghai was torn out.

On the evening of April 18 Chiang Kai-shek held a banquet at his headquarters in Nanking. He invited his Soviet military advisers to attend. They sat at the main table at his right. His leading generals were also in attendance. After a long feast Chiang made a speech. At the end he raised a glass of wine and shouted, *"Ta tao kung chang tan!"* ("Down with the Communist Party!") The sixty-odd generals present rose, lifted their glasses and shouted, *"Ta tao kung chang tan!"*

The Soviet advisers left the room. Within days they were gone from Chiang's headquarters. The Chinese Revolution was over and would not regain momentum for two decades. Chiang Kai-shek the revolutionary military commander had come to power and turned into Chiang Kai-shek the reactionary military dictator.

★

There were other acts to be played out: Wuhan would not fall until late summer. The illusion that revolution was still alive would linger. Borodin would plot and strain and seek to keep something going. International revolutionary cadres would try to relight the flames. But it was no good.

In Moscow a great debate would arise. Trotsky was still free and able to speak. For months he had been warning that Stalin's policy of coalition with the Nationalists and reliance on Chiang would lead to disaster. China had become the key issue of Stalin's conflict with Trotsky. Stalin, his principal supporter, Bukharin, and the others had closed their eyes to every sign that Chiang had, in effect, broken with the Communists on March 20, 1926, that he was just one more in the succession of ambitious Chinese warlords. Stalin would not *permit* Chiang to be considered anything but a loyal supporter of revolution. Even if Chiang did not support revolution (and Stalin finally had to admit that perhaps he did not) Chiang was a supporter of Russia, a vehicle for Soviet policy; he was—and in the future, Stalin insisted, would continue to be—a reliable instrument and an ally of Moscow. So Stalin insisted, and *so it had to be*. Stalin's position was predicated on it. If Chiang was not reliable, then he, Stalin, had committed a colossal error, and neither he nor his supporters would admit any error, let alone one of such magnitude.

So until the denouement at Shanghai, Chiang's reputation had been preserved in Moscow; even after Shanghai, for his own political purposes Stalin pretended that the Revolution was still alive and well and on the road to victory in Wuhan.

Any view of Trotsky's, any realistic appraisal of China was swept under the table.

It was this imperative of Stalin's in his struggle with Trotsky that had plagued the Chinese Communists ever since the earliest moment, the period of March 1926. It had prevented them from mustering their forces (actually very powerful as they gained momentum on the Northern Expedition) and kept them from trying to sweep Chiang from the scene. Borodin, whatever he thought privately (and he made enough remarks so that many realized his personal assessment of Chiang did not match his public pronouncements), was gagged by Stalin. Borodin could not have moved against Chiang had he wished. He was compelled to restrain his Chinese Communist colleagues. Stalin did everything he could to prevent Borodin or the Chinese Communists from letting the Chinese people gain a clear image of what Chiang was up to.

Stalin—and his servants, in which number Borodin must be counted—kept up to the last the fiction that Chiang was the valiant leader of the Chinese Revolution.

"Events might prove Trotsky right," Isaacs concluded, "but the struggle against Trotsky had to go on." The Chinese Communist leaders, in Malraux's opinion, were terrified of expressing an attitude that might seem to link them to the Trotskyite opposition, and "in the name of unity with the Kuomintang they had led the workers to the slaughter."

Not even the fall of Shanghai brought a glimmer of truth to Moscow's voice. On April 21 Stalin simply declared that Shanghai had "fully and entirely proved the correctness of the Comintern line."

In Wuhan there was a small end game, desperate and romantic, idealized by Vincent Sheean in his *Personal History*, involving long-odds gambling by Borodin; bravery by Madame Soong Ching-ling, Dr. Sun's young widow, true to the Revolution to the end; naïveté and devotion by young Americans like Anna Louise Strong and Rayna and Bill Prohme; brave declarations by Dr. Sun's Foreign Minister, Eugene Chen. But it could not last long.

By August Madame Soong, Eugene Chen and the Prohmes were en route to Russia, smuggled out of Wuhan by steamer, then up to Vladivostok and on to Moscow. Chiang Kai-shek offered to send Blyukher home by naval cruiser but the Russians did not trust the plan. Blyukher and his wife, accompanied by an old czarist general named Shalavin who had become devoted to Blyukher, slipped away from Wuhan in disguise aboard a Japanese boat. There was a price of sixty thousand yuan on Borodin's head in Shanghai, but he left Wuhan in style aboard a special train for northwestern China accompanied by Miss Strong, Eugene Chen's two sons, Jack and Percy, and a rather large entourage. The party went to Chengchow by special train. There they were entertained by General Feng Yu-siang, the so-called Christian general. After Percy Chen turned over many thousands of silver dollars for "road repairs," General Feng saw the party off. His military band played "Onward, Christian Soldiers." Borodin rode at the head of the column in an eight-cylinder convertible Buick with a canvas cover and mahogany fittings. Percy Chen followed in a Dodge laden with spare parts and sixty gallons of gasoline in tins. Anna Louise Strong and Jack Chen rode in Percy's car. Anna Louise developed a crush on Borodin. Once Percy came upon her crooning to Borodin "When the Shepherds Watched Their Flocks by Night." After two verses Borodin said, "For God's sake, woman, sing the 'Internationale.' " Anna Louise dissolved in tears.

Madame Borodin had been shanghaied by warlord troops who seized the Soviet steamer *Pamyat Lenina*. She was thrown into jail in Peking. The Russians bribed a Chinese judge to set her free and spirited her to an old Buddhist temple. There she lay low for weeks and finally was taken back to Russia via Mongolia.

Borodin's hand in China had played out. He went back to Moscow and obscurity. He was given a room at the Hotel Metropol and badgered unmercifully by official party critics who placed upon him the blame for Stalin's mistakes. He was browbeaten and slandered. He went to work on a book about China's revolution but never finished it. He wouldn't have been allowed to publish it if he had. He hardly saw his old China comrades, even though many lived in the Metropol (Soong Ching-ling was in the room next to his). They quickly realized he was under orders to stay aloof.

In November 1927 Rayna Prohme, the young American woman who had epitomized the Revolution in the eyes of Vincent Sheean (who became her lover), died in Moscow of encephalitis. On Thanksgiving Day, November 24, Rayna was buried. It was cold. The snow fell. A hundred mourners followed the cortège across town to the crematorium, among them Sheean, Soong Ching-ling, who refused a Russian limousine and walked with the others, Dorothy Thompson, who happened to be in Moscow, Anna Louise Strong, the Chens, Madame Borodin—but not Borodin. Bill Prohme had left months earlier for Manila, where in time he would kill himself.

The mourners walked to the slow pace of Chopin's Funeral March. They committed Rayna's casket, covered with golden chrysanthemums and the red flag, to the crematorium furnace. It was the funeral of a thirty-three-year-old American woman, born in Chicago, whose flaming red hair billowed to her hips. It was the funeral of Borodin's revolution.

That night Borodin came to see Sheean in his room at the Savoy Hotel. It seemed to Sheean, lying on a narrow bed in a narrow room, that Borodin looked down on him from a great height. He spoke with deep emotion. "What is needed," he said, as he had said so often in China, "is the long view. Take the long view. A wonderful friend and a wonderful revolutionary instrument have disappeared together . . . China . . . Russia. . . ."

Borodin did not disappear. Stalin gave him the Red Banner of Labor. Jack Chen always believed that was why his name was not on the list of China specialists whom Stalin disposed of by prison or execution in the 1930s. Borodin got a prosaic job running the English-language propaganda paper, the *Moscow Daily News*. But he was frozen out of Chinese affairs. Never again was he consulted on China. In the mid-thirties Stalin sent some of his China advisers back to help Chiang Kai-shek (he never lost his soft spot for Chiang) during the United Front period. But not Borodin.

Stalin executed another large group of China hands, including Blyukher and most of the military advisers, in the late 1930s. Borodin survived that. During World War II he occasionally was seen in Moscow, gaunt and silent and gray. But in the postwar years Stalin finished the job and wiped out most of the survivors.

Borodin was arrested, along with Anna Louise Strong and the staff of the *Moscow Daily News*, in January 1949. Strong was released after a few days in the Lubyanka, branded an agent of the CIA. It would be the mid-1950s before she made it back to China. Borodin went to prison camp. There he perished in a Yakutsk installation on May 29, 1951. He was sixty-seven.

★

One name is missing from the recital of the revolutionary debacle. It is that of Mao Tse-tung. This is no accident: Mao played no role in these dramas. Once again he returned to Hunan, once again he went back to the old farm at Shao Shan; once again he ventured into the countryside to talk to the peasants. Early in 1927 he spent thirty-two days traveling through five counties interviewing hundreds of peasants, and came back to write a classic document: *Report on an Investigation of the Peasant Movement in Hunan*.

The picture he painted remarkably resembled the pictures that would be painted of events in China's countryside after 1949 and during the Cultural Revolution. Images of a world turned upside down: peasants ruling the roost and landlords paraded in dunce caps, driven from their estates, and executed by peasant courts, their houses pillaged and burned.

"In a very short time," Mao wrote, "several hundred million peasants will rise like a mighty storm, like a hurricane, a force so swift and violent that no power, however great, will be able to hold it back."

The peasants, he forecast, would throw off their bonds and surge forward to liberation. "They will sweep all the imperialists, warlords, corrupt officials, local tyrants and evil gentry into their graves. There are three alternatives. To march at their head and lead them; to trail behind them, gesticulating and criticizing; or to stand in their way and oppose them."

Only the first course was worthy of consideration. "Every revolutionary," he said, "should know that the national revolution requires a great change in the countryside." Nor should there be worry about excesses. Proper limits would have to be exceeded in order to right a wrong, or else the wrong could not be righted. "A revolution is not a dinner party or writing an essay or painting a picture or doing embroidery; it cannot be so refined, so leisurely and gentle, so temperate, kind, courteous, restrained and magnanimous. A revolution is an act of violence, an insurrection."

Mao brought his report to Wuhan. It was not liked. Not by his Communist Party associates, not by his Nationalist Party associates (he had retained his close connections with the Kuomintang). He was seen as too radical. His slogans were not admired: "Anyone with land is a bully; no member of the gentry is not evil"; "In correcting a wrong we must be excessive in upholding the right." Under the influence of Mao's slogans the elderly, gentle father of Li Li-san, Mao's party associate, was killed by the peasants of his local village. This made Mao's party comrades nervous about him. He presented his views to the party plenum and was removed as head of the peasant department. Then he returned to Hunan to try to organize the peasants against Chiang's warlord ally, who was slaughtering them. He was ordered back to Wuhan—the party was not yet ready to break with the Kuomintang. By the time he got back Borodin was packing his bags and the break was a reality.

In their final agony the Communists lashed out with a series of violent ventures—the Nan-chang rebellion, in which Chou En-lai and Lin Piao participated; the Autumn Harvest Uprising led by Mao; and the Canton Commune.

Each was doomed. Each was the product of desperation. Moscow had to have victories to demonstrate to Stalin's Trotskyite opponents that his revolutionary policies were still valid, that China was still bursting with revolution.

A post-mortem of the Nan-chang rebellion by its leaders gives the flavor of these operations: "Neither food nor drink could be bought. When thirsty we drank from the ditches in the fields and therefore a great many of the soldiers died of disease; men fell over and died along the road constantly. . . . During only three days' march we had lost more than one-third our actual strength, almost half the ammunition was abandoned, all the mortars were thrown away, and several of the large cannon were also lost. The soldiers who deserted or died of illness approached four thousand." The campaign started September 5 with about twelve thousand men. It dissolved three weeks later with fewer than two thousand troops. The men simply slipped away and disappeared in the countryside.

The Canton Commune, a last gasp of surviving Communists, flickered a few days and then was ended in a bloodbath that even by Chinese civil-war standards was extraordinarily brutal.

Mao's efforts to raise the flag of rebellion in Hunan fared much the same. Even before he got into the vicinity of Chang-sha to assemble his forces he was at loggerheads with his Communist Party chiefs. They denounced his program of carrying out the uprising under the Communist flag (he had designed his own: a red field, a hammer and sickle within a gold star) rather than the blue-and-white Kuomintang banner; the creation of rural Soviets; the raising of a mass peasant army from among these millions that he had reported a few months before were burgeoning with revolution; the dispossession of the landlords—all of this seemed to the party to smell of adventurism and "leftism." Mao, they said, wanted to rely too much on military organization; he was a military "romanticist," a military deviationist.

Mao ignored the critique and went ahead but his uprising sputtered out. He was captured near Heng-yang and was marched off for execution. He borrowed some money from a fellow prisoner and tried to bribe a guard to let him go. The guard refused. Two hundred yards from the execution grounds, Mao dashed into the heavy undergrowth. Night fell before search parties could find him. He slipped away, used the seven dollars he had borrowed to buy a pair of shoes and an umbrella (Mao was never to be long without an umbrella) and rejoined his troops.

Mao had started his venture with fewer than 4,000 men. His hopes for a peasant rising were not fulfilled. Chiang's warlords had massacred 330,000 peasants in northern Hunan by September 1. The peasants were too dazed and bloody to fight again. Mao found no food in the countryside. His wounded had to be left behind, to certain death. Spies and informers dogged him.

On September 20 he gathered the remnants of his forces at the foot of the remote Chingkang Mountain and shouted to his troops: "Do we dare to carry forward the Revolution?" His troops, down to a thousand men, shouted, "We do." But when the climb began the next morning only eight hundred went up the mountain. On the barren ridges of Chingkang the peasants were so backward they had no wheeled vehicles. They started fires by striking flint against steel. Most were Hakkas, the same Hakkas who had provided the first recruits for the Taiping rebellion. On the mountain crest Mao found two tribes of Hakka bandits, six hundred men with a hundred twenty rifles. He persuaded them to join his band of eight hundred men and eighty rifles.

It was a ragtag army. Most of the soldiers were rural tramps, what the Chinese call *yu-min*, vagrants and déclassé elements, not even proper peasant soldiers. There was absolutely nothing in Marxist thought to suggest that this riffraff was a suitable medium for creating a revolution. The group included, in Mao's words, "soldiers, bandits, robbers, beggars and prostitutes."

"They each have a different way of living," he observed. "The soldier fights, the bandit robs, the thief steals, the beggar begs and the prostitute seduces. But to the extent that they all must earn their living and cook rice to eat they are all one."

The déclassé element in Chinese society was enormous. Mao thought it might number as many as twenty million, possibly more. They were bound together in secret societies, the Triads, the Ko-lao-hui (particularly strong in Hunan), the Big Sword Society and, in Shanghai, the Green Gang. These were elements from which the Taipings had drawn much strength, although Mao did not mention this. Nor at that time did he draw any inferences regarding Chiang's connections with the Green Gang. He was simply talking about the basic facts of Chinese society as it existed and he insisted that "these people are capable of fighting very bravely and if properly led can become a revolutionary force."

Those words were written by Mao before he found himself at Chingkang Mountain. Now he had to rely upon the *yu-min* if the Revolution was to be kept going. The Central Committee of the Communist Party, strongly urban-oriented, believing literally in Marx's proletarian revolution and never at ease with Mao's theories drawn from the stubborn facts of Chinese life, was horrified when it discovered what Mao was up to. News did not travel very fast to and from Chingkang Mountain but the Central Committee ordered Mao reprimanded, deprived

*(Text continues on page 145.)*

George Bernard Shaw visits China. From left to right: American writer Agnes Smedley, Shaw, Soong Ching-ling, Tsai Yuan-pei (liberal intellectual), Lu Hsan (famous radical writer). Photograph taken after luncheon on February 17, 1933, at Madame Soong's Shanghai home. EAS

The Soong sisters inspect bomb damage in Chungking, 1940. Left to right: Soong Ching-ling (Madame Sun Yat-sen), Soong An-ling (Madame H. H. Kung) and Soong Mei-ling (Madame Chiang Kai-shek). WW

*Overleaf:*
Chinese youth rebel against the Manchu-imposed pigtails in the early 1900s. BET

*Opposite:*
Soong Mei-ling with her older sister, Soong Ai-ling. Photo from the late 1920s. CUL

Soong Mei-ling (Madame Chiang Kai-shek). Photo from the late 1920s. CUL

Dr. Sun Yat-sen, China's first President, in Japan in 1916. Sun is seated in the center of the first row; his new wife, Soong Ching-ling, is at his right. MIL

Dr. Sun Yat-sen (second from left) forming the democratic revolutionary organization in Hawaii in 1894. SYS

*Opposite:*
Dr. Sun Yat-sen and Soong Ching-ling at Whampoa Military Academy, Canton, June 16, 1924. Chiang Kai-shek, Chou En-lai and many famous Kuomintang and Communist military leaders were trained at the academy, founded by Dr. Sun and largely staffed by Russian military advisers. CPS

Dr. Sun Yat-sen, leader of the Chinese Revolution of 1911, founder of the Canton revolutionary regime and of the Kuomintang. EAS

Soong Ching-ling, widow of Dr. Sun, in the early 1960s. She had become a supporter of the Chinese Communist regime and Vice-Chairman of the People's Republic of China. EAS

*Opposite:*
Dr. Sun and Soong Ching-Ling en route to Peking in 1924; Dr. Sun died shortly after arriving. EAS

Wedding portrait of Chiang Kai-shek and Soong Mei-ling, Shanghai, December 1, 1927. WW

Chiang Kai-shek betrays the Communists in Shanghai, April 12, 1927. Workers are arrested and executed by the thousands. MRV

*Opposite:*
Generalissimo Chiang Kai-shek in the mid-1930s. WW

Chinese forces moving north from Mukden to meet the attack of the Japanese in Manchuria, 1932. UPI

*Overleaf:*
Two soldiers guard the armored locomotive of a Chinese troop train during the campaign against the Japanese in Manchuria in 1932. UPI

Starvation's victims in the wake of the devastating famine of 1928 and 1929, witnessed by Edgar Snow and Rewi Alley. MRV

The Japanese attack Shanghai, 1937. Fighting in the workers' district of Chapai. LC

Chou En-lai (second from left) playing a woman's role in a play at the Nankai Middle School in his home city of Tientsin. MRV

*Opposite:*
The overseas founding group of Chinese Communist Party in Paris, 1924, including Chou En-lai (front row, fourth from left) and Teng Hsiao-ping (back row, third from right). MIL

Winners of school competitions at Nankai Middle School, Tientsin. Chou En-lai is seated in the middle. MRV

Chou En-lai (born in 1898 to a mandarin family) as a schoolboy of thirteen in 1911. MRV

*Opposite:*
Chou En-lai as a student in Paris, 1922. MRV

一九二四年攝於巴黎

KAETE 4
3 Hers

Chou En-lai at Yenan, 1936.
MIL

Chou and his wife, Teng Ying-chao, in Chungking, about 1940. MRV

Chou returning to Yenan from Sian in 1936, at the time of the kidnapping of Chiang Kai-shek. CPS

Lin Piao leading Chinese Communist forces in Manchuria, 1948. WW

Mao Tse-tung and his family
at the time of his mother's
death, about 1918. Left to right:
Mao's younger brother, Mao
Tse-tan; his uncle; his father,
Mao Jen-shen; and Mao. MIL

Mao in Shanghai, 1924. CPS

*Opposite:*
Mao at Chang-sha in 1918,
aged twenty-five. CPS

Mao Tse-tung addressing peasants in the revolutionary base area in Kiangsi, 1933. CPS

Mao's office in one of the Yenan caves. MIL

Mao's first wife, Yang Kui-hui, with their sons, Mao An-ching and Mao An-ying. She was executed at Chang-sha by Chiang Kai-shek's forces in 1930.

Ho Shih-chen, Mao's second wife, at Yenan after Long March, 1937.

Mao and Chiang Ching presented this photo to the Soviet representative P. P. Vladimirov in Yenan in November 1945.

*Opposite:*
Mao and Chiang Ching (Lan Ping) in Yenan. EAS

Photograph taken after triple wedding ceremony at Star Movie Studio, Shanghai, spring, 1934. Left to right: film actor Ku Er-yi and wife, Tu Chian-huan; unknown man; in the foreground, Chao Tan and his wife, actress Yeh Lu-shi; to rear, Lan Ping (later better known as Chiang Ching, Mao's last wife) and her husband, actor and critic Tang Na. Lan Ping was divorced from Tang Na in 1937. According to some accounts she had an affair with Chao after leaving Tang. LEX

*Opposite:*
Mao and Chou En-lai in Yenan in 1945. CPS

Otto Braun in the early 1970s. Braun, a German Communist, representative of Comintern and Stalin's liaison with Mao Tse-tung, was the only foreigner to make the Long March.

Chinese warlord's house where in January 1935, during the Long March, the famous Tsunyi conference was held, which confirmed Mao's *de facto* leadership of the Chinese Communist Party. MIL

Mao addresses the Lu Hsun Art Academy in Yenan in May 1938, not long after the enrollment in the academy of a young Shanghai movie actress, Lan Ping, whom Mao would soon marry. CPS

Mao and his son Mao An-ying (born in 1921) in Yenan. Anying was to die in the Korean War, serving with the Chinese forces. MIL

*Opposite:*
On May 25, 1935, Mao's Red Army forces seized and crossed this swinging bridge at Liu Ting Chiao across the Tatu River in southwestern China, the most difficult and daring undertaking of the Long March. MRV

*Left:*
Crossing the desolate great Snowy Mountains on the Long March. EAS

*Left:*
Forcing the way across the Wu River. CPS

*Opposite:*
Chinese guerrillas in Shansi-Chahar-Hopeh area destroy rails behind Japanese lines. CPS

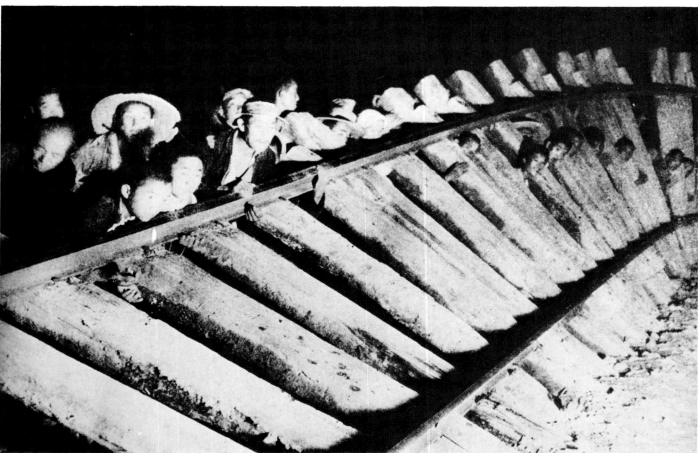

Chinese commanders in the Long March. Second from left, Peng Te-huai, later dismissed in a quarrel with Mao. Third from left, Chu Teh, long-time commander of the People's Liberation Army. Fourth from left, Chen Yun. On extreme right, Teng Hsiao-ping. CUL

In Yenan, an ambulance donated by the Chinese Laundrymen's Alliance of New York. People's Liberation Army Commander Chu Teh is on the right. WW

Chu Teh addressing troops, Yenan, 1937. WW

The Yenan caves where Mao established his headquarters. WW

*Opposite:*
A People's Liberation Army soldier on guard in Yenan. WW

Chinese forces on guard against the Japanese at the Great Wall, 1942. CPS

U.S. Ambassador Patrick J. Hurley arrives in Yenan in 1944 and is greeted by Mao Tse-tung. Chu Teh is sitting beside Hurley. UPI

*Overleaf:*
Chinese Red Army troops in action against the Japanese in North China. MRV

*Opposite:*
Dr. Norman Bethune, a Canadian volunteer, operates in Yenan. CPS

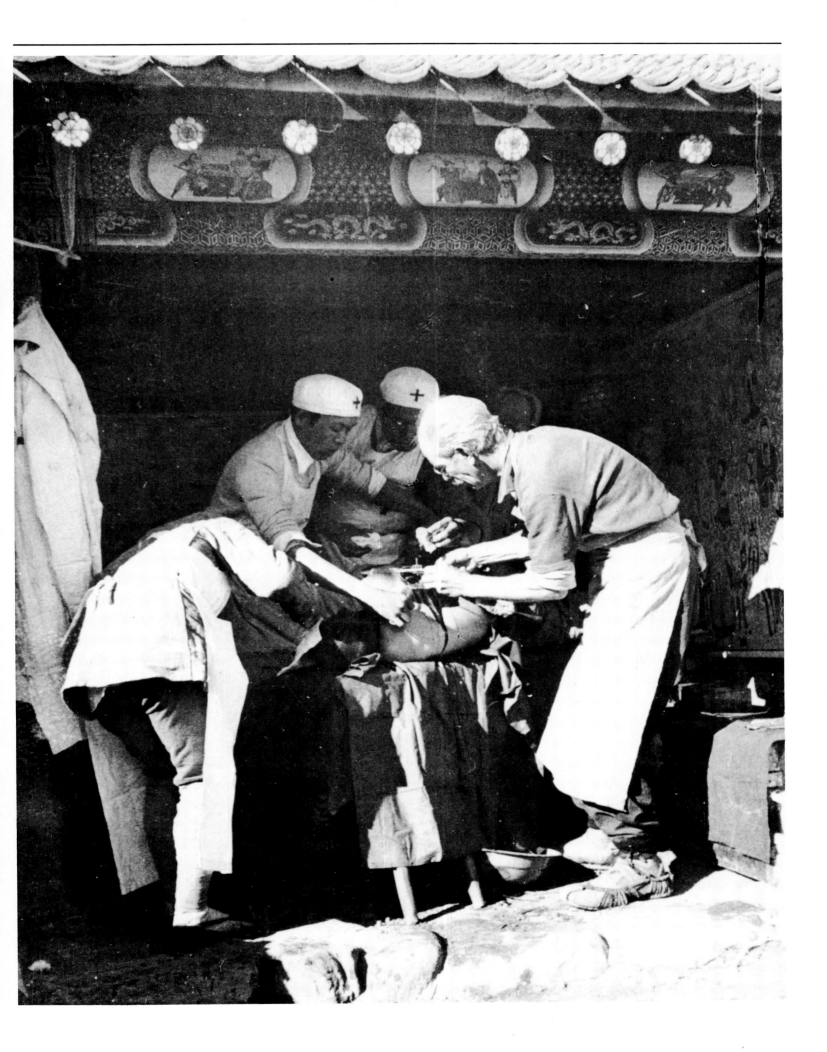

Nationalist forces parade in Kun-ming, Yunnan Province, on "Double-Seven," July 7, 1944. ROT

Hardly worth the notice of a passer-by, a coolie dying of starvation on the pavement in Hengyang, July 1946. ROT

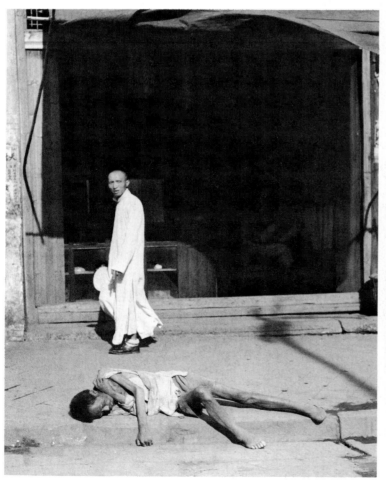

Nationalist soldiers stand under a Nationalist wall painting, as the civil war with the Communists is about to break out. ROT

Life goes on as usual for Chuan Kao-chai, dealer in antiquities on Nanking Road in Shanghai, 1946. ROT

*Opposite:*
Shanghai, Christmas 1945, liberated from the Japanese. The poster of Chiang Kai-shek dominates Nanking Road from the wall of the Sun Department Store. ROT

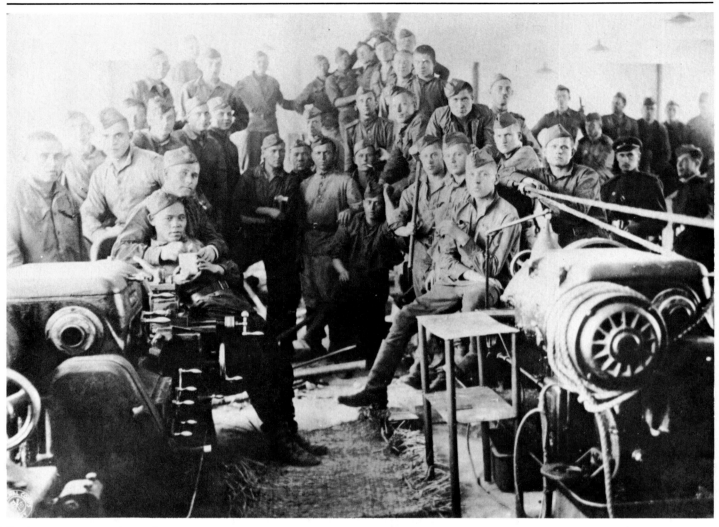

Soviet troops remove heavy industrial equipment from a Manchurian factory in 1946. LC

The wall of this coal hydro-
genation research laboratory in
Mukden, Manchuria, was
blasted out by Soviet troops, to
facilitate their removal of
equipment for transport back
to the Soviet Union. LC

In Mukden, Manchuria, Russian soldiers letter a warning on a Japanese pillbox, quoting Prince Aleksandr Nevsky's saying that those who come to the Russian land with a sword will be met by the sword. LC

*Opposite top:*
Mao on the march against the
Nationalists in northern Shensi
in 1947, after abandoning Yenan. CPS

Nationalist conscripts, roped
together and led to the assembly point. LC

*Opposite:*
Chinese Communist forces
battering their way toward
Nanking in 1948. CPS

Mao enters Peking, March 25, 1949. MRV

Henry Pu-yi, last of the Manchus, puppet Emperor of Manchukuo under the Japanese, lives on in the Communist regime, finally working as a gardener at the palace he once occupied. UPI

of his place on the Central Committee and removed from the Hunan party committee. Once again Mao was in disgrace. The party feared that Mao and his little band in the mountains might become a modern version of the heroes of *Shui Hu Chuan,* the tale of the 108 bandits.

Far back in the hills, Mao did not learn of the party's action for three months. Not until late February or early March 1928 did he discover that he was in official disgrace. By this time he had been joined by his two brothers, Tse-min and Tse-tan, and his adopted sister, Tse-hung. His wife, Kai-hui, and their two (possibly three) children were still at Shao Shan. Mao was not to see her again before she was killed by Chiang's execution squads in Chang-sha in 1930. In the battles of Chingkang Mountain Mao met an eighteen-year-old woman named Ho Shih-chen. Her father had been a small landowner who became a Communist. She had fought in the Nan-chang rebellion. They fell in love, and Shih-chen was to bear Mao two children. After the death of Kai-hui the two were married.

In April 1928 Chu Teh arrived at Chingkang. Chu Teh was probably the most capable military commander the Communists possessed and his partnership with Mao would be long-lasting. Chu brought with him a substantial army: between them Mao and Chu now had about ten thousand men. Among those who arrived with Chu was a brilliant twenty-one-year-old officer named Lin Piao. Chu's political commissar was Chen Yi, later to become a celebrated commander, still later Foreign Minister under Mao and eventually hounded to death during the Cultural Revolution.

Chu Teh had been sent to take over from Mao. Instead, the men formed an enduring partnership. Occasionally their views would differ—Chu Teh was a blunt, open military man. Mao was much more political. But in the battles of Chingkang Mountain an alliance began that would endure through the years.

Later Chingkang would become part of the legend of Mao Tse-tung. But in 1928 it was a backwater, southeast of Chang-sha, between the rivers Hsiang and Kan. Few Chinese could have located it on a map.

It was distant from the embers of the Chinese Revolution. When the Sixth Congress of the Chinese party met that summer, it was held not in China but in Moscow. Supposedly, there was no place in China secure enough for such a meeting. Actually, it gave Moscow a chance to dominate and pick leaders. Nikolai Bukharin was very much Stalin's viceroy for international questions, and Pavel Mif, a twenty-six-year-old doctrinaire whose real name was Mikhail Aleksandrovich Fortus, had replaced Borodin as Stalin's China expert. Mif was young, pliant and ambitious and knew how to take orders. Like so many of Stalin's China specialists Mif would vanish in the 1938 purges. Now he oversaw the Sixth Congress. Among those who attended were Chu Chiu-pai (who had replaced Chen Tu-hsiu as head of the party and would now be replaced by Li Li-san), Chou En-lai, Chang Kuo-tao (later to break with the party and leave as a legacy an intimate and revealing account of these years) and Liu Shao-chi (for years one of Mao's closest collaborators but ultimately the principal target of the Cultural Revolution).

Mao, of course, was not present. Nor was Chu Teh. Li Li-san was quoted as saying, "What kind of Marxism can there be on the Chingkang Mountain?"

The Sixth Congress put Mao back on the Central Committee, but the emergence of Mao's fellow Hunanese Li Li-san as party secretary ensured that Mao's conflict would continue. The two men shared the hot Hunanese temperament. They had never gotten along. They would not now. But, typically, it would be five months before Mao learned of the Sixth Congress's decisions (the meeting concluded in September 1928) and by this time he and Chu Teh had moved their base from Chingkang Mountain to a more fertile region of hills and mountains in Kiangsi Province near the boundaries of Fukien and Kwangtung provinces. Communications into and within the region were difficult, and this gave Mao a chance to build up his strength. He and Chu began with a nucleus of four thousand troops. They set up their capital at Juijin, started to train forces, gradually extending the area under their control.

★

There was constant conflict in the next two or three years between the Communist troops of Mao and Chu and satellite Communist areas, and the forces of Chiang Kai-shek. There were fierce struggles between Mao and Li Li-san and his Shanghai-based, city-oriented party headquarters. Again and again Li tried to get Mao to come out of the countryside and capture cities. Mao fell ill for a while. *Imprecor*, the Comintern bulletin, reported his death—an indication of how remote he was from the center.

But it was the remoteness that enabled him and the revolutionary forces under his command to put a little flesh on their bones, to provide a core from which the Chinese revolutionary cause might yet emerge. For China as a whole the notion of revolution had virtually vanished. Chiang had solidified his power. The threat in Chinese minds these days was that of the Japanese, deepening their penetration, ceaseless in their encroachment. The Chinese public was hardly aware of the existence of Mao and Chu and their base areas in Kiangsi. Chiang Kai-shek, of course, knew very well of the existence of the Communist areas. When he had the time and the forces available, he would attend to them.

In 1930 Li Li-san won Moscow's approval to launch an offensive out of the base areas. Mao and Chu went along with this, as did another able Red Army commander, Peng Te-huai (who later would become China's Defense Minister). Peng succeeded in capturing Chang-sha but lost the city after ten days. Mao and Chu tried to take Nan-chang but could hold it only twenty-four hours. Then all three, on Li Li-san's orders, tried for Chang-sha again, with an army of twenty thousand men, the largest force the Communists had ever mustered. They failed and returned to Kiangsi. In the ensuing Chang-sha bloodbath Mao lost his wife, Kai-hui, and his adopted sister, Tse-hung. His two sons were saved, but Shao Shan was seized and the graves of his parents desecrated.

Li Li-san lost his post as general secretary because of the Chang-sha fiasco. He was sent back to Russia. But this meant no immediate boost for Mao. Power in the party fell into the hands of the disciples of Pavel Mif (rector of the Sun Yat-sen University in Moscow), twenty-eight young Chinese Communists who were sent back to China after a couple of years of study at Mif's university, the "twenty-eight Bolsheviks," or "Stalin's Chinese," as they came to be known. Two of these "Bolsheviks," Wang Ming and Po Ku, both twenty-four years old, took over direction of the Chinese party after a plenary session in January 1931. Contrary to party rules, neither Mao nor Chu was invited to the meeting. Once again, as so often, Mao was absent from the inner circle when a party decision was made. Within months police raids, informers and traitors had turned the party's Shanghai headquarters in the French Concession into a place of doom. The "Bolsheviks" determined to move to Mao's Kiangsi base, the only place in China where a Communist was more or less secure. Then Wang went back to Moscow, to stay there until 1937, attempting to organize a new Chinese Revolution by letter and telegram as Chinese representative in the Comintern.

China was in turmoil that year of 1931. The Japanese invaded Manchuria. Chiang's warlord alliances were in some disarray. He had launched three massive expeditions against Mao and the Communist base areas. In the first he used a hundred thousand troops against thirty thousand on Mao's side, in the second the odds were two hundred thousand to thirty thousand and in the third he employed three hundred thousand. Mao and Chu Teh beat him each time. Many of the defeated troops and some of Chiang's generals came over to the Communists.

On November 7, 1931, the First Congress of the Soviet Republic of China was held in Juijin. Mao was elected chairman, receiving the most votes. Wang Ming came in fourth. Mao was later to write: "From 1931 to 1934 I had no voice at all at the Central [Headquarters]." Mao was exaggerating but he certainly had no influence in the Shanghai center, or among the "Bolsheviks." By 1932 he was again being discredited, thanks to their work. At a plenary in August, at the height of Chiang's fourth "bandit" extermination campaign, Mao was relieved as Red Army political commissar and as party secretary for the forces. Chou En-lai (not yet in alliance with Mao) replaced him as political commissar. Mao no longer had a voice in Communist military operations. His land-reform program was criticized (not radical enough). He was attacked for "right opportunism" and "procrastination." He was still chairman of the Soviet, however, and in April 1932 managed to issue a declaration of war against Japan. No one paid much heed to it but later on it looked good on the record. His influence was at a nadir. He puttered about with economic questions and again fell ill of malaria, this time critically. His temperature rose to 105 degrees. His life was saved by Dr. Nelson Fu, a Chinese Christian who had thrown in his lot with the Communists.

The deciding word on military operations had now passed to a rather serious-looking man with horn-rimmed spectacles, a scholarly air, no command of the Chinese language and no knowledge of Chinese conditions, political, economic, cultural or psychological.

This was Otto Braun, also known as Otto Stern, Karl Wagner, Hua Fu and Li Teh. He was an agent of the Comintern, a onetime schoolteacher, a sometime newspaper correspondent and a graduate of the Frunze Military Academy, the top Soviet military institution.

Braun set foot in China in the late spring of 1932, within a month of graduating from Frunze. He traveled on the Trans-Siberian, crossed the border at Manchuria Station and went on to Harbin, where he spent some weeks briefing himself on China. No one would have guessed that this solid, sober-looking German carried a marshal's baton in his knapsack. Braun was thirty-two years old and a professional revolutionary. He had long been a member of the German Communist Party, having fought on the barricades for the Bavarian Communist regime in 1919. He was imprisoned by the Weimar Republic but escaped in 1928 to the Soviet Union, where he was trained as a professional revolutionary and sent to Frunze to become a military specialist. His arrival in China signaled a new effort by Moscow to control and direct the remnants of the Chinese Revolution. The "Bolsheviks" would handle the political side; Braun would handle the military.

After a bit of travel Braun made his way to Shanghai and checked into the Astor House, an excellent old English hotel. Later he moved to an American pension, which he felt enabled him to blend better into the background.

The Comintern already had a military representative in Shanghai named Arthur Ewert,* and another military operative, a man named Manfred Stern, who went under the pseudonym of "Fred," was supposed to become the chief of station. Fred didn't get on the scene until 1933. Later, in Spain, Fred became famous as "General Kleber," one of the chiefs of the International Brigades. (Not a few of the Comintern agents and military specialists in Spain got their training in China; eventually Stalin wiped out almost all of them.)

There was little or nothing for a Comintern military expert to do in Shanghai except second-guess what Mao and Chu Teh were doing in Kiangsi. Well, there was one thing. Braun could and did report to Moscow information about Nationalist Chinese and Japanese military strength, using intercept data which were relayed to him from Kiangsi. Mao and Chu had established a highly efficient intercept operation. Braun soon knew more about Chiang Kai-shek and the Japanese than he did about Mao's army.

Communist Party affairs in China were controlled by Po Ku, only twenty-five years old, and Lo Fu (the pseudonym of Chang Wen-tien), a onetime San Francisco newspaperman, two of the "Bolsheviks." Wang Ming, in Moscow, passed on orders from Pavel Mif, who in turn got them from Bukharin (until Stalin displaced, arrested and executed him). The orders actually, of course, originated with Stalin and his immediate entourage.

The fatal effects of long-distance control by the Kremlin had already been demonstrated in the 1927 Shanghai disaster and Chiang's switch of sides. But this experience did not change Stalin's attitude. What he wanted and intended to have was a Chinese party that was a tool of Russian policy. If that meant further disaster for China's revolution—so be it.

Stalin's instrument was Braun. His assignment could not have been simpler: by whatever means, mobilize China against Japan. The Soviet Union felt threatened by the rising aggression of Japan on her Siberian frontiers. Already the Kremlin envisaged what soon became a reality—the tripartite Axis of Germany-Italy-Japan.

Writing his memoirs forty years after his mission to China, Braun made his priorities amazingly clear: he was there not to aid China's revolution but to help Moscow.

"Already in 1932–1933 the chief enemy for us—and I want especially to emphasize this—" Braun wrote, "was aggressive Japanese imperialism."

In contrast, Mao and most of the Chinese Communists thought their primary task was to defeat Chiang Kai-shek and win the Chinese Revolution.

Mao, Braun said, contended that the center of world revolution had shifted to the East, to China, just as in 1917 it had shifted from Germany (where Marx thought it would begin) to Russia (where it actually occurred).

The Comintern, the Kremlin and Stalin, however, believed the chief conflict still lay between the Soviet Union and the capitalist world.

Mao, said Braun, thought that the big crisis was between Japan and China and he believed

CHINA
100 Years
of
Revolution

148

---

*Arthur Ewert, a German Communist, was active in the Comintern in the late 1920s and was close to Bukharin. Curiously, he employed the cover name "A. Braun" in Moscow and "Grey" in the United States. A man called "A. Braun" was said to have been arrested and tortured to death in Brazil in the mid-1930s, but whether this is the same man is not certain.

that the Soviet Union should give number-one priority to helping China, even if this led Russia into war, because Mao felt that victory in the Chinese Revolution would aid world revolution.

But the view of Stalin, the Kremlin, Moscow, the Comintern, Braun and the "twenty-eight Bolsheviks" was that the chief threat was not to China but to the Soviet Union, and decisions about China must be subordinated to Moscow's needs.

Braun initially spent much time trying to estimate the anti-Japanese mood of Kuomintang troops and their generals, in line with the Kremlin's search for allies against Japan. (Stalin had not given up hopes for Chiang Kai-shek.) He sent reports back to Moscow by courier and microfilm.

Braun thought Mao's ideology all wrong, in that Mao believed the chief revolutionary force in China was the peasant, not the working class, as Marx (and Lenin and Stalin) proclaimed. To Braun, Mao's concept of the proletariat was unsound—Mao wanted to base himself not on urban factory workers but on artisans, small traders, peasants, migratory labor and even beggars.

The slogan the Comintern advanced was "Hands Off the Soviet Union," reflecting Moscow's fear of Axis attack. The Chinese party's slogan was "Help the Soviet Union." Braun thought that wasn't too bad. But Mao's slogan couldn't be worse. It was "Help China."

Braun couldn't wait to get to the "Soviet Republic" in Kiangsi and put things on the right (Soviet) track. Po Ku, Lo Fu, Chen Yun and others of the Shanghai center got away in the spring of 1933. It was September 1933 before Braun reached Kiangsi. He carried a secret code enabling him to communicate with Fred. Fred's last words before Braun boarded a little English boat that was to take him to Swatow were that he, Fred, was the chief Comintern military representative in China, and that Braun was to carry out his orders without fail. Moscow would tell Fred, Fred would tell Braun and Braun would tell the Chinese.

The departure of Braun from Shanghai was not to lessen in any way Moscow's iron hand on the Chinese Revolution. It served, rather, to extend even further the tenuous line of communications.

Braun boarded his ship at midnight. In his moneybelt he had what he later was to call "not a few hundreds of dollars." More likely a good many thousands.

★

Chiang Kai-shek's Fifth Campaign against the Communists was getting under way by the time Braun reached the Soviet zone. Von Seeckt's tactics were working well. Braun had his job cut out for him. Chiang was personally directing operations. He had massed ten divisions and five hundred planes. The Communists were taking heavy losses, and von Seeckt's strategy of ringing the base area with concentric circles of blockhouses was destroying mobility and pinching off supplies.

Mao was playing no role in this. He was ill and did not attend the fifth plenary in January 1934. Po Ku claimed it was a diplomatic illness but that seems doubtful. Mao was no longer in the Politburo, though he still held his post of chairman of the Soviet Republic.

But even Braun had to concede that Mao was "the most significant" figure among the Communist leaders. He was a straight, trim, thin forty-year-old man. Braun thought he looked more of a thinker and a poet than a soldier or politician. Mao spoke in aphorisms, often with a bite. He would observe that "red peppers are the food of a real revolutionary" or that anyone who doesn't eat red peppers "isn't a real soldier." Braun couldn't eat the hot Hunan food. He thought that Mao was giving him the needle.

By late summer it was apparent that something had to be done or Chiang would whittle the Soviet zone to bits. The area had withered from seventy counties and nine million people to six counties and possibly three million in population. It was decided that the Red Army must break out. The first task was to smash through the von Seeckt blockhouse system, then to try to join the famous Communist Fourth Route Army in Hunan. No one knew exactly where the Fourth Army was, but no matter.

This was Braun's plan and it was approved by Po Ku and the "Bolsheviks." Chou En-lai drafted it in detail. It was agreed upon by the party Politburo, then communicated to Shanghai, which submitted it to Moscow, where in turn the Comintern, after consulting Stalin, gave general approval.

Military affairs were in the hands of a troika, Braun, Po Ku and Chou, but Mao's influence remained enormous. In fact Chou secretly consulted Mao on the eve of the breakout. Mao was rusticating at Yütu near the First Army headquarters of his protégé, Lin Piao, in the autumn of 1934 when he was visited by Chou and Chu Teh. Later Mao hinted that he had been sent to Yütu under house arrest by Braun and Po Ku. Braun violently denied the charge but there seems to be substance to it. Chou and Chu Teh told Mao they were concerned about the "Bolsheviks" and Braun's direction of military operations. Should they abandon Kiangsi? Mao proposed a carefully prepared strategic retreat—so it was said. Later he would criticize the haste with which preparations to leave Kiangsi were made.

Chiang was on the verge of another attack, and the Red Army command knew this from wireless intercepts. Preparations for the breakout had to be made in a week or so. It was decided to leave a third of the force behind, especially those who could not move rapidly. Mao left his two children by Shih-chen with a peasant family because no toddlers were permitted. He never saw them again. His brother Tse-tan stayed behind, was captured and executed a few months later. Chu Chiu-pai, the displaced party leader, ill with tuberculosis, suffered the same fate. Several hundred women started the march but only thirty-five concluded it—Shih-chen, Mao's wife, among them.

A new Military Council was formed. Mao had a place on that, along with Chu Teh, Chou En-lai and, of course, Braun. Chu Teh commanded the march and Peng Te-huai was his deputy.

The size of the main force is the subject of some argument. Braun placed the number at 75,000 to 81,000, of whom 57,000 to 61,000 were organized troop formations with 41,000 to 42,000 guns, the others being, for the most part, porters and other noncombatants. The usual figure given is 100,000 to 120,000, but Braun claimed this was a "propaganda figure." Each soldier, he insisted, carried two weeks' supply of rice. Others reported that many soldiers had only three days' supply.

Certain it is that the column had no winter clothing and that most of the troops had no idea where they were going. Braun attributed this to strict security. Of course, the fact is that wherever they intended to go—they didn't get there. Plans were to change again and again and again.

Mao's orderly told Han Su-yin: "We received orders to equip ourselves lightly in preparation to go to the front to fight the Japanese. Some other units apparently did not get this information; they thought they were going to open a new base and fight landlords. Others thought they were going on a parade."

The main force left on October 16, 1934. Mao joined the columns on October 18 with his special bodyguard. He brought along two blankets, a worn overcoat, a wool sweater, an umbrella and a rice bowl. He used his horse to carry supplies.

So the Long March began. But no one called it that. No one knew it would be the Long March. They didn't know they would go on for seventy-five hundred miles. Mao had no role in the command. He was not even, as he had been in the past, the political commissar to his old comrade, Chu Teh.

## 8

## THE LONG MARCH

**T**HE LONG MARCH—THE "MARCH
of twenty-five thousand li," as Mao Tse-tung was still calling it when Edgar Snow held his
talks with him in Pao-an in 1936—began slowly. The troops were laden with supplies, crates,
carts, files, paper. If it was not, as Edgar Snow later described it, something like a "nation
on the move" it was very much like a government on the move.

True, a force of possibly twelve thousand troops had been left behind to defend the Kiangsi
base, to hold it open if possible, to provide a shelter and continuity, to maintain a presence.
Still, the main body of the Chinese Soviet Republic was on its way, destination unknown. The
hope was that it would break through von Seeckt's concrete rings, join up with the Fourth
Army and establish a new regional center somewhere near the intersection of Kweichow and
Hunan or possibly Szechwan. True, they were off to fight the enemy, off to fight Chiang Kai-
shek and ultimately, perhaps, the Japanese. But they had nearer-term tasks. The first was to
crush the rings of blockhouses.

This was no small obstacle. Von Seeckt's strategy had been well thought out, and Chiang
Kai-shek had provided the troops and money to set up the fortifications. Chiang Kai-shek had
correctly deduced that the Red Army would try to make a juncture with the Fourth Army.
Chiang had positioned an army between the two Communist forces and he had divisions strung
out along the flanks of the Communist route to assault them as they marched.

Chu Teh had no air force and no anti-aircraft guns. There was nothing he could do to prevent
low-flying German-piloted Nationalist planes from strafing the Communist columns as they
slowly moved westward.

To preserve some security of movement and protect his forces from air attack, he ordered
night marches for the first ten days. But there was little cover and the German pilots had no
trouble locating the resting columns by day. Losses were heavy.

Chiang may have had more exact information about Communist plans than Chu Teh realized.
Just before the start of the Long March, Chiang's secret police raided the party's Shanghai
Central, the liaison office through which the Soviet zone communicated by wireless with
Moscow and the Comintern. The heads of the bureau, Slavin and Mitskevich,* also known as
Li Chu-sheng and Shen Zhung-lian, were arrested. They gave Chiang's police much detail
about party operations in China. Braun believed they revealed the breakout strategy.†

Chiang was shrewd enough to put two and two together. The direction of the Red Army
forces was quickly apparent.

---

*Braun gives the name as Mitskevich; this may be, in fact, O. A. Mitkevich, a veteran Soviet party member who served as Comintern representative
in China as early as 1928.
†Eugene Dennis, later to become secretary of the American Communist Party, was stationed in Shanghai as a Comintern operative in 1933–1934.
Apparently his carefully camouflaged and luxurious flat in the French Concession was not affected by the Kuomintang raids.

The wiping out of the Shanghai communications post was to have a more profound effect: it cut the Communists off from the rest of the world and severed the umbilical link to Moscow and the Comintern. Not for eighteen months would communications be restored. Every military move since the "Bolsheviks" and Braun had taken over had been dictated from or cleared by Moscow. Now they were on their own. Now it would be the word of a German Communist who spoke not a whisper of Chinese, who had never been under gunfire before, against that of the veteran Mao Tse-tung, who had been fighting this way for years and years. Mao was at home in China's backcountry. He knew every unit and every commander, had appointed many of them and had led them through peril to ultimate victory. A real Hunan red pepper plopped into Braun's rice bowl.

The route of march took the army westward in a fairly straight line. Later Mao would contend that Braun was at fault for failing to employ feints or diversions to throw Chiang off the track. The point was a good one, although the Communists knew by radio intercepts (many of them passed on by the Fourth Army) that Chiang had three or four divisions moving on parallel lines on both flanks. And they knew by bloody losses that Chiang's divisions were in close pursuit, engaging the Communist rear guard repeatedly. Mao later charged that Braun didn't even possess maps of the terrain. This may have been true but the Communists captured some adequate French maps from local Kuomintang troops.

The strength of the Red Army dropped rapidly. A hard battle was fought driving across the Hsiang River, where Kwantung, Kwangsi and Kweichow provinces met. This battle and the fight past the sturdy von Seeckt blockhouses cost twenty-five to thirty thousand casualties. Mao's influence grew daily. No longer could Braun or Po Ku invoke Moscow's authority. Years later Braun would whine that Mao refused to maintain his assigned position in the line of march. Instead he moved up and down, talking with one commander after another, assessing the situation. Mao didn't criticize Chu Teh, commander-in-chief; he criticized Braun and he criticized Po Ku. Arguments broke out over a change of course. Braun blamed Mao. Mao blamed Braun. By the time the Red Army captured Liping, in eastern Kweichow, the army was, by Braun's admission, down to half its original strength. It had lost 75 percent of its reserves. It now mustered not more than forty-five thousand men, probably fewer. It had marched five hundred kilometers, had fought ten major engagements and had broken through the von Seeckt lines. But it was still an army in search of a goal.

At Liping they paused for four days. There were new arguments about tactics and strategy. Mao's views were beginning to gain ascendancy. Much unneeded furniture was junked here. The lumber of a temporary government capital began to be discarded. The route of march was shifted to the northwest in almost a direct line for Tsunyi, an old and wealthy country town in north-central Kweichow. On December 19, after four days of rest, the advance to Tsunyi began, a three-hundred-kilometer march made, in Braun's words, under extremely favorable conditions. There were no enemy fortifications. Foggy weather protected the troops from bombing and observation by Chiang's German pilots. The troops were deep in the backcountry but found food supplies plentiful. In fact, they requisitioned more than they needed. The surplus was distributed to poor peasants. The only opposition came from provincial troops, badly armed, badly trained, who scattered at the first Communist shots.

One serious obstacle was the River Wu, six hundred feet wide, with a rapid current. All boats and ferries had been taken to the opposite shore. Advance parties quickly knocked together bamboo rafts, crossed the river and chased away the defending troops so the army could follow in their path.

Tsunyi was captured by Lin Piao on January 5. He used an old military trick. Lin Piao had captured some outpost troops. Now he dressed his advance guard in their Nationalist uniforms and marched them up at night, blowing bugles and pretending to be Nationalists returning from beating back the Red Army. The gates of the old walled city were opened. Lin Piao's men were inside before the trick was discovered. In no time he controlled Tsunyi, an easygoing town of ten thousand, a city of parks and palaces, of green and quiet. A twelve-day rest was ordered. The troops relaxed. The generals and political leaders slept on beds, ate good food and debated the future of the Long March.

★

At Tsunyi they were actually debating the future of China, though no one knew it. Tsunyi proved the most significant event of the march. Its shadow would fall forward across the years of the Chinese Revolution. It was the great divide, the fork in the road determining what came after.

Historians have argued over Tsunyi for years. They are still examining the scanty records to discover exactly what happened. One puzzle is that two years later, when Mao Tse-tung, Chou En-lai, Chu Teh and the rest sat down at Pao-an to give Edgar Snow their history, particularly the history of the Long March, Tsunyi was not even mentioned. Nor did Agnes Smedley, the doomed American writer who fell in love with Chu Teh and chronicled his version, say a word about Tsunyi.

What happened at Tsunyi is that Mao Tse-tung took over the Chinese Communist Party, took control of military and political affairs—took them into his hands, where they would remain for the rest of his life. He would be challenged occasionally, sometimes critically. But from Tsunyi on, Mao was in charge. Not Braun, not Po Ku, not the "Bolsheviks," not the Shanghai center, not the Comintern, not Moscow or Stalin. Mao was in charge. He would remain in charge. It would be *his* Chinese Revolution, made in the pattern of his thinking, his ideas, his tactics, his strategy, a revolution that would differ profoundly from the Soviet Revolution, a revolution that would carry the Chinese Communists so far away from the Russian Communists that Moscow would finally call Mao Tse-tung a madman and a Hitler, his revolution an Oriental satrapy. And Peking would call the Soviet leaders imperialists and capitalists who had nothing in common with Communism.

All this was determined in talks that lasted from January 6 to January 8, 1935, on the first floor of what Han Su-yin described as the gracious house of a small warlord, a two-story dwelling with wide verandas and a paved courtyard, across an attractive old bridge over the Tsunyi River. A merchant of soybean sauce occupied the lower floor. In a large room, finely paneled in dark wood, the Tsunyi meeting was held, a so-called widened session of the party Politburo, with thirty or forty participants, including seven or eight Politburo members, the "Bolsheviks," the generals.

The meeting was a confrontation. On one side were Braun and Po Ku, on the other Mao. Mao put blame for the high casualties, the difficulties, the mistakes on Braun, Po Ku and to a lesser extent Chou En-lai. There was no criticism of Chu Teh, Lin Piao and the commanders. There were wrangles about errors made in handling Chiang's Nineteenth Route Army, which had been ready to defect to the Communists but did not because of Communist arrogance and bureaucracy. Mao called Po Ku's leadership style "shocking." He contended that Braun had bypassed the Military Council and taken the whole conduct of military matters in his own hands.

The recriminations were the kind that commanders level at one another when things go wrong in a hard campaign. But the attack was deadly. There was no way Braun could counter Mao. He was, he recollected with some self-pity forty years later, "the one and only foreign adviser with limited powers, no knowledge of the [Chinese] language and no connection with the outside world."

There wasn't, Braun recalled, a word said about the international situation, about Japanese aggression, about mobilizing China against the Japanese—that is, about the matters in which Moscow was interested.

Chou En-lai played the critical role. He had already swung to Mao's side, and when he told the meeting that Mao "had been right all the time and we should listen to him" the game was over. With those words Chou formed a partnership with Mao which was to endure to the end of their lives, in 1976—or almost the end.

Mao emerged from Tsunyi in charge of the Red Army and in charge of the party. There is still uncertainty as to exactly what his title was, but it made no difference. He was the leader and would be from now on. Lo Fu replaced Po Ku as general secretary. Braun was relegated to the baggage train—what was left of it after another cleaning out of the files.

With Mao in charge the Red Army set off anew on what would become a long, long march, but one that would end with the total victory of Mao and his comrades on October 1, 1949.

Whatever words would be used to paper over the differences with Russia, Mao and the Chinese Communists had embarked on a new course: no orders from Moscow, no dictation by the Comintern. Stalin could put this in his pipe and smoke it.

These decisions were made in total ignorance of what was happening in the Soviet capital. The rugged band of Red Army survivors did not know that on December 1, 1934, just a month before Tsunyi, Sergei Kirov, the Leningrad party leader, had been murdered on Stalin's secret orders; that already the first of Stalin's great purges was under way; that Stalin would sweep away almost all surviving Old Bolsheviks, all the men whose names were known to the Chinese—Bukharin, Zinoviev, Kamenev, Radek, Grigorii Pyatakov and all the rest, down to the Soviet advisers who had been coming to China since 1921. They would all go. A new course for Moscow. A new course for China. Stalin's in Russia, Mao's in China.

★

The Red Army's fortunes took no sudden turn for the better under Mao's direct control. He darted back and forth, trying to confuse Chiang Kai-shek and clear a way to move north. It wasn't easy.

Mao's problem was to get across the Yangtze River. He could not move north without crossing the Yangtze. Chiang Kai-shek knew this. He knew the points at which Mao might cross and he planned accordingly. Mao found his northward path blocked and perceived that Chiang was trying to squeeze him westward, where he would surely perish in the barren wastes of the approaches to Tibet.

Suddenly Mao switched directions and sent Lin Piao on a strong push south toward Kunming, capital of Yunnan Province, where, as it happened, Chiang and Madame Chiang were vacationing. Panic seized the provincial capital. Chiang and his wife fled down the railroad into French Indochina. Meanwhile, Mao and his main force scouted the banks of the River of Golden Sands, as the Yangtze was called in these distant hills. He assigned a battalion to build a bamboo pontoon bridge with great ostentation, making certain that Chiang's aerial reconnaissance would spot it. They did, and Chiang rushed his forces to meet the threat.

Then one of Mao's commanders, dressed in the uniform of a high Nationalist officer, his troops wearing the blue-and-white emblems of the Nationalists, persuaded a stupid provincial officer to give him some junks to take his troops across the river. Once across, they overpowered the small garrison, and in the next nine days Mao managed to get his troops over the stream.

Mao was in Szechwan now but he was hardly free from trouble. There was another river to cross—the Tatu—and it was two hundred miles away. The distance to the Tatu was across tribal country, the Lolos, Black Lolos and White Lolos, and the Yi.

Here, in the course of marching back and forth, Mao and his men discovered *maotai*, the fierce, high-proof beverage that became the national drink of China after the advent of the People's Republic. The name comes from the small town in Szechwan where *maotai* is distilled from rice and the limestone water of the village. The going was not too bad. Not only was there *maotai*. There were no hostile troops. Food supplies were adequate. But no one made light of the test that lay ahead. Chiang Kai-shek had flown back to Chungking to direct operations. He was determined that Mao was not going to cross the Tatu. This was a river famous in Chinese lore. It was here that *The Romance of the Three Kingdoms*, one of Mao's favorite classics, was set. And here the Taiping leader Shih Ta-kai had been run to earth in the 1860s and sliced to death by the Manchu generals. Chiang's planes dropped leaflets on the Communists saying that Mao would suffer the fate of Shih Ta-kai.

Mao's troops reached the banks of the Tatu, a narrow, extraordinarily swift river at the medieval town of An Jen-chang. They captured a boat there but it carried only fifty men. They could not take more than a battalion a day across the river. Chiang Kai-shek's bombers quickly appeared overhead. It would never be possible to get the army across.

Again and again the Communists attempted to throw a bridge over. Each effort miscarried. The bamboo pontoons were swept away by the current.

Several more small boats were finally rounded up and it was decided to divide the force: one division, the First, would cross the Tatu by boat and fight its way up the riverbank while the main force, under Lin Piao and headed by the Fourth Regiment, would move parallel to it on the near bank of the Tatu through mountain forests.

Both columns would head for the only bridge on the Tatu within hundreds of miles, the only bridge east of Tibet. It was ninety miles away. It had been built early in the eighteenth century by an engineer named Liu, and across it passed the ancient Imperial highway that linked Tibet and Lhasa with Cheng-tu, the capital of Szechwan. The bridge was called Liu Ting Chiao—the bridge that Liu built.

As the First Division began to ferry across the river, Chu Teh, the commander-in-chief, arrived. The troops had requisitioned some pigs from landowners, sharing them with the poor peasants. An officer approached Chu Teh, told him they had reserved the pigs' livers. Could he advise them how to cook them?

Chu Teh was delighted. "Cut it into pieces and I'll come and cook it," he responded. Soon they were eating Chu Teh's treat. "I can really cook liver," he boasted. "If you get another pig save me the liver and get me some red peppers, and I'll make you a real dish."

Once across the Tatu the First Division fought through territory largely inhabited by the Mantzu people. They lived in tiny reed huts perched on the steep riverbanks like swallows' nests. They grew corn on the terraced cliffs. Giant dogs guarded the little habitations. Veterans of the march remembered the extraordinary quiet of the Mantzu villages. Most of the villagers fled their approach and for some reason the dogs did not bark.

The Fourth Regiment, half exhausted after fierce battles and hard marches, struck into the mountain forest. Tsiao Lun, a member of the regiment, recalled that their orders were to march the ninety miles in three days. The trail began along the Tatu, then mounted a crest, where they encountered fierce enemy resistance. As they came down the other side they met enemy fire from across the Tatu. Several times they found that small bridges over mountain streams had been destroyed, but they still managed to get across. Finally the road narrowed and they were halted by an enemy blockhouse defended by a Nationalist battalion. A Communist company slithered up the mountainside. Half an hour later it appeared behind the blockhouse, capturing the Nationalist commander, a hundred soldiers and more than a hundred rifles. Also a hundred opium pipes and a hundred opium lamps.

The column went on in the gloom until they encountered a second blockhouse, perched on a cliff. There was no way around it. They approached in total silence and tossed grenades through the windows. The defenders were dozing in opium-drugged sleep. In minutes the position was taken.

At eight the next morning the troops were on the road again. At 11:00 A.M. an urgent message arrived from army headquarters. It ordered that Liu Ting Chiao be taken, "within one day." The Fourth Regiment was 240 li from the bridge—between 60 and 70 miles. In eighteen hours they had to march 240 li over mountain terrain and carry out a sudden and desperate attack on what surely would be a heavily defended strong point.

"We were already late," Tsiao Lun recalled, "but the task had to be carried out. The commissars shouted out the orders to the troops. There was no time for a meeting."

As dusk fell they were still thirty miles from the bridge. It was raining. No one had eaten since morning. Now they dumped all their equipment, everything not urgently needed—horses, gear, baggage, personal belongings. Only guns and ammunition for the attack was carried forward. Three light battalions were ordered to dash to the bridgehead. The road was slippery as grease. They noticed lights flickering on the other side of the river. The Nationalists were racing, too, trying to get to the bridgehead first. What to do? Stumble ahead in the dark or light torches, increase speed and give away their location? Commissar Yen ordered torches lighted. If the soldiers across the river shouted an inquiry they would identify themselves as Nationalists and say they had just beaten off an attack by "Red bandits."

At 5:00 A.M., May 25, 1935, the troops were still struggling forward. Many had fallen beside the trail in exhaustion. Some had slipped from the cliffs to their deaths. An hour later, at dawn, the first scouts saw the outlines of Liu Ting Chiao in the early mist. It was nearly three hundred feet long, suspended a hundred feet over the rock-carved walls of the Tatu by thirteen iron chains cemented into the stone on either side of the river. The bridge was defended by two brigades of Nationalist troops. They held the approaches, the riverbank, and the mountain behind. They had machine guns and mine-throwers in place, and when they spotted the Fourth Regiment scouts they opened fire. The planking on the bridge halfway across had been removed, leaving the naked chains. Between bursts of gunfire the Nationalists taunted the Communists.

"Hey, Communist bandits," they shouted. "Come on over to us. Come on over by air. We want to lay down our arms to you. Why don't you come over to our side?"

"We need your bridge, not your guns," the Communists shouted back.

Some Fourth Regiment men began looking for wood to make planks. They wrenched doors out of huts, pulled down roof poles, scavenged wood from barrels and chests.

Twenty-two young soldiers of the Second Company volunteered to lead the attack, to climb out the naked iron chains and clamber along these precious links to the planking at mid-bridge. The Third Company was deployed to lay down covering fire. Behind them every man who had a gun, a grenade or a mortar-launcher was positioned.

At the signal to attack a heavy covering fire was directed toward the enemy across the bridge. The young volunteers inched out on the chains. Each carried a dozen grenades, a carbine and daggers or hatchets. The chains swayed downward. The most frightening moment, Tsiao Lun recalled, was at the middle of the river, where the chains swung just above the raging water that leaped up like angry dragons trying to sweep the men from their perches. The volunteers clawed forward, some pitching to their deaths in the Tatu. As they reached the comparative safety of the planking, the Nationalists set fire to a wooden enclosure that covered the approach to the bridge on their side. The Third Regiment was already laying down new planking. "Straight forward!" the commander cried. "Straight through the flames." The exhausted men plunged through the flaming shed. Their clothing caught fire. Their hair and eyebrows were singed. But the bridge was in Communist hands.

Of the twenty-two volunteers, seventeen died in the attack. More than a hundred men won decorations for bravery. The defenders fled in panic. A hundred Nationalist soldiers who had witnessed the taking of Liu Ting Chiao volunteered on the spot to join the Red Army.

The Snow Mountains were next, sixteen-thousand-foot peaks, with unfriendly Fan tribesmen, deaths by hunger, cold or falls from precipices, while Braun still grumbled about Mao's attitude toward the Soviet Union. What Mao wanted, Braun said, was war between the Soviets and the Kuomintang—a policy epitomized by an old Chinese saying, "Sit on a hill and watch the two tigers fight in the valley." There was wireless communication with the Fourth Route Army now. Later Chang Kuo-tao, its leader, would tell of sitting by the wireless set from 7:00 P.M. to 3:00 A.M., waiting for Mao's radio to come on the air so he could relay intelligence reports. Chang had begun moving the Fourth Route Army, positioning it to meet Mao's main force. He had about fifty thousand troops. Official histories say Mao had forty-five thousand. Han Su-yin puts the figure nearer twenty thousand. It may have been lower. Mao had lost his artillery. He had few machine guns left. His riflemen averaged fewer than five shells for each gun.

At 5:00 P.M. on a day in mid-June 1935, Chang Kuo-tao, on horseback, accompanied by a cavalry escort of thirty men, arrived outside the little market town of Fu-pien ninety li north of Mao-kung. There Mao, Chu Teh, Chou En-lai and others of the main army group were waiting. Han Su-yin described them as huddled in their rags "under a tarpaulin by the roadside." It was raining. The contradictions in the details of what followed mirrored the contradictions that would arise between Mao and Chang.

One of Mao's officers said Chang, riding a fat horse, didn't even dismount to greet Mao until he had practically reached his side. Chang recollected leaping from his horse as soon as he saw Mao and running full tilt to embrace him. One witness heard Mao observe to a companion as he saw the well-fed horses, "Don't envy the horses." Chang remembered that he and Mao walked into Fu-pien together, arms around each other's shoulders.

Whatever the details, it was evident that trouble lay ahead. There was a great banquet that evening. Chang didn't think his comrades (he and Mao hadn't seen each other for eight years; they had never been close) were interested in his accounts of the Fourth Route Army; Mao's historians thought Chang had no interest in the perils overcome by the main army. Mao brought out his cliché about hot peppers: those who didn't like hot peppers, he said, didn't make good revolutionaries. Po Ku rose to the bait and said he didn't care for chili. Chang didn't disclose his opinion.

That night Chu Teh followed Chang back to his quarters and the two spent the night talking about their campaigns. Chu Teh said of his army, "[It] can fight no more. It used to be a giant but now all the muscles are gone, there is only a skeleton left."

The question was what to do next. On this there was a radical difference between Chang and Mao. Chang wanted to move to the northwest, northern Szechwan or Sinkiang, where there would be a chance of communication and support from the Soviet Union. Mao wanted to go north, possibly to Shensi. He wanted to have Outer Mongolia at his back and he wanted to engage the Japanese.

The argument was not resolved. The two armies split apart, the Fourth going northwest, Mao going north. For reasons still not clear Chu Teh went with Chang. Bitter recriminations broke out by wireless, but each held to his course, Mao to the north, Chang to the northwest.

It was not easy going for Mao. Later many were to speak of it as the worst trial of the Long March. At the start Mao had built up his force again, possibly to thirty thousand, but the total was swiftly reduced. A substantial group turned back and joined Chang. But the heaviest and most painful losses came in the Kansu marshes. There was hardly any food except some *kaoliang*, a kind of millet. Although it was only August the nights were freezing. It rained all day; by night soft melting snow fell. Mules vanished into the bogs before the men's eyes. So did men who strayed off the paths. Many died of starvation. Each morning the soldiers awoke to find comrades stiff in death beside them.

By the time the column reached Basi it was down to nine to twelve thousand men, of whom only seven to ten thousand were fit for fighting. The wildest rumors circulated. There was talk that Chang had plotted to wipe out Mao and his leadership group, one of the legends that would persist for years, though there was never substantiation. The countryside was inhabited by the hostile Mantzu minority. The Mantzu queen threatened to boil alive any Red Army soldier who fell into her hands. Mao's columns had to break with their custom of requisitioning supplies only from the wealthy and paying poor farmers for what they needed. They foraged into the Mantzu territory, killing and looting to gather food, taking it as they could, sometimes shooting down the Mantzu people to get cows and sheep.

Later Mao was to tell Edgar Snow about this, adding, "This is our only foreign debt and some day we must pay the Mantzu and the Tibetans for the provisions we were obliged to take from them." There is no evidence that Mao ever did so.

On October 20, 1935, Mao and his vanguard arrived at Wuchichen County, in northern Shensi Province, just south of the Great Wall. It was twilight. Through the dusk they heard the sound of gongs and drums. A crowd emerged from the city walls to meet the vanguard of the Red Army. A man stepped forward and Mao moved up to him.

"Is this Comrade Hai-tung?" Mao asked. Yes, was the reply. It was Hsu Hai-tung, leader of the Communist "Fifteenth Corps," sometimes called the "Pioneer Corps" since so many of its soldiers were youngsters of fifteen and sixteen.

"Thank you for having taken so much trouble to come and meet us," Mao said.

Mao had about seven thousand men left. The Long March had ended. It had carried him and his men more than seventy-five hundred miles, over eighteen mountain ranges, half of them snow-topped, across twenty-four rivers, into eleven provinces, through sixty-two cities and towns. Uncounted and uncountable were the men and women who had given their lives. It would become the legend on which the Revolution was based, a shining example of bravery in a world of danger, death and disillusion.

On the eve of completing the Long March, Mao sat down one night in his temporary hut and wrote a poem. Here, in Han Su-yin's translation, are a few lines:

*High is the sky and clear the clouds. . . .*
*On the crest of Liupan our banners waft in the west wind*
*Today we hold in our hands the long rope to bind the dragon*
*When shall we bind fast the gray dragon?*

# ★ 9 ★

## THE YENAN WAY

**I**N THIS RICH LOESS COUNTRY OF northern Shensi—dry, remote, lightly populated, a region that had access to the rest of China only by trails and primitive cart tracks beaten across the desert and climbing the wind-carved sides of mountains, a region without large cities, with an illiterate population, a region less than sufficient in food and almost totally dependent upon its own meager resources for clothing and the necessities of life—the Chinese Revolution was born again.

They set up headquarters first at Wayaopao, then moved to Pao-an and finally to Yenan. Yenan was to give its name to the period and, in a sense, to the movement. Here in the loess hills, relatively secure from Nationalist attack, living a spartan life on the barren land, Mao, the other survivors of the Long March and the thousands who gradually joined in set the tone that would carry them to victory. It was, in many ways, a grim, almost puritanical way of life. The Red Army, commanders and soldiers alike, sewed their own clothes, patched their own boots, cooked their own food, cleaned their quarters. It was an egalitarian society, forged in danger and hardship. Its ways were simple. There was little distinction between private and general, not in dress, not in custom, not in life. In northern Shensi, wood was scarce. Almost everyone lived in caves hewn out of the hill and mountain walls. The caves were comfortable, secure from air attack, cool in summer, warm in winter (although Otto Braun complained of rats and fleas). There was no question of requisitioning food from the peasants. They were as poor as the Communist troops; everyone was in the same fix. Mao worked a garden at the entrance of his cave. The troops were set to breaking the land, digging new irrigation ditches from the stone-strewn River Yen, sowing and tilling crops. If Mao's men did not grow enough to feed themselves they would go hungry. They farmed, they learned to spin and weave, to husband every resource. The diet was skimpy—three or four cups of barley or millet and a little cabbage made a day's meal in Yenan for soldier and peasant alike.

Yenan was, in every sense, a poor and backward area, as poor and backward as could be found in China. The climate was bad: sandstorms off the Gobi, very dry, not too cold in winter and little or no snow, but a wind that tore the skin from a man's face. Pure air and sunshine in summer but water in short supply.

At the start Mao had a base area of twenty-five thousand square miles. His fief ran from the border of Kansu eastward almost to the Shensi line, and from the Great Wall on the north to Fuhsien on the south. The larger towns were held by Chiang Kai-shek, as was the single automobile road that linked Yenan with Sian. About half a million people or a little more lived in the area controlled by Mao.

To a resident of Paris, London, New York or Shanghai, Yenan would be the bleakest of hells. To Mao's men and the handful of women who had survived the ice storms of mountaintops, the fiery deserts, the perilous river crossings, the unspeakable terror of the Great Marshes, the battles, the guerrilla attacks, the desperate foraging for food, Yenan seemed like paradise.

Here what would be called the Yenan spirit came into being. Here they started schools. Here they began to attack illiteracy—95 percent of the army and 95 percent of the poor peasants could not read or write. Here Mao once more became a schoolmaster, schoolmaster-to-be of a nation. Here he began to think about the nature of the society he was going to create. Here there was time to confront the political problems that had piled up: the question of relations with Russia, attitudes toward Chiang Kai-shek and the Nationalists, the growing threat of a war in Europe, the implications of the Anti-Comintern Pact that linked Berlin, Rome and Tokyo, the Japanese assault on China, relations within the Communist movement, the deep frictions between Mao and Chang, the fate of the "twenty-eight Bolsheviks," the Comintern— the whole agenda that could not be resolved by Mao and his army on the march. Of course, some of these questions could not be resolved—Chang, for example. Eventually, Chang and the battered remnants of his army would make their way to Yenan, but ultimately Chang would make his way out of Yenan to Chungking, joining Chiang Kai-shek for a while, and then spend the rest of a long life in exile, in Hong Kong and finally Canada, writing bitter memoirs.

In Yenan Mao was in communication with the world again—tenuously, to be certain, but he was not totally cut off, as he had been on the long cavalcade from Kiangsi. For the first time in more than a year, messages began to trickle in and out of Mao's headquarters. Little as he and his comrades knew about the outside world, that world knew even less about them. To the people of China Mao was the invisible man. The Communist movement had vanished from the cities. Of course there were said to be small Communist bands, miniature armies, many of them little more than bands of "Red bandits," as they were called by Chiang, operating in remote, unheard-of parts of the countryside. What Mao might be doing, where his army might be—if indeed it existed—not a handful knew or cared. An occasional rumor appeared in the press. Chiang moved troops around and again and again proclaimed that the "Red bandits" had been wiped out. Most people knew this wasn't quite true. But they could not have told you where Mao was. They hadn't heard of the Long March. They did not know Mao had set up headquarters and was consolidating his movement in Yenan.

Moscow knew no more than the rest. Its representative, Otto Braun, had made the Long March without a single communication to or from Moscow. He was the only foreigner on the Long March. Now Moscow was the first outside force to reestablish communications—but very precarious they were. An agent, Chang Hao, a member of the Chinese Central Committee, was parachuted into China somewhere south of the Great Wall and got to Pao-an in December 1935, still wearing a light summer coat made in Moscow. He carried no documents, for fear of being seized by the Nationalists. From him the Communists learned that Russia had sent an earlier party carrying wireless equipment. It traveled from Outer Mongolia disguised as a caravan of traders but was captured in Inner Mongolia and executed. It would be June 1936 before a new Soviet communications team managed to reach Pao-an.

Chang Hao brought word of the political situation in Moscow (Stalin's purges were gaining momentum) and of Moscow's continued refrain: Don't fight the Kuomintang; collaborate with Chiang against the Japanese. This news produced long and indecisive discussions, with some supporting the Moscow line. Mao did not want to break openly. He was still hopeful of getting Russian arms and support for fighting Japan. But when Braun wrote a long letter protesting plans for an operation against Chiang Kai-shek, Mao told him, in effect, to shut up. Later, in Moscow in 1939, Mao was to bring charges against Braun. Braun felt Mao wanted him shot and was ever grateful to Stalin for sparing his life.

The international situation was changing so swiftly that it was taking decisions out of the hands of men like Mao, like Chiang Kai-shek, even like Stalin.

European war had begun to loom over the world. The Spanish war had flared up. Japan was on the move in China. More than ever Stalin's policy reflected his perception of military dangers to the Soviet Union. He wanted Chiang Kai-shek and Mao to fight side by side against Japan, not against each other, and if that slowed down China's revolution, so be it. In China, Chiang was under increasing pressure to fight Japan—not the "Red bandits." This pressure came not only from the public; it came also from some of the warlords. The "Young Marshal," Chang Hsueh-liang—son of old General Chang Tso-lin, who had ruled Manchuria—was an ally of Chiang Kai-shek's. But Chang was on the firing line against the Japanese. Now he began to talk privately with the Communists. He made secret arrangements—he would not fight them; they would not fight him. He let them send underground representatives into his capital at Sian. Secretly, Communist specialists began to train some of his men. The Communists were able to move clandestinely from Yenan in and out of Sian and into the rest of China. For the first time in years Mao made contact with Communists in other parts of China, including Peking, Shanghai, Wuhan, Canton.

Edgar Snow had been living and working in China for nine years by the summer of 1936. He and his wife, Helen (later to write under the name Nym Wales), lived in Peking. Snow had an intimate knowledge of China and Chinese politics. He was writing about China for *The Saturday Evening Post* and sometimes for *Life*. There were few better-informed men in China.

The rest of China, the rest of the world might be ignorant about the Chinese Communists. Not Snow. He had heard of the arrival of Mao Tse-tung in northwestern China. Not one foreign journalist, not one American journalist had visited the Communists. To a man like Snow the Chinese Communists were *the* story. He had many friends among Chinese radicals, Chinese students, secret sympathizers with the Communists. They kept him informed.

In June 1936 Snow was told about the arrangements the Communists had made with the Young Marshal. There was, he was told, a chance that a correspondent might reach the Red base area. Snow went to Shanghai to consult his old and close friend Soong Ching-ling. Through the years Madame Soong had not wavered in her support for the Communist side. She was no Communist, but the Communists, she felt, came closer to carrying on the heritage of Dr. Sun than did her brother-in-law Chiang Kai-shek. Madame Soong lived in the French Concession. Years later it would be revealed that she had given refuge in her big house or in other quarters to Communists on the run. This was known to Chiang Kai-shek and his police. There was constant danger that Madame Soong might be assassinated.

With the aid of Madame Soong, arrangements were made for Snow to penetrate to the Red areas. He returned to Peking and one midnight boarded a shabby train to Chengchow. In his pocket was a letter of introduction to Mao written in invisible ink. Snow was returning after nearly ten years to that ancient birthplace of the Han people, the lands at the bend of the Hwang Ho, the Yellow River, where he had first learned of the disasters, the catastrophe of drought, the area where millions had starved in the years 1929–1930 without the world's doing more than shrugging its shoulders.

Snow dozed all night in a compartment with two Chinese, an old man with a wispy gray beard and a young man who began to talk about the Communists in his home province of Szechwan. He was sympathetic but said, "They kill too many people."

"*Sha pu kuo*," the graybeard snapped. "Not nearly enough."

Snow had to leave the train before he could find out what the old man meant.

Another day's ride brought Snow to Sian. There he had conspiratorial meetings with a Chinese who called himself "Pastor" Wang, and he met Teng Fa, chief of Mao's secret police, who was staying with the Young Marshal in his house. There Snow discovered that he was not to be alone on his trip to meet with the "Red bandits." Another American was going, too: George Hatem, a young, idealistic doctor from North Carolina, fed up with treating cases of syphilis in Shanghai, hopeful of putting his life to some more useful purpose by helping the medically famished Reds. The two sat in the Sian Guest House and played rummy for two weeks, waiting for arrangements to be completed. One morning, before dawn, Snow and Hatem, escorted by one of the Young Marshal's officers, set out in a big military truck toward the "front." At Yenan, which was still held by the Nationalists, Snow and Hatem dropped off, made contact with their guide and found their way to the Communist lines. A day and a half later, at a little town called Pai Chia Ping, a rather slender young Communist officer with a black beard walked up to Snow and said in English, "Hello. Are you looking for somebody?"

It was Chou En-lai.

Snow's arrival in Red China proved to be a little like the landing of Man on the Moon. At a single step it established the reality, the importance, the *presence* of Communist China. The personalities of Mao Tse-tung, Chou En-lai, Chu Teh and the others, delineated in intimate detail—their lives, their philosophy, their origins, their conduct, their aspirations, their goals for China—and the superlative epic of the Long March caught the imagination of the world in a way that is almost impossible to recapture.

At a stroke, the balance of forces in China was changed. No longer was China a jungle, a wilderness in which only the flawed figure of Chiang Kai-shek and the bright image of Madame Chiang were visible. China became three-dimensional. The focus shifted, because for the first time the Chinese themselves had a picture of what the "Red bandits" were, who they were, their names, their programs, their history, their plans and ideas for China. Snow's words were translated and almost every literate Chinese read them.

It is not often that a journalist's report changes the world, and it cannot do so with mere words and pictures. It must present a reality, a reality that is absorbed by public opinion. This proved true in Snow's case. Once he had written *Red Star over China* the world changed, because the Chinese Communists were seen by the public and by foreign offices in a totally different perspective, and, being thus perceived, they began to change, began to move onto the world stage—their leaders accepted the role that had, in effect, been spelled out by Snow's book.

*Red Star* appeared in 1938 in the United States but excerpts and articles were published as much as a year earlier, at a time of full-scale war between Japan and China. Global attention was focused on the surging Japanese forces, bombing, pillaging and ravaging China's cities and villages.

The drama was heightened by an event that stemmed from the symbiotic relationship that had developed between the Communists and the Young Marshal at Sian. Chiang Kai-shek, despite the Japanese, despite the rising national fervor, had gone to Sian to tighten his blockade against the Communists, to initiate a full-scale offensive and to bring to an end the secret collaboration of the Young Marshal and the Communists.

On the night of December 12, 1936, as Chiang was relaxing at the ancient hot springs of Lintung, a Tang-dynasty resort not far from Sian, a detachment of the Young Marshal's troops surrounded his villa. Chiang leaped out his bedroom window (leaving his false teeth behind, as the Communists never tire of reminding visitors) and dashed up the craggy mountain path in nightshirt and bare feet. He tried to hide in a crevice in the rocks but a patrol ferreted him out. "I'm your commander-in-chief," he said stiffly. "Yes," said the sergeant in charge, "but you are also our prisoner."

The Young Marshal brought Chiang Kai-shek back to Sian under guard. The sensational news flashed around the world. What would happen? Chou En-lai was rushed to Sian to take part in the negotiations. Mao and the Chinese Communists were elated. They hoped that Chiang would be publicly tried and executed for his barbarous crimes against thousands of Chinese, including, of course, so many Communists. Then, perhaps with the Young Marshal at the head, a United Front government of Kuomintang and Communists would take up the battle against the Japanese.

The Great Powers feared Chiang would be executed and that, without Chiang, China would fall into anarchy and the Japanese would sweep ahead to victory. Moscow shared the fears of England, France and the United States. Now that communications with Mao had been restored he was sent the bluntest of messages, a message that Edgar Snow attributed to Stalin himself, flatly ordering Mao to abandon any plans for a trial and to arrange for Chiang's release immediately. The message was probably sent in the name of the Comintern, if Otto Braun is to be believed. Snow reported that Mao flew into a rare rage. He cursed, stamped his feet and tore up the cable. Be that as it may, Vyacheslav Molotov later contended that the cable saved Chiang's life.

The affair developed like a classic of the Peking Opera. Madame Chiang Kai-shek flew into Sian and joined the talks. So did her brother T. V. Soong and W. H. Donald, Chiang's Australian adviser. Chou negotiated for the Communists. Messages flew back and forth—Moscow to Yenan, Nanking to Sian, Washington to Peking. The Japanese watched warily.

Finally Chiang agreed not to renew the civil war against the Communists, to throw his resources into the struggle against the Japanese. Chiang told Chou he was "glad to be working again with him" (they had last worked together at the Whampoa Military Academy in Canton; Chou had narrowly escaped death in Shanghai at the hands of Chiang's thugs) and a more or less united front was promised. Chiang was released on Christmas Day and flew back to Nanking. The Young Marshal went with him and, as it developed, was to remain in "protective custody" for the rest of his life. A day or two later Mao's troops occupied Yenan, which was to be the Red capital for the next ten years.

**W**ednesday July 7, 1937, was a beautiful day in Peking, not too hot, blue skies, no wind from the north to fill the air with dust, the wheat in the irrigated fields near the capital beginning to turn from lush green to harvest gold. The Japanese north of the city were, as so often, engaging in small maneuvers, parties of troops, machine-gunners and cavalry roaming the dusty roads. That evening, after the town gates had been closed for the night, a Japanese detachment appeared outside the walls of Wanping, beside the ancient marble bridge described by Marco Polo. They routed out the night watchman and demanded that the gates be opened so they could search for a missing soldier. The town's commander refused. The Japanese opened fire. The Chinese fired back. Instantly the affair became known as the "Marco Polo Bridge" incident. By July 25 Japanese troops were advancing on Peking from Tientsin, and on August 8 Japanese troops marched into Peking as foreigners stood on the Tartar wall and watched. The Sino-Japanese War had begun.

By September a united front, or at least as much of a united front as might be expected from two men who bitterly and personally hated each other, had been forged by Chiang Kai-shek and Mao Tse-tung. The Communist area was formally designated a "Special Region" and part of the Chinese Republic headed by Chiang Kai-shek. A joint military council was established, headed by Chiang's number-one deputy, Chen Cheng. Chou En-lai became number two to Chen Cheng, and a Communist mission was set up at Chiang's headquarters, first at Nanking, later at Wuhan and finally at Chungking.

Communist forces grew rapidly. The Eighth Route Army was established with Liu Shao-chi as chief political adviser. Stationed in the northwest, it occupied a key position behind the Japanese lines. Chiang's troops opposed the Japanese with genuine determination and considerable skill. They had had good training under a German mission headed by General von Faulkenhausen, and when the Japanese compelled the Nazis to pull out their advisers (Tokyo didn't think it quite cricket for her Axis partner to be helping her chief foe) the Russians rushed in to fill the gap. "You are occupying warm beds," a Soviet diplomat told the first group of Red Army men to arrive.

There was a rapid flow of Soviet arms and equipment. The Russians built a road from Lanchow to Hami in northwestern China and pushed a highway out from Alma-Ata (in northeastern Kazakhstan) to Urumchi. With the approval of the local warlord in Sinkiang they stationed a brigade of Soviet troops in Hami (dressed in Nationalist uniforms) and sent into China more than two thousand military advisers, including such men of later fame as Marshal Georgi K. Zhukov, Marshal Vasily I. Chuikov (the hero of the Battle of Stalingrad) and survivors of the 1924–1927 days. Five Soviet air wings came to China and actively fought the Japanese. Soviet trucks brought in Soviet guns and ammunition.

Stalin had finally gotten what he wanted—a union of the contending Chinese forces—and he was prepared to pay for it. This he did with military-aid loans of a hundred million dollars in 1938 and a hundred fifty million in 1939, and a nonaggression pact—all with Chiang Kai-shek. Not a kopek went to Mao Tse-tung.

Not that Stalin neglected Mao. He had no guns for the Communists but he did send in two planeloads of medical supplies and surgical equipment and a large, very large, shipment of Communist literature translated into Chinese—Marx, Lenin and many of Stalin's own speeches. Also stacks of *Pravda* and the latest pamphlets of the Comintern. He sent back to Yenan Wang Ming and as many of the "twenty-eight Bolsheviks" as could be rounded up. Otto Braun was delighted, particularly to get *Pravda*, although he complained that it didn't arrive regularly. Mao got the message. It was hard not to get it. In Yenan they began to say that the new Moscow slogan was "To the bourgeoisie—guns; to the proletariat—books."

The Japanese began to bomb Yenan regularly, pulverizing most of the buildings. All activities were shifted into caves. There was even a corridor dug under a mountain, about three hundred feet long, where shops, markets and a little restaurant were set up. Lanchow, in Nationalist territory, was more fortunate: Soviet fighters shot down so many Japanese planes they stopped their bombing.

But all of this was trivial. The important fact was that China was swept by a surge of national patriotism and that within the United Front the Communists rode the crest of a wave. Despite the Japanese, despite Chiang Kai-shek, despite Stalin and his open favoritism for the Nationalists, Mao's revolutionary movement was on the rise. It had national and international recognition. The nationwide party network was rapidly reconstructed. The Communists were gaining a priceless advantage. They were growing so rapidly they could hardly count the numbers. The Eighth Route Army more than doubled from 1938 to 1939 to reach a total of more than 150,000. By 1940 it totaled 400,000. It was not heavily armed. In mid-1938 it possessed 31,000 rifles, 108 heavy machine guns, 750 light machine guns, 50 mortars, 2,400 Mausers and 26 cannon of mixed size and origin. It had about 100 cartridges per rifle and 300 per machine gun. An arsenal outside Yenan turned out 150 rifles and 50,000 cartridges a month. The chief source of weapons was the battlefield, and procurement rapidly grew. Red Army men drew a pay of one yuan (about five U.S. cents) a month. Chu Teh, their commander, was paid five yuan. The Fourth Route Army, operating south of Nanking, had 10,000 men in May 1938, of whom only half were armed. By 1939 it had 40,000 and by 1940 an estimated 136,000, about half of them equipped with rifles. By 1945 the Red Army would number 900,000 men and the Red militia more than 2,000,000.

The virtue of these years—and this would be true until the end of the war in 1945—was that the Communists and the Red Army were constantly on the move, constantly spacing out farther behind the Japanese lines, filling the interstices in the great Chinese land, carrying the joint appeal of nationalism and revolution.

Wherever the Red Army went it performed as a living object lesson. It did not prey upon the peasants. It played the role of Robin Hood. It took from the rich landlords and wealthier peasants and it gave to the poor. It encouraged the peasants to do what came naturally—to take the land. It was rigorous in paying for food and supplies. Agnes Smedley watched in amazement one evening when the Red Army company with whom she was traveling had no food and no money to buy millet from the peasants. The soldiers sat in a circle and listened to their captain lecture them on Mao's three rules and eight sub-rules about not taking anything from the peasants. Mao put the rules into the form of doggerel. The evening ended with the hungry soldiers chanting the rules—then to bed, unfed.

Behind the Japanese lines in the Red areas, collectives or cooperatives—particularly the Indusco movement sponsored by Edgar Snow's onetime companion in the starvation areas of the northwest, the New Zealander, Rewi Alley—sprouted like mushrooms after rain. Reading and writing, personal hygiene, public sanitation were taught in classes set up in bare dirt courtyards. Again and again the lesson was hammered home: Stand up to the Japanese invaders, stand up to the landlords and other exploiters.

China had seen nothing like it. The Communist soldiers were role models against the thousand-year Chinese tradition that "You do not use good iron to make a nail; you do not make good men into soldiers." The traditional Chinese soldier was impressed, forced into the army, unpaid, never decently fed, untrained—the dregs of humanity, cannon fodder.

The Communists changed the whole psychology. True, they had from the beginning taken into their ranks the riffraff, the beggars, the idlers. They took anyone they captured or anyone who volunteered. Their ranks were filled with teen-agers. But they turned the poorest human material into brave and proficient fighting men and women, and they made these soldiers personal ambassadors to the poor peasants of China. Their discipline and dedication constantly astonished foreign observers.

★

Not everything was austere in Yenan. Mao was busy in his cave, or more often at a plank table outside the cave, pondering and writing and discussing the issues with his comrades; new works poured from his pen like leaves in the autumn: *On Protracted War, On Contradictions, Problems of Strategy in the Anti-Japanese Guerrilla War, Problems of Strategy in China's Revolutionary War* (it was during these days that he uttered his famous aphorism usually translated as "Political power grows out of the barrel of a gun").

But it wasn't all work. A stream of foreigners (mostly Americans) was finding its way to Yenan: Agnes Smedley, the obsessional and talented radical writer; Helen Snow, wife of Edgar; George Hatem, now known by the Chinese name Ma Hai-teh (improbably rooming in the same cave with Otto Braun); Evans Carson, a remarkable U.S. Marine officer and Red Chinese sympathizer (regarded by the Russians as an American intelligence agent—as, in fact, they considered all the Americans); Anna Louise Strong; the English writer Gunther Stein; and ultimately, as World War II developed, the extraordinary group of wartime Americans, John Service of the State Department, Colonel David Barrett of the U.S. Army, head of the famous Dixie Mission to Yenan, and many, many more. Bright young Chinese figures from the worlds of the theater and literature were now appearing in Yenan, among them the famous writer Ting Ling.

Life was not all lectures and study in the caves of Yenan. There were long hours to pass. Chinese love to play cards. Anna Louise Strong played bridge almost every evening, often with Chou En-lai. Once, when Chou didn't appear for the nightly game, she went to the cave where he was attending a Military Council with Mao. When Chou saw her he rose and with great firmness escorted her out, saying sternly, "Anna Louise, I have played cards with you three nights this week. This is too much." All the way back to her cave Anna Louise muttered to herself, "Why, he was really angry with me! Chou En-lai really was angry!" She seemed to cherish his anger like an icon.

Even Otto Braun, most morose of foreigners, played cards, often poker, with foreigners and high party men. When Americans made their way into Yenan they brought the latest dance records, the newest jazz.

Yenan was very much a small town: everyone knew everyone else's business. Everyone in Yenan knew that Mao suffered from chronic constipation. His bowels moved only once every seven or eight days. Sometimes at even longer intervals. Tension built up day by day. Mao grew moody. The community grew nervous. When the great moment arrived there was enormous relief. Word of mouth passed the news swiftly: "The Chairman's bowels have moved!" Spirits lightened. There were those in later years who sought to correlate Mao's political writings with the status of his bowels.

Not unnaturally, some of the unions among those who had made the Long March began to break up. This happened to Mao. Ho Shih-chen had survived the Long March but at the cost of her health and equanimity. She had been badly wounded, her body pierced by many fragments of shrapnel. Now she was a bundle of nerves. She and Mao quarreled and there were not many in Yenan who did not know of this.

Two beautiful, talented young women from Shanghai arrived in Yenan about this time, Li Li-yang and Lan Ping, accompanied by Huang Chin, an important Communist underground figure. The women were good friends. Li Li-yang was a singer, Lan Ping an actress. Lan Ping had appeared in many Shanghai movies, mostly second-rate features. In Yenan the two entered the Lu Hsun Art Academy and appeared in traditional Chinese opera and modern propaganda plays.

Sometimes Li Li-yang and Lan Ping dropped in at the cave of Otto Braun and George Hatem on Saturday nights to join other young people. They drank wine, played music, danced, talked, gossiped. Soon Lan Ping left the circle, but Li Li-yang kept on coming and Braun, having discarded the Chinese woman who had accompanied him during the Long March and borne his child, asked for and got permission to marry Li Li-yang. This caused criticism of Braun, who was not liked by either foreigners or Chinese. (When he met Helen Snow for the first time he told her, "I am maximum antisocial.") Braun's marriage with Li Li-yang was not destined to last long. In 1939 he quit Yenan for Moscow, leaving her behind, and never saw her again.

Agnes Smedley came to Yenan in 1937. She was writing the biography of Chu Teh, the big, bluff, gifted Red Army commander. Smedley was a hero worshiper. She had long sympathized with the Chinese. Now she was devoting all her time and emotion to Chu Teh and his story. In fact, Chu had become a kind of father figure to her. Helen Snow, wife of Edgar Snow, competitive, energetic, determined to learn even more about Yenan and its leaders than her husband, arrived about the same time. In May 1937 the two were living together in the same cave. Lily Wu (Wu Kuang-wei), a stunningly beautiful Shanghai woman of twenty-six, an actress who had played the lead in Gorky's *Mother*, very fluent in English, had been assigned to Smedley as her interpreter.

One evening, unexpectedly, Mao dropped into the Smedley-Snow cave. The two women and Lily Wu were having supper. They invited Mao to stay. He accepted. They had some wine. They drank and enjoyed themselves. Before the evening was over Mao and Lily were holding hands, and they left the cave together.

What happened next? There is no doubt that Mao and Lily had a fling. Smedley, according to the not necessarily reliable Braun, encouraged the romance by suggesting that the cave shared by Braun and Hatem was unoccupied during the daytime hours. Whether the couple employed that cave for an occasional rendezvous or not, Mao's wife became convinced that this was so. Shih-chen blamed Smedley for the whole thing and had a tremendous row with Mao. As she told a friend, "He grabbed a bench, I grabbed a chair." Word got to Smedley that Shih-chen had threatened to have her killed by her bodyguards. In panic Smedley made Helen Snow take the bed beside the window. "If the bodyguard had come," Helen said years later, "he would have shot me, not Agnes."

The scandal grew when Mao insisted on having an official party inquiry into the matter. By this time Lily Wu had quietly been sent away from Yenan, back to her native Szechwan, some said, never to play an international role again. Shih-chen, accompanied by her daughter and Mao's first son by Yang Kai-hui, Mao An-ying, was sent off to the Soviet Union for psychiatric treatment. The party granted Mao a divorce.

Presently the reason why the third young Shanghai woman, Lan Ping, had stopped showing up at the Braun-Hatem cave came to the surface.

At one of the lectures at the Lu Hsun Academy Lan Ping had met Mao Tse-tung and quickly

CHINA

100 Years

of

Revolution

won his interest. One morning she returned to her dormitory at the academy and, so it was said much later, announced to her startled classmates, "I have good news for you. I am now sharing the bed of Comrade Mao."

Romantic tittle-tattle from the caves of Yenan. Perhaps. But these were the words of a woman who began to call herself Chiang Ching, a woman who was to play a fateful role in the Great Proletarian Cultural Revolution and the strange drama of Mao's last years revolving around the Gang of Four.

★

Chiang Ching was born in March 1912 in Shantung Province into a lower-middle-class family. Her name at birth was Li Chin. She was one of a large family, her father a carpenter and handicraftsman with, Chiang Ching was to tell Roxanne Witke in a famous series of interviews, a vicious temper. He beat his children, including Chiang Ching, and their mother, sometimes with a spade.

Chiang Ching grew up in poverty, her mother having left her husband because of his cruelty. Her school name was Li Yun-ho (Cloud Crane). In 1929, as she told Witke, she was admitted to the Shantung provincial dramatic school in Tsinan and her profession was chosen. In Shanghai she appeared on the stage (the role of Nora in Ibsen's *A Doll's House* was a high point) and in films. She had, it seems clear, many affairs and one or two husbands: Tang Na, a film critic who later ran a restaurant in Paris, was one, and possibly Huang Chin who accompanied her and Li Li-yang to Yenan was another. Huang was a regional party figure of some consequence. By Chiang's account she dabbled in leftist politics and became an underground Communist. She was good-looking, with dark intense eyes and a dramatic carriage, bold and direct in conduct. What motivated her journey to Yenan is not certain. She, quite naturally, later insisted it was political conviction; some of her peers thought her desire for adventure and excitement played a stronger role. She came at a moment when many young Chinese women were making the pilgrimage.

She and Mao began to live together in 1938 and were formally married in 1939. In giving Mao permission to marry Chiang Ching the party executive enjoined that Chiang Ching was not to participate in political or party affairs. Some accounts suggest that a twenty-year ban was imposed. In her meetings with Roxanne Witke, Chiang Ching denied this by implication. She also denied a story believed by many Chinese that Mao Tse-tung himself chose her new name. Her acting name of Lan Ping, which she bore on arrival in Yenan, means Blue Apple. Chiang Ching, in her own words, means "Rivers of Azure." In choosing it Chiang Ching said she wanted to make a clear break with her bitter childhood as Li Chin and Li Yun-ho and with her theater life as Lan Ping. It would be as Chiang Ching that she would go down in history. Americans met Chiang Ching during the Yenan years. Some of them, including Brooks Atkinson, then the *New York Times* correspondent in China and before and later the *Times* drama critic, sometimes danced with her at Saturday-evening socials. He thought her a pretty and attractive young woman, surely not a great actress, but a woman of talent. He never dreamed the day would come when she would for a time hold the fate of China and its revolution in her nervous, restless, delicate hands.

# ★ 10 ★

## THE RED STAR RISES

**T**HE EYES OF YENAN IN THE SUMMER of 1939 were not turned, as were those of Europe and America, to the dramatic events that led to the signing of the Nazi-Soviet pact, the invasion of Poland and the outbreak of World War II.

Yenan's attention was fixed on a remote corner of Outer Mongolia where war had broken out between Japan and Soviet Russia. It was not called war. It was described as a "border skirmish" but it was war, all right.

Japan had tested Russia the year before in a clash near Lake Hassan in the Russia-China-Manchuria triangle. The Japanese had been driven off. Now a far more important conflict had developed near Khalkin Gol in eastern Mongolia. More than thirty thousand Japanese troops had invaded Mongolia with tanks, heavy artillery, planes. The Russians moved in powerful forces under the command of Marshal (then General) Georgi K. Zhukov, who had seen service as a military adviser in China and would go on to become the Soviet's number-one commander in the war against Hitler.

The Mongolian fighting raged all summer long. But in an offensive launched on August 20, 1939 (just as Soviet and Nazi emissaries were preparing to sign their nonaggression pact), Zhukov defeated the Japanese, crushing the Sixth Army and sending them reeling back to the Manchurian frontier.

It was a battle with far-reaching consequences. The Japanese would not again attack the Soviet Union. Instead, on the eve of the Nazi assault on Russia on June 22, 1941, Tokyo would sign a nonaggression pact with Stalin. Japanese armies in China would remain on the defensive (for the most part) while Japan turned its attention to the spectacular attack on the United States and Southeast Asia, beginning at Pearl Harbor in December 1941.

Yenan would have a breathing space. True, Mao would test out the Japanese in what came to be called the "Hundred Regiments Offensive," launched by the Eighth Route Army. But this would prove a disaster, involving heavy losses and causing the Japanese to attack the Communist area. But the action died away. Chiang Kai-shek did launch an assault on the Communist new Fourth Route Army in February 1942 (his first response to Pearl Harbor) but the Fourth Route Army remained in being. Chen Yi was sent in as commander and Liu Shao-chi as chief political commissar.

But when Hitler invaded Russia on June 22, 1941, Moscow sent hysterical demands to Yenan, calling for the Communists to attack the Japanese at any cost. Moscow desperately feared that the Japanese would stab her in the back, since the Russians had to transfer strong reserves from Siberia and the Far East in order to mount the counteroffensives which saved Moscow in December 1941 and won victory at Stalingrad a year later.

The first urgent Soviet message went to Yenan in early July 1941. The appeal was repeated in autumn 1941, when Stalin feared that both Moscow and Leningrad would fall. He called for help again during the Stalingrad crisis in 1942. But, as the Soviets were later to reveal, Mao promised aid but did nothing. Moscow said he proposed that they abandon Europe, retreat beyond the Urals and continue to fight from Siberia.

In truth, a major offensive by Yenan on the Japanese (as the Hundred Regiments operation had demonstrated) would have been a disaster. Later, in the frenzy of polemics against China, the Soviet Union would contend that at this time, and even as early as the late 1930s, the United States and Mao had forged an anti-Soviet alliance. This, of course, was nonsense.

If Mao was worried about Moscow, Tokyo or Chiang Kai-shek during the World War II years, he showed no sign of it. He occupied himself preparing for the struggle for power which he was certain (as was Chiang Kai-shek) would come once the Japanese had been defeated. Soviet propagandists later would say that Mao directed 10 percent of his strength against Japan and 20 percent to fighting the Nationalists and reserved 70 percent for the postwar struggle. In fact, the percentages were probably 30–40 percent to fighting the Japanese, 10 percent to holding off the Nationalists and the remainder for postwar operations.

★

That was the military side of things. What chiefly preoccupied Mao in this time was politics. This was the period of his "rectification movement," of the writing of a new introduction to the classic study of the Peasant Movement in Hunan which had launched his career as a Communist leader, and of his lectures on literature and the arts to artists and writers at what became known as the Yenan forum. The Yenan talks would reverberate in the People's Republic to the present day. Mao advanced the principle that the creative talents should be put to the service of the Revolution, to the service of the people. Art for art's sake was out. He gave a jolting response to Ting Ling, the marvelously talented writer of the pre-Yenan period who had undergone long imprisonment and house arrest by the Kuomintang, had lost her lover by execution and who had finally made her way to Yenan. There she was the center of a sparkling group of young, talented, liberated women, women as diverse in style as Agnes Smedley and young actresses like Chiang Ching, Li Li-yang, Lily Wu and the beautiful wife of George Hatem, Chou Su-fei. These were liberated women who had little in common with the peasant puritanism of the Long March. If they had an inspiration it was Aleksandra Kollontai, the Russian revolutionary who denounced bourgeois and peasant morals and boldly proclaimed that "love is like a drink of water."

Ting Ling was the boldest. She attacked Mao head on. She had no use for marriage, no use for convention. Mao might be inclined to unconventionalism in his private life but publicly (possibly with a bow to his peasant constituency) he was foursquare for the traditional virtues. He had his picture taken with Ting Ling but before long she entered a long calvary which turned into personal hell by the time of the Cultural Revolution. Only after Mao's death and Chiang Ching's arrest did she emerge rehabilitated, once again honored as China's most talented twentieth-century woman writer.

There was nothing original about Mao's Yenan-forum views. They were reminiscent of the lectures that Stalin had read to Soviet writers a decade earlier, when he proclaimed the thesis that they must be "the engineers of human souls" and established the cult of "socialist realism" controlled by the Union of Soviet Writers. Mao and Stalin clearly perceived the danger of free creative minds.

This was the period in which the doctrine of "Maoism" was formally born: Mao's own theory of Communism, drawn from Marx, modified to China's needs and tradition and strained through the close net of Mao's personal philosophy.

Sometimes Mao's language was less than elegant. Ross Terrill quoted him as saying to his party opponents: "Your dogma is less useful than shit. Dog shit can fertilize the fields, man's can feed the dog. But dogmas? They can't fertilize the fields or feed dogs. Of what use are they?"

In his late years Mao said that of all his honorifics the only one he wished to endure was that of Teacher. He was a teacher. Chou En-lai once said, "All we know we have learned from Chairman Mao. He is our teacher and we are all his pupils." This was a courtier's exaggeration, but there was deep truth within it. Mao's calling was that of a teacher, and he put his calling to revolutionary purpose. In the Yenan days this was clear. But he was a curious teacher. He had no use for dogma, no use for tradition, no use for authority (except perhaps his own). He was forever exhorting students to rebel and he was forever criticizing teachers for narrowness, pedantry, dedication to books, failure to understand the practical; in the end, he would exhort his whole nation that it must learn not from books but from work in the fields, the factories, the army. This would be his consistent theme throughout the Cultural Revolution. But it was not a new theme. He harked on it again and again at Yenan. Mao embodied both the rebellious student (revolting against his father and the schoolmasters) and the schoolmaster himself.

In these Yenan days, another trait came to the fore—his deep, deep roots in Chinese classics and tradition. He never halted reading them, and although he was often to cite Marx or Lenin, a frequency study of his speeches would show the supremacy of Chinese classics among his examples.

By the time Mao had concluded his "Rectification Movement" he had successfully purged the party of all the elements he considered to be a challenge, either bureaucratic or ideological. The "twenty-eight Bolsheviks" were in rout, as were all the others who had opposed him. He had been in command of the party since Tsunyi. Now he formalized his control by eliminating all possible challengers. Many wandered off or slipped back to Moscow. Chang Kuo-tao was long since gone. Wang Ming stayed on a while, praising Mao regardless of what he thought in private, then returned to Moscow, never to see China again. He headed a small anti-Mao brain trust for the Kremlin. Interestingly, Wang was not removed by Mao from the Chinese party's Central Committee until the late 1950s. By then, of course, the party battalions were ranged solidly behind Mao—Chou En-lai, Chu Teh, Liu Shao-chi, Lin Piao, all the others.

The membership was purged, the bureaucracy refreshed. Mao now possessed a coherent and comprehensive body of doctrine by which to test his fellow party members and on which to draw, should need be, in the polemics of the future. It was—and he openly proclaimed it so—a Chinese brand of Communism. No matter that the Soviet doctrinaries had insisted that there could be only one Marxism—their own. World War II was on. There was no time for ideological conflict. Meanwhile Mao was taking advantage of political opportunities as they developed. Those opportunities were largely colored red, white and blue.

**D**avid Barrett was, in 1941, a balding, rotund, irreverent middle-aged Coloradan who had gone to war in 1917, two years after college, and spent his life thereafter in the U.S. Army, largely in China. He had come to Peking in 1921 as a military language officer and spent the next four years learning Mandarin. He served with the Fifteenth Infantry in China and for many years as a military attaché. For practical purposes his life from 1921 onward *was* China. Generals George C. Marshall and Joseph W. Stilwell also saw service in the Fifteenth Infantry and both knew and valued Barrett.

As John K. Fairbank pointed out, Barrett, like the typical American army officer of his day, loved to scout out the terrain. Like Stilwell he was forever on the go, always exploring China, on the road, walking, having a bowl of noodles in a street stall, swapping stories with the local innkeeper, a robust, rollicking, self-reliant, earthy man. Like Stilwell and many, many other Americans he *loved* China and the Chinese. He knew the Chinese faults and virtues. He spoke almost perfect Peking dialect, the best of the army language scholars. The army in these times took great pains at teaching Chinese to officers assigned to China and sent them back for tour after tour, respecting and valuing their expertise. When his army career was over, Barrett looked forward to settling in China. He couldn't think of living anywhere else. He considered it a tragedy that Chiang Kai-shek refused to let him live in Taiwan when he retired in the 1950s.

Barrett, also like Stilwell, was in the best U.S. Army tradition, as John S. Service of the State Department was in another American tradition, the missionary tradition—born in China (in Cheng-tu), speaking perfect and fluent Chinese, the embodiment of a skilled Foreign Service officer, cool, careful, educated in Chinese nuances.

To read the reports of Barrett, Service, Stilwell and the others and match them against the diaries, journals and reminiscences of Russia's "China hands" is to perceive the advantage the United States possessed through its years of intimate, understanding, open association with China.

Leaving aside the deliberate tendentiousness of many Russian experts, they are (for the most part) men without a feeling or knowledge of China; more often than not without the Chinese language; men on pick-up assignments, reading background books while traveling on the Trans-Siberian or on planes from Alma-Ata to Urumchi and Lanchow. In no period was the contrast so marked as during World War II. Small wonder that the baffled, semi-literate, frustrated Soviets concluded the Americans were all spies and that Mao himself was Washington's cover man. By this time Stalin had shot or sent to prison almost all of his genuine China specialists.

But neither Russia nor America had much contact with Yenan in the early war period. Yenan had been sealed off by Chiang Kai-shek since 1939. Americans couldn't get in. Russia, struggling to survive, had neither time nor interest for Yenan. Stalin maintained his contacts with Chiang. Until a man who called himself Pyotr Vladimirov arrived in Yenan on May 11, 1942, the Comintern's link to China was Wang Ming, whose relations with Mao were badly strained.

There were three low-level Russians in Yenan from about 1939 to 1942, a Tass correspondent named Igor Yuzhin, radio operator Leonid Dolmatov (known as Li Wen), and Boris Aleyev, a translator. Vladimirov brought in Andrei Orlov, a military surgeon, and Nikolai Rimmar, a radio operator. The others went home.

The Russians found themselves in the hands of Mao's security man Kang Sheng, for whom they developed a violent antipathy. There was little in Yenan (if Vladimirov's posthumous and "edited" diary has any validity) that they enjoyed. The Russians had no affinity for the Chinese, nor did Mao and his associates show them much respect. Vladimirov got the impression that the Chinese did not think the Russians had handled themselves well in the early phase of the war.

Chou En-lai had warned Stalin of the impending Nazi attack (as had Roosevelt and Churchill and Stalin's own extraordinary intelligence agents in Berlin and Tokyo) but Stalin had paid no heed. The war's course in 1941 and 1942 convinced Mao that even if Russia beat Hitler (and of this he was not always certain) there was small chance of China's getting much aid from the Soviet Union after Japan was defeated and Chiang Kai-shek crushed.

This calculation—and an American calculation that the Chinese Communists could be a powerful ally against Japan—is what brought, on July 27, 1944, a U.S. Army C-47 transport plane to the rough and dusty landing strip just north of Yenan. It made a jolting landing in which the propeller blade was splintered and cut through the pilot's cabin, missing the head of Captain Champion by an inch.

So Dixie Mission arrived in Yenan—nicknamed Dixie in part because it was a mission to the Chinese "rebs," in part because of the song "Is It True What They Say About Dixie?" It was up to Dixie to find out if it was true, if the reports about the Communists—that they were good fighters, well trained and resolutely engaged against the Japanese—had any substance.

Dixie Mission entered the task with enthusiasm, ability and know-how. The reports sent back by Barrett and John S. Service remain core documents in the study of the Chinese Communists. Ultimately a score of Americans were stationed in Yenan, augmented from time to time by others, who were flown in specially from Chungking, and by a shifting group of American correspondents, men like Theodore White, whose book with Annalee Jacoby, *Thunder Out of China*, would become a classic; Brooks Atkinson; Harrison Forman; Harold Isaacs, who would write *The Tragedy of the Chinese Revolution*; and others.

Mao, Chu Teh, Lin Piao, Liu Shao-chi and Chou had long talks with the Americans. Colonel Barrett and his men watched the Eighth Route Army engage the Japanese in combat. They were impressed by the fighting spirit and discipline of the Communist troops in contrast with the ill-trained, ill-led Nationalist forces. Here were men who knew what they were doing, not like the bedraggled Nationalist recruits the Americans had often seen being led to the barracks, tethered together so they would not escape. The Communist officers did not beat their men with rifle butts. The Red soldiers got on well with the peasants. Colonel Barrett, years later, after the waning of the McCarthy era but before U.S. rapprochement with China, was still worrying a little about his judgments but he did not think he should change them. He was, he said, impressed with the Communist troops and their leadership.

The Communists were equally impressed with the Americans and the U.S. stress on pragmatic measures for fighting Japan.

**A**nd then there were the Saturday-night dances at the grove of fruit trees called the Pear Orchard. Top Chinese leaders turned out, including Mao Tse-tung, wearing white shirt and dark trousers, no tie, no jacket. Dapper, agile Lin Piao, in army fatigues, was the best of the Chinese dancers (in the opinion of John Paton Davies). Chu Teh sat on the sidelines in faded blue cotton uniform watching the proceedings. Chinese girls, pigtails down their backs, Barrett recalled, would come up to Mao and say, "Chairman, please dance with me." Mao danced. Davies found it a little difficult to tell the girls from the boys, all in cotton padded jackets and trousers. The band was Chinese, three violins and some curious percussion

CHINA

100 Years

of

Revolution

175

instruments. It played "Marching Through Georgia" and "Yankee Doodle" and the dancers fox-trotted. No one ever forgot the Pear Orchard hops.

On other evenings there were sometimes plays, sometimes traditional Chinese opera, sometimes modern realistic plays. Very well done, said Brooks Atkinson. Once in a great while there were movies: a film or two was sent up to the Dixie Mission, a film or two provided by the Chinese.

★

The intimacy of the Communist leadership and Dixie Mission drove the Comintern man, Vladimirov, to fury. (By this time Stalin had dissolved the Comintern, as a gesture to his Western allies, but Vladimirov doggedly continued his reports; he thought dissolution of the Comintern made the Chinese feel they had no international obligations—that is, no obligations to Moscow.) He was particularly displeased when Mao participated in a ceremony at which Barrett was presented with the U.S. Medal of Merit by an American military delegation flown in from Chungking. Vladimirov complained that he wasn't invited to Chinese-American gatherings, where, he insisted, liquor flowed like water. He spoke of quantities of Johnny Walker, but none of the Dixie survivors recalled any Scotch in these puritanical precincts. Many entries in Vladimirov's diary sound like those of a small boy who hasn't been invited to the party.

When Mao began to use Vladimirov's wireless set for messages to Moscow he was not pleased. He thought it a trick to undercut his critical comments. Once Vladimirov happily noted that Mao had spent eight hours talking with him. Then he decided it was a scheme by Mao to cover up his real antipathy.

The agony of the Comintern man peaked when President Roosevelt sent Patrick J. Hurley to China as his special emissary, tasked with bringing Chiang and Mao into a dual government. The Hurley mission was the climax of what had gradually been building up between the Americans and the Communists—a growing sense that they could work together with profit. The Americans wanted the Communists as reliable fighting allies against the Japanese. The Communists wanted the Americans to give them equal status with the Nationalists and thus gain an advantage for the intra-Chinese struggle that lay ahead.

Hurley's arrival in Yenan was a totally unexpected event. He had come to Chungking but sent no warning that he would visit the Communist area. Colonel Barrett was standing beside Chou En-lai at the airport when a C-47 landed, the door swung open and Barrett perceived Hurley, "tall, gray-haired, soldierly, extremely handsome, wearing one of the most beautifully tailored uniforms I have ever seen," standing at the top of the steps. "Who is that?" Chou inquired. It was, Barrett told the startled Chou, the President's special representative. "Please hold him here until I can bring Chairman Mao," said Chou, disappearing in a cloud of dust. Within minutes the converted Chevrolet ambulance, marked "Gift of N.Y. Chinese Laundrymen's Association," which was Yenan's only civilian vehicle and Mao's pride, brought the Communist Chairman to the spot. An infantry company appeared as a guard of honor. Hurley returned the salute, drew himself up and emitted a Choctaw war whoop that almost lifted Mao off his feet.

It was a bizarre moment but there was nothing bizarre about Hurley's purpose. He was, unlikely as it seemed, President Roosevelt's chosen instrument for achieving a coalition between Chiang and Mao, a coalition that would bring the Communists into the war against Japan as full-fledged allies alongside the Nationalists, receiving American aid and fighting shoulder-to-shoulder against the common enemy.

CHINA
100 Years
of
Revolution

176

(Text continues on page 193.)

醒獅

每月一回朔日發行

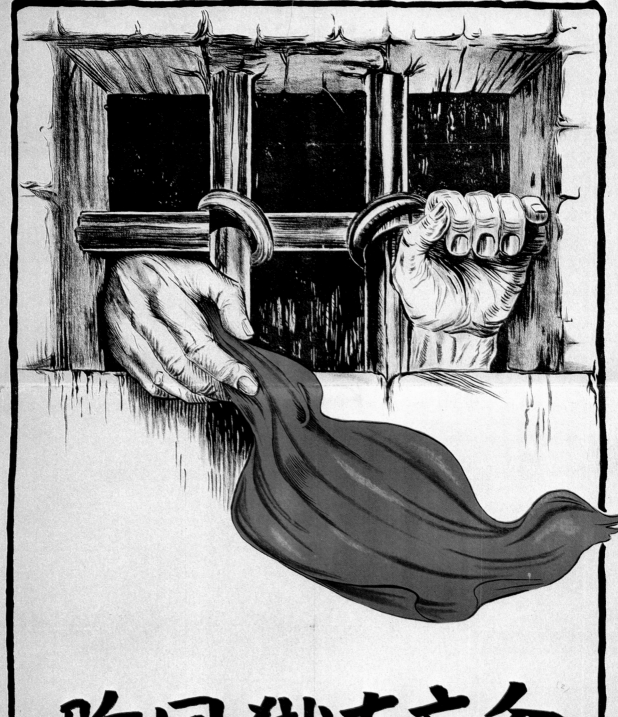

*Overleaf (preceding):*
Chinese students' pre-1911 radical monthly, called *The Awakened Lion*. MRV

*Opposite:*
"Don't forget your brothers in jail!" A poster issued after the May 30, 1924, incident. LC

*Above:*
A call to Chinese citizens to support the war effort against the Japanese just as Chinese soldiers are backing it with their lives. A poster from the mid-1920s. LC

*Overleaf (following—left):*
A propaganda poster issued by the revolutionary army in the 1920s. It exhorts the Chinese to keep fighting against foreign imperialists. LC

*Overleaf (following—right):*
Chinese peasants, workers, soldiers, merchants and students are called to unite against warlords and imperialists. A leftist poster from the mid-1920s. LC

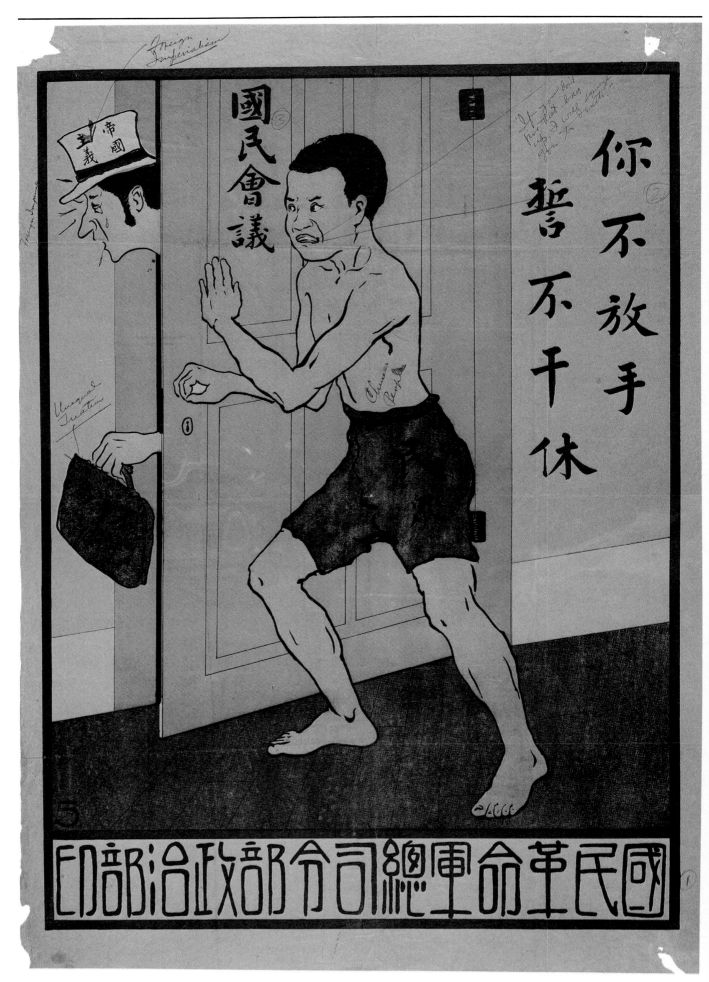

敵軍反戰圖 軍委會政治部

*Overleaf (left):*
An anti-imperialist poster in which the worker swears to fight to the end against the unequal treaties imposed upon China by European powers; it probably dates from the Northern Expedition of 1927. LC

*Overleaf (right):*
A Chinese hero puts to death the "Devil of Communism." A Chinese Nationalist poster of 1941–1942. LC

*Above:*
A Japanese recruit turns his sword against his officer. A Chinese Nationalist cartoon from the mid-1930s. LC

*Opposite:*
Mao Tse-tung and the People's Liberation Army entering Peking, January 1949. A Chinese wall poster. GRA

*Above:*
Peasant women organize medical aid for the countryside. A wall poster from the 1960s. LC

*Opposite top:*
A peasant couple register their marriage under the new Communist regime. A wall poster from the late 1950s. LC

*Opposite bottom:*
Peasants sign a world peace petition. A wall poster from the 1960s. LC

*Overleaf:*
Mao Tse-tung in July 1966 at Wuhan, scene of his famous swim in the Yangtze River. A contemporary painting. LC

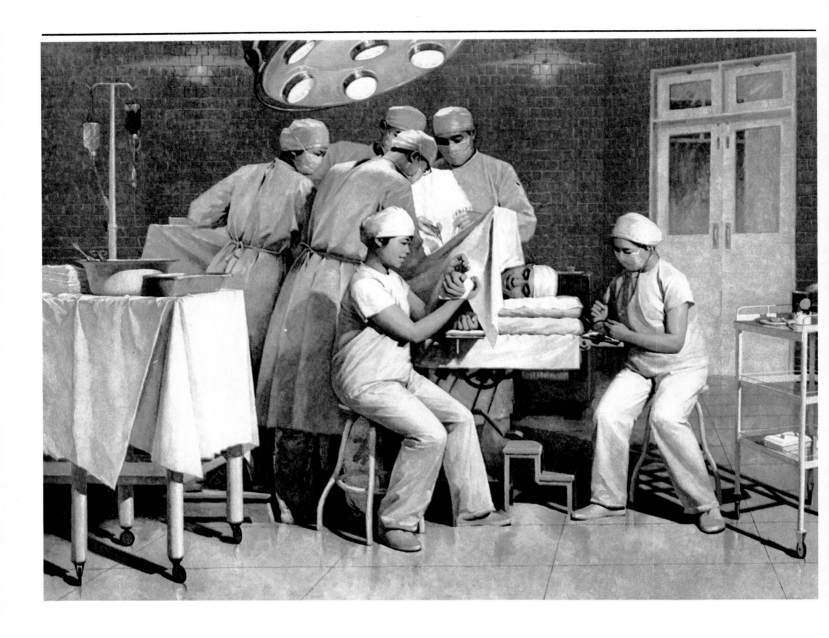

*Above:*
A Chinese medical team prepares for a surgical operation by reading the "little red book," during the Cultural Revolution. A contemporary painting. LC

*Opposite:*
Chairman Mao, icon of the Chinese Communist Revolution. A contemporary painting. LC

After the Cultural Revolution—Chinese students relax, turning their backs to a propaganda slogan. DEL

Mao had already spent long hours in conversation with Service, Barrett and the other Americans. Thousands of words of reports had gone back to Washington. The groundwork had been laid.

Now, this most unlikely of individuals, Oklahoma businessman, Republican politician, part Choctaw Indian, had been sent to clinch the deal. Success seemed at hand. Hurley and Mao knocked together a declaration for a coalition government, an amalgamation of Nationalist and Communist armed forces under joint direction, the whole to be carried out under a policy that was described thus:

"Designed to promote progress and democracy and to establish justice, freedom of conscience, freedom of the press, freedom of speech, freedom of assembly and association, the right to petition to the Government for the redress of grievances, the right of the writ of habeas corpus, and the right of residence."

This idealistic declaration, drafted basically by Hurley, was at his suggestion countersigned by Mao and Hurley. He carried it back to Chungking for Chiang's signature. Naturally, this was never forthcoming.

The American military, representatives of General Albert C. Wedemeyer, special emissaries of the OSS (the wartime predecessor of the CIA) and Colonel Barrett, acting for the China-Burma-India command, discussed with Mao, Chou and Yeh Chien-ying proposals for joint operations with the Chinese Communists—large-scale U.S. guerrilla operations with the Communists behind the Japanese lines, major landings of American forces on the Shantung peninsula (protected by Communist armies), a cornucopia of mutual projects. John Paton Davies explored with Mao and Chou the prospects of postwar economic collaboration.

So heady was the talk that in January 1945 Mao and Chou made a secret proposal that they fly to Washington to discuss with President Roosevelt China's future, their role in it and relations with the United States.

Because of a bureaucratic mishap and the unpredictability of Hurley, the message never reached the White House: Hurley intercepted it (it had been addressed to General Wedemeyer) and refused to transmit it to Washington; Roosevelt never heard of the idea; Mao and Chou never got a reply and never knew why. The very existence of the Chinese initiative remained unknown for twenty-five years, after which it was brought to light by the historian and China specialist Barbara Tuchman.

Even the Russians played an oblique role in this tragedy of errors. Stalin and Molotov each assured Hurley (and other Americans as well) that they had no interest whatever in the Chinese Communists in Yenan. In fact, said Stalin to Hurley, they are margarine Communists, not the real thing. He couldn't care less what became of them. There was much truth in Stalin's lack of interest in the fate of Mao. But it had quite another motive, and it would be decades before Stalin's intense hostility toward Mao and consistent preference for Chiang Kai-shek would be documented. Stalin's reasoning was characteristically pragmatic. He regarded Chiang as weak and believed a weak China which he could manipulate was in Moscow's interest. He had had a dozen bitter quarrels with Mao and was certain that in power Mao would be difficult or impossible to deal with. Stalin was right. Thus, the reality of the Soviet position was the opposite of what most American observers in Yenan, Chungking and Washington tended to fear: that is, that by supporting the Chinese Communists the United States would be playing the Soviet game and putting Stalin's man in charge in China. Mao was not and never would be anyone's man.

Naturally, no one was going to tip off the United States to the reality, neither the Chinese

CHINA
100 Years
of
Revolution

Communists nor the Russians, and when, occasionally, an American observer suggested that there did not seem to be a strong connection between Yenan and Moscow or that the Chinese Communists were taking a very independent course, the observer loaded such tentatives with heavy qualifications. No one wanted to stray too far from the common assumption that the Communists all belonged to the same camp and that its capital was Moscow. It was much simpler (and more usual) to assume that Yenan was a stalking horse for Moscow.

As the disarticulated discussions between the Americans and the Chinese Communists went forward, Mao and Chou concluded that for whatever reason (and the American conduct was too contradictory to analyze) Washington had come down on the side of Chiang Kai-shek. The diplomats with whom the Chinese had been dealing—Service, Davies and the rest, Colonel Barrett and many other officers—began to vanish. They were posted to Washington, Moscow or elsewhere. Hurley continued to preach coalition of Communists and Nationalists but by now his proposals bore the stamp of Chiang Kai-shek and T. V. Soong. It seemed to the Communists that they could expect nothing from the Americans; they did not believe they would get anything from the Russians. It was to be, they decided, once more a case of go-it-alone. That would make things more difficult. But they had done it before; they would do it again.

In that judgment Mao and Chou were correct. To be sure, there would be one more major effort by the Americans to find a middle way. They would send in the best of them all, General George Marshall, in 1946 to try to achieve a *modus vivendi* between the Communists and the Nationalists. But it would not work. Each side was positioning itself for civil war by the first months of 1945.

There would be a Russian move in total secrecy to try to deter civil war, a move that faithfully reflected Stalin's perceptions for China. At some point in 1945, as Mao later revealed, Stalin specifically advised him not to engage Chiang in civil war but instead to accept a role in a coalition government and dissolve the Communist armed forces. Stalin's prescription was almost identical with the proposals Hurley offered Yenan at the instigation of Chiang Kai-shek and Madame Chiang. Immediately after the Yalta Conference in February 1945, Stalin entered into a postwar treaty with Chiang, regulating Soviet relations with China, obtaining from Chiang the concession of Outer Mongolia's "independence" (in other words, subservience to the Soviet Union) and renewal of Russia's old special rights in Manchuria—all this as a preliminary to Soviet intervention in the war against Japan. The treaty was designed to lay the foundation of postwar relations between Chiang and Moscow.

None of this would impede in any way the triumph of the Chinese Revolution. It would, however, change the Revolution's direction and emphasis. Like one of the periodic upheavals of the Hwang Ho, the preposterous failure of the United States and Communist China each to understand what the other was talking about would inflict terrible wounds—on China, elsewhere in Asia and on the United States. Out of these ingredients would be compounded the great fictions of McCarthyism, the "loss" of China, the martyrization of a generation of skilled American China hands. Had the course advocated by the American specialists been followed it is possible, as one of them said much, much later, that there might have been no Chinese civil war, no Korean War, no Vietnam War. A different world.

★

It was not to be. Both the United States and the Soviet Union tried to make it possible for Chiang Kai-shek to take over China in 1945 and 1946. The United States put planes and ships at his disposal, which enabled him to shift Nationalist forces to Nanking, Tientsin, Peking and Manchuria. The United States moved two hundred thousand Nationalist troops to Manchuria alone. The Japanese were ordered to surrender only to the Nationalists, not to the Communists. Chiang asked Moscow to keep its troops in Manchuria until he could take over from them. The Soviets obliged. They turned over the area to Nationalist, not Communist troops. Instead of leaving the great Japanese industrial installations of Manchuria for the Communists, the Russians dismantled the factories and shipped them back to Russia. Stalin was demonstrating publicly on which side he had put his bet.

During Marshall's patient peace efforts in 1946, Chiang and Mao positioned themselves. By the time the battle opened in late 1946, Chiang controlled areas of China populated by 340 million people; the Communists about 110 million. Chiang had armies estimated at 4 million with another 1 million irregulars. The Communists had an army of 1.2 million and about 1.5 million irregulars. By June 1949 the figures would be reversed: Chiang, 1.5 million; Mao, 4 million.

On paper Chiang had an excellent position. He controlled China's larger cities and had cleared wide areas around Shanghai and Nanking of Communist troops. He drove Marshal Chen Yi's Fourth Route Army into the mountains of Shantung. What wasn't immediately apparent was that the Communists simply sat on Chiang's communications. Chiang had the cities. No links in between.

By January 1947 came the first clues to what would happen. The Communists attacked the Twenty-sixth Kuomintang Division, entirely U.S.-equipped. It immediately surrendered and turned over the equipment to the Reds. Again and again and again this would happen. The Communists had no need of help from the Soviet Union or anyone else. Chiang Kai-shek provided them the best in U.S. arms.

The countryside began to turn against Chiang's troops because of their pillage and rape. Villages and cities organized against the Nationalist marauders. Chiang closed a gap in the dikes along the Hwang Ho, to create a water barrier between Chen Yi and another Communist army led by Liu Po-cheng, a one-eyed general. The move made a hundred thousand people homeless, threatened another four hundred thousand, destroyed twelve hundred villages and swung the area over to the Communists.

Chiang moved a big army away from the Hwang Ho and sent it up to capture the Communist capital of Yenan. When the Nationalists arrived they found the valley bare: the Communists had decamped to the north without loss of a single platoon. Then Lin Piao and Liu Po-cheng took advantage of Chiang's troop displacement to move over the Yellow River and into the valley of the Yangtze.

In Shanghai the first portents of doom appeared. The government insisted the Communists were retreating and retreating. But the exchange rate dropped to three hundred thousand yuan to the dollar. A few months later it was two million to the dollar. Correspondents drank at their club on the eighteenth floor of Broadway Mansions, Jack Belden recalled, and began to worry what to do with their White Russian mistresses. Gambling and opium-smoking were everywhere.

Chiang Kai-shek had five U.S.-equipped armies in Manchuria, but no firm communications between Manchuria and North China. The Nationalist position began to crumble. In September 1948 Tsinan, Shantung's capital, fell. Nationalist General Wu Hua-wen turned over his Ninety-fourth Army to the Communists. In Manchuria the Nationalist generals began to hole up in the cities. They were waiting, it was said, for the Presidential election victory of Governor

Tom Dewey in November, which, they thought, would bring a lot of U.S. aid. Dewey lost. No aid came. Colonel Barrett and John Melby of the American embassy in Nanking went to the airport one day. They watched planes land from Peking, one after another. Finally Barrett said to Melby, "John, I have seen all I need to see. When the generals begin to evacuate their gold bars and concubines the end is at hand."

Lin Piao besieged Chang-chun, capital of Kirin in Manchuria. His men called out on loudspeakers to the Nationalist troops to join them. No more ropes, no more beatings. The Nationalists began to desert. Their colonels rushed prostitutes up to the lines but this did not keep the soldiers from melting into the Communist lines. In September and October Chiang Kai-shek lost four hundred thousand troops and fifty generals, almost all by desertion. By October 30, 1948, Mukden fell, most of Jehol was gone, the road was opening to Peking. In November and December Generals Chen Yi and Liu laid siege to Suchow, a hundred eighty miles north of Chiang's capital of Nanking. The city fell on January 17, 1949, and cost Chiang five hundred fifty thousand men. On January 31 the Communists entered Peking. The city surrendered without a shot.

The end was obvious but the Communists did not rush it. They simply let Chiang's forces disintegrate. They set up shop in Peking. Manchuria was established as the Northeast Autonomous Region and by June 1949 Kao Kang, a veteran member of the Politburo, was in Moscow, negotiating a special economic agreement with Stalin.

Later Kao Kang's role would come under special scrutiny. He bossed Manchuria until after Stalin's death, in March 1953; then, under mysterious circumstances, he and an associate, Jao Shu-shih, were arrested. Kao Kang was charged with having conspired with a foreign power to set up an independent "kingdom" and detach the province from China. He committed suicide, and this was regarded by Peking as a specially traitorous act, designed to foil his just punishment. At first the Russians followed the Chinese line. Kao Kang became a nonperson, his name deleted from the Soviet encyclopedia. Later, however, he was restored to full Soviet favor, characterized as a true and loyal Communist and an "internationalist"—that is, a supporter of the Moscow line—and a victim of a plot by Mao. The curious turns of Soviet propaganda support Mao's suspicions that Kao Kang was, in fact, Stalin's secret man. Mao's feeling may have been strengthened by other Soviet intrigues. There was a curious episode in 1949 in the distant border province of Sinkiang. Secret negotiations went on between the Russians and Chiang Kai-shek, almost up to the proclamation of the People's Republic, for a deal that would have established an "independent" Sinkiang government under Soviet protection. Russia had plotted and schemed in Sinkiang since the mid-nineteenth century, and for many years the Kuomintang governor there had been a Soviet puppet. However, in the end the Soviet-Kuomintang deal fell through.

★

There was one last flicker of the spark that had been lighted at Yenan by the Americans. It was June 1949. The Communist regime was well established in Peking. Colonel Barrett was still on the scene, serving as assistant military attaché assigned to Peking. One day he got a message from Chou En-Lai, a message of such secrecy that the emissary said Chou did not even wish his name attached to it.

The message had the flavor of the Dixie Mission era. Chou said that two wings had developed in the Communist Party, one radical, one liberal. Mao held a place in the center. The "radicals," headed by Liu Shao-chi, were oriented toward the Soviet Union, wanted a close military alliance with the Russians, wanted to proceed swiftly toward a Soviet system and elimination of private business. They were anti-U.S. and anti-West. The "liberals," headed by Chou, believed China must go through a transition period and undertake an enormous reconstruction without ideological bonds. They wanted aid from the United States or possibly Britain. They took the view that the United States had evolved into something outside the categories of Marxist theory. Chou depicted his group as feeling that Soviet policy (this was 1949, height of the Cold War) was "crazy" and carried a high risk of war. They felt Russia was unable to help them; they needed aid badly and were prepared to negotiate with the United States to get it, in return for which China would not become Communist for a long time and would serve as an intermediary between the West and the Soviet Union.

Chou emphasized that he was speaking for himself and that he hoped the United States would resume contacts with those they had worked with at Yenan. He and his associates wanted "peace in our time" and were prepared to work in every way to move the Soviet Union away from policies directed toward war.

It was a remarkable declaration but, like so many initiatives between the Communists and the United States, it came to nothing. A gingerly effort was made by the Americans to follow it up, but this effort petered out and the episode was classified top secret and buried deep in the archives, not to emerge until half a dozen years after President Nixon's 1972 trip to Peking.

There was a curious aftermath to this last effort to revive Yenan. In July 1951 Peking announced that a plot to assassinate Chairman Mao at Tien an Men Square had been uncovered and that Colonel Barrett was its instigator. A half-dozen Chinese were accused of participating in the conspiracy. Twenty years later, Premier Chou spoke personal words of apology for these charges, which he said were unfounded and had been inspired by dubious personalities. There were those who wondered whether this "plot" might not, in fact, have been invented by opponents of Chou, trying to tar him with the brush of association with so dangerous an American enemy.

★

Slowly, almost sedately, the great change moved forward. The People's Liberation Army had occupied Nanking on April 21. It took Wuhan on May 17, Sian on May 20, Shanghai on May 27.

Chiang Kai-shek scuttled ahead. He gave up the Presidency. He took it back. His government fled to Canton, to Chungking, to Cheng-tu. Finally to Taiwan. Faithfully the Russian ambassador, an impassive man named Roshchin who had several times proposed that Moscow mediate between the Communists and the Nationalists and who had even asked Chiang Kai-shek to take over Dairen and Port Arthur and the South Manchurian Railroad (was Moscow fearful the Communists might take back these Russian concessions?), tagged along.

All the other powers kept their embassies at Nanking. Only the Soviets were faithful to the end. They broke off when Chiang left the mainland.

So finally the day came. October 1, 1949. Mao had long since taken up residence in the Imperial City, in an old Ming-dynasty house. He had been in Peking since March 25. From his doorstep he had a view of South Lake and of Central Lake. It was a quiet spot. He read and wrote a lot. Emperors of China had trod the cool courtyard stones.

Then, on October 1, he finally proclaimed the People's Republic. He left the pleasant old

Ming house and rode in a great open limousine into Tien an Men Square. A Sherman tank preceded him, one of those the United States had given to Chiang Kai-shek. Mao stood on a platform at Tien an Men and spoke to a million people.

"The Chinese people have stood up . . ." he said.

It had been a hundred years since it started, a hundred years since the Opium War and the Taipings, he reminded the crowd. Time had moved slowly, in the Chinese way. But surely. The mantle of heaven had fallen from the Emperors. Now it rested across the shoulders of a Hunan middle peasant's son. Mao Tse-tung.

# ★ 11 ★

## R E V O L U T I O N   V I C T O R I O U S

**T**HE REVOLUTION WAS VICTORIOUS.
The struggle of one hundred years had ended. Communism, born in China in 1921, had come to power after twenty-eight years of struggle and sacrifice. The long fight was over.

Or was it? As time passed it became more and more evident that when Mao mounted the steps of Tien an Men on that bright October day in 1949 it marked not the end of the Revolution but one more beginning in the Long March of the Chinese people toward a New Day. True, as Mao said, the people had risen up. True, their backs no longer bowed to Emperors, nobles, tyrants, landlords or foreigners. But the end was not in sight, nor was it even certain what that end might be.

In 1949 Mao was a sturdy man of fifty-six. He had put on weight. No longer was he the lean, tall, wiry, tousled youngster with the high-cheekboned face of the 1920s and early 1930s. His frame had fleshed out. His face took on a softer mold. He seemed a bit ponderous, spoke a bit solemnly; the beginnings of the Wise Man of China could be detected. He did not often appear in public. In private, in inner party circles, Politburo sessions, plenaries, his air of dominance was plain. He spoke in earthy, often rude terms. The courtyard of his Hunan farm was never distant from his similes. There was a weight to his humor, a vinegar bite that was stronger than before. He was conscious that it was *his* Revolution, and the consciousness showed in the oracular quality of his speech. He had made the Revolution. Now he must administer it. The task would not be easy, and many of his problems were embodied in the divergence between the views of his comrades of the Long March and his. This gap would widen.

The tasks lay everywhere. Not all of China was under Mao's sway by October 1, 1949. The Communist writ was tenuous in South China, the remote areas of the northwest and west, Sinkiang, Szechwan, Tibet, the far reaches of Yunnan, the fringes of the western and northern deserts. And there was the countryside. Mao and his Communists held the cities but China was a land of villages. Far from all of the villages had been penetrated. Far from all knew what Communism or Mao was about. At the core China was still medieval.

The problem of the countryside was tackled by "work teams," bands of activists who spread through the villages and the countryside, organizing the peasants, encouraging them to speak the bitter tales of their lives, encouraging them to attack landlords, moneylenders, merchants as the "class enemy." Youngsters from the cities headed by a few cadres ventured into China's roadless depths. It was a tedious process, a bloody process. How many landlords were killed? The tally has never been taken. Probably a million or more. As Mao once said: "Whom have we executed? What sort of people? Elements for whom the masses had great hatred. If we did not kill some tyrants, or if we were too lenient to them, the masses would not agree." Yet he warned against indiscriminate killing. "People's heads are not like leeks. When you cut them off they will not grow again."

When the bloody ritual was over the landlords had lost their property, if not their heads. They had been declassed. Visitors twenty years later would look in vain for a surviving landlord, and when the term was mentioned an expression of revulsion would pass over the face of a Chinese. He would say, "There is no such thing as a good landlord. It is a contradiction in terms." The survivors were set to work at the lowliest tasks—collecting excrement, driving the "honeywagons," carting night soil from city to countryside.

The People's Liberation Army fanned out into the farthest regions, gradually bringing them under control. In remote Tibet a compromise was struck with the Dalai Lama. A quasi-collaborative regime was established. Not until ten years had passed—in 1959—would the PLA take Tibet from the hands of the Dalai Lama, who fled to India with many of his followers.

The question of relations between the United States and China was put on hold. Mao had concluded that the United States was not to be trusted. President Truman, beset by Republican criticism over the "loss" of China, had decided to "let the dust settle." He refused military support to Chiang's regime on Taiwan and deferred diplomatic relations with the Communists in Peking.

But the problem of China and the Soviet Union could not be deferred. China needed economic help at once. Mao had no illusions as to his relations with Stalin. They had been facing each other down for twenty years. Mao had defied Stalin again and again. He had engaged Chiang in civil war against Stalin's orders. He had pursued the civil war to victory despite repeated representations from Moscow. Only six months before he took the podium at Tien an Men, Mao had received a final message from Stalin. Once again, according to Han Su-yin, Stalin was trying to slow Mao down, to narrow his revolutionary objectives, to create a foothold where Chiang Kai-shek could hold on. Sometime in the spring of 1949 Stalin sent a telegram to Mao: "Leave South China to Chiang." Mao ignored this as he had all the other recommendations of the Kremlin.

Now Mao had no alternative. He had to consolidate power in China and he needed Stalin's support. Mao had founded his movement on the peasants, not the proletariat—against Moscow's theories. He had driven Moscow's factions out of his party. True, he retained Wang Ming, Stalin's man, on his Central Committee. Wang had a voice but no power. Mao's break with Moscow's strategy and Moscow's ideology had been total. He did not advertise this, nor did Moscow. But both knew it. Now Mao and Stalin had to talk.

Mao Tse-tung arrived in Moscow by train on a cold gray December 16, 1949. Snow was falling. There was, contrary to protocol, not a word of advance notice to the Soviet public, and little notice after Mao got to Moscow. He was taken to the Bolshoi Theater on December 21 not to celebrate his arrival as Russia's great ally but to honor Stalin's seventieth birthday. Mao was cast in the role of a senior vassal bringing tribute from a distant land to the great Slav Emperor. The spectacle for the evening was a revised version of an old Soviet ballet called *The Red Poppy*. Its central character was a Russian sailor who organizes the Shanghai coolies in revolt. The Chinese had a difficult time concealing their distaste—was this a deliberate insult by Stalin or a gesture born of ignorance?

Talks with Stalin went on and on and on. Mao's visit vanished from the Soviet press. Western correspondents went to the Chinese embassy to inquire whether Mao had secretly left the country. When the Chinese gave a reception for their Russian hosts they were compelled to use the dining room of the Hotel Metropol, where Rasputin had once staged his revels. Not until February 15, 1950, was a communiqué issued announcing an agreement on a treaty of aid, assistance and mutual defense (but only against Japan!). The agreement was notable for its stinginess—sixty million dollars a year in aid (loans not grants). In the old colonial pattern, it established joint-stock companies (Moscow held the deciding vote) for exploitation of the mineral resources of Sinkiang, for air service, for oil exploration. Mao was obliged to confirm Russia's special position in Manchuria, her rights to the ports of Dairen and Port Arthur, and the Chinese Eastern Railway. Years later Mao described the agreements as setting up "two colonies," Manchuria and Sinkiang, where no one of a third country was permitted to live. There had been a real struggle over the 1950 treaty, he conceded; Stalin had not wanted to sign it, had suggested that "China might degenerate into another Yugoslavia" and that Mao might "be another Tito." Stalin had called the Chinese Revolution "a fake." No treaty might have been concluded had not Chou En-lai flown into Moscow at the last moment and managed to ease tensions enough to permit the signing of a document that both he and Mao regarded as demeaning—but necessary. Stalin made Mao pay a heavy price for his lifetime of conflict.

Typically, Western diplomats circulated texts of imaginary secret military protocols to the "Sino-Soviet Alliance" under which the Chinese placed their armed forces at Stalin's service in return for Soviet aid and equipment—the reverse of the real situation.

If Mao had been compelled to pay a heavy price to Stalin in Moscow, this proved to be only a down payment.

On June 25, 1950—before President Truman's "dust" had settled, at a moment when China and the United States had not yet regularized their relations—North Korea burst into South Korea. Within days the United States, under the banner of the United Nations, was at war to defend South Korea. The Seventh Fleet had been sent to protect Taiwan from Chinese Communist interference.

Thirty years after the event, the origins of the Korean War remain an enigma. But there has been an accumulation of evidence that the conflict was part of an elaborate plan by Stalin to strengthen Russia's Far Eastern position and complicate China's relations with the United States. In fact, it may have been part of a plot by Stalin to undermine or destroy Mao.

None of this was obvious at the time. The United States assumed that Peking had put the North Koreans up to attacking the South, not realizing that Kim Il Sung was a Soviet puppet and that the Chinese did not even have a diplomatic mission in Pyongyang at the time war started. The American suspicions seemed to be confirmed when, in December 1950, General MacArthur's troops approached the Yalu River. The Chinese, one million strong, poured over the frontier, and the conflict became a direct war between the United States and China.

Did Stalin anticipate this? Was he provoking war between China and the United States for his own purposes? Possibly. The Korean conflict poisoned Washington-Peking relations for nearly a quarter-century. More likely, however, the Kremlin dictator had another purpose in mind. The United States, through declarations by Secretary of State Dean Acheson, had widely advertised that Korea lay outside its defense perimeter. It is probable that Stalin took these declarations at face value, did not anticipate U.S. intervention, and saw a chance for a power play to give Russia a stranglehold on China. The Soviet Union already dominated Outer Mongolia. It dominated Manchuria through control of Dairen and Port Arthur and the South Manchurian railroad. If Korea could be placed under the Soviet puppet Kim Il Sung, Russia would hold Peking in a nutcracker.

It was a much stronger nutcracker, moreover, than was visible on the surface, because of the special relationship of China's Manchurian boss, Kao Kang, to Stalin. The relationship was so warm that Stalin, as Mao later recalled, gave Kao a fine motorcar. Every August 15 (the date of the signing of the Soviet-Manchurian economic pact) Kao sent a personal telegram of congratulations to Stalin.

The evidence seems convincing that Stalin had plotted with Kao Kang against Mao. Stalin was trying to put an iron collar around Peking. Had his plans worked out he could have tightened his ring in Mongolia, Manchuria and Korea and choked the life out of Mao.

The plot failed. North Korea did not take over South Korea. Korea remained divided, and as a result of China's massive intervention, Kim Il Sung switched allegiance from Moscow to Peking. And China's war against the Americans had an unexpected effect. It rallied the Chinese people around the new regime in a way that might not have been possible without it. Young Chinese fought in Korea. The nation was exhilarated by its ability to stand up to General MacArthur. And Stalin's plotting (China received no more advance warning of the Korean attack than did Washington) confirmed to Mao the dangers that lurked in the hug of the Polar Bear, as he began to call the Soviet Union.

No hint of this deep rift in the Communist world escaped the Kremlin and Peking's Forbidden City, although Mao once quizzically noted that Chinese artists, when they painted him with Stalin, "always painted me a little bit shorter." Stalin was a short man, only five feet four inches; Mao was six or seven inches taller, a "big" Chinese, strongly built though a bit stooped in his later years.

There was a remission in Chinese-Soviet antagonism with the death of Stalin. Moscow and Peking sought to find a basis for a new relationship. The oppressive Stalinist agreements were revoked and Moscow announced it was sending thousands of specialists to China to help in constructing hundreds of aid projects. The collaboration was short-lived, however, and Mao soon knew that China would have to go it alone.

★

Stalin had been dead three years in 1956; the Korean armistice had been in effect for two years; the Revolution was seven years old and China had moved into the task of creating its new shape. Mao had been giving much thought to the subject, and in February 1956 he began to discuss the ideas that had been taking form in his mind, ideas about shaking up China's internal life in order to release more productive forces, cutting back on the defense budget drastically (it had been taking as much as 32 percent of Chinese resources), giving intellectuals more freedom of action, loosening red tape, cutting through the dead weight of the bureaucracy, chopping the civil-service list by two-thirds, lightening the tone of ideological propaganda.

(The questions with which Mao was trying to cope were almost identical with those that possessed Lenin in 1922, the fifth year of the Bolshevik Revolution, Lenin's last year before illlness incapacitated him; they amounted to the problem of why the Revolution had not brought about the *Revolution,* the failure of expectations.)

Mao first began to voice his ideas late in 1955 and placed his program before the Politburo in a major speech in April 1956. What China needed was economic growth, a clean break with her feudal past and the marshaling of all forces for the new goals.

Just as Mao's ideas were crystallizing, Nikita Khrushchev, in Moscow, was exploding a bomb that would shake the whole Communist world, China along with it.

On the evening of February 25–26 Khrushchev delivered what came to be known as his "secret speech" about the crimes of Stalin. Chu Teh and Teng Hsiao-ping heard the speech as Chinese delegates to the Twentieth Congress of the Soviet Communist Party. Quickly they brought the news back to China. On their heels came Anastas Mikoyan, dispatched by Khrushchev to explain to Mao what the denunciation implied. Mao (and his associates) were shaken. Not that Mao had any illusions about Stalin. But he disapproved of Khrushchev's technique, feared for the consequences of the destruction of Stalin's image.

Yet, possibly stimulated by Moscow's action, Mao pushed forward what he called a campaign to "Let a Hundred Flowers Bloom, Let a Hundred Schools of Thought Contend" within China. For the first time in a Communist country, for the first time since Lenin carried out the Bolshevik coup of November 7, 1917, in Petrograd, a Communist regime invited, urged, called upon its citizens to speak out freely, frankly, openly, what was in their minds and hearts.

Mao's colleagues showed little sympathy for the "Hundred Flowers." Mao's speech to the Politburo has not been published to this day, but regardless of his comrades and regardless of the disorder within the Communist camp fueled by Khrushchev's revelations and the eruption of revolt in Hungary and Poland, Mao pressed ahead. He called in leaders of non-Communist groups and urged them to express their criticisms publicly. No one would suffer for speaking up. "Listen to opinions, especially unpleasant ones. Let people speak up. The sky will not fall. If you don't let people speak you will lose. Don't think you are always right," he exhorted the party leaders, "as if you alone had the truth, as if the earth would stop spinning without you. Some comrades are allergic to criticism. They intimidate others."

Mao's words were sharp. Despite the opposition of party leaders like Liu Shao-chi and Peng Chen, mayor of Peking, the campaign moved forward, and by spring 1957 a gusher of criticism was pouring forth, particularly from intellectuals, professors, students—and lower-rung party members. Posters went up on the walls of Peking and other cities. But by June the Hundred Flowers had begun to wither. Those who had expressed the strongest criticism fell into disfavor, some were arrested, more lost their jobs. Some exclaimed bitterly that it had been just a trick to expose malcontents. They were wrong. Mao's purpose was far deeper, but for a time the waters closed over and the Hundred Flowers seemed never to have been, a vagrant episode in the unfolding drama of China's revolution.

History would demonstrate that this was a premature evaluation. The Hundred Flowers would take its place as the first in a series of endeavors by Mao to create, as Régis Debray later was to christen it, the "Revolution in the Revolution." It was Mao's first experiment in loosing the people against the apparatus, in thrusting a thunderbolt at the party itself, against the bureaucrats and, as would later become apparent, against his enemies and rivals in the leadership. The Hundred Flowers was a failure but Mao learned from it—even though to many in China it appeared an aberration.

What should have been apparent (but was not) was that a fundamental division was emerging between Mao, on the one side, and a more conventional party leadership, headed by Liu Shao-chi, on the other. Not for ten years would this division burst into full public view, but when it came the violence of the Cultural Revolution would make the confusion of the Hundred Flowers seem like a tea party.

★

**H**ardly had the Hundred Flowers faded, hardly had the last protesting intellectual been sent down to cleanse the poisonous blossoms from his brain by tending pigs, when a new revolutionary concept by Mao swept China—the Great Leap Forward!

It is difficult now to recapture the enthusiasm of the Great Leap, a pure evocation of mass spirit. With bare hands China would erect its own future. By sheer labor it would transform itself. One night's work in the factories would produce more than China had built in one thousand feudal years. "We shall teach the Sun and the Moon to change places," clarioned a slogan. People believed this. They toiled at their lathes until they dropped in exhaustion. They worked all day and all night and the following day. China would transform itself within a single season. How? No one asked. It was an article of pure faith, a belief in muscle and élan. The Great Hall of the People in Tien an Men was thrown up in a few months by volunteers. Thousands of Peking residents worked on it. The capital turned out to build dams and irrigation works beside the Ming Tombs, Premier Chou En-lai at their head with pick and shovel.

The whole countryside organized itself into Communes. Men and women entered barracks life. The era of the "blue ants" dawned, men and women unrecognizable in their identical blue costumes, their sexless dedication to physical toil, their sharing of a mutual rice bowl. Nothing was beyond the power of China's hundreds of millions of hands, her millions of sturdy backs. Did China need steel? Let every Commune erect a small steel furnace in the backyard. Did China need rice and grain? Let all of China's Communes grow rice and wheat. Forget anything else. Within China was a power never before tapped. It would conquer all.

Did Mao believe his rhetoric? Almost certainly. He was a pragmatic leader but within him burned a deep spirituality. To a man who had led his army through the Long March it did not seem unreasonable that six or seven hundred million people could transform China and transform the world.

Mao's idea probably derived from his Hundred Flowers crusade. That, too, was designed to release China's creative and productive forces. Now he was trying a different tack. He may have been inspired by his attendance, in the autumn of 1957, at the assemblage of Communist parties in Moscow, a meeting held in the aura of the Soviet Union's launching of the first Sputnik into outer space, an achievement accompanied by the test of an intercontinental ballistic missile with a hydrogen warhead. Mao's imagination was overwhelmed. He proclaimed: "The East Wind prevails over the West Wind!" That is, the Communists now possessed military superiority over the United States and the capitalist world. In this heady atmosphere anything seemed possible.

Khrushchev and the Russians were more cautious. They did not believe that the world balance of power had been turned, as Mao did. Russia had promised China help in developing nuclear weapons. In his enthusiasm Mao sought to storm the barricades of China's historic backwardness. At this moment he believed nothing could halt the East Wind. "Right now," he said, "there is a ten-force typhoon of enthusiasm."

Alas, not even a ten-force typhoon could paper over the sad results of the Great Leap. Once Mao died the Great Leap was officially categorized as one of his gravest errors. Its immediate results were dreadful. Grain production fell heavily. By 1960 there was famine in China, real famine, for the first time since the Communists had come to power. Industrial production sagged. Later it was estimated that the Great Leap cost China five years of industrial output. Mao had told his people that within fifteen years they would surpass Great Britain in industry. China would be making its own automobiles. Steel output would multiply eight times, all of this through China's own, original Marxism, Marxism-plus-China, or Marxism-plus-Maoism. A whole new world was opening up, Mao said. Marx could not have understood it because Marx did not know China.

To be certain, Mao acknowledged, his radical program stimulated widespread disagreement within the party. But disagreement was good. Out of it grew a healthy party. The party would emerge stronger because of the debates, the disagreements, the splits.

It didn't work out that way. After a year of excitement, rhetoric, violent work, campaigns against the "four pests"—rats, flies, mosquitoes and sparrows (sparrows were dropped from the list after it was realized that they ate insects)—dreams of organizing all of China in "one big Commune," the whole thing sputtered out. Mao quietly went off to the countryside, relinquishing his role as chief of state but retaining chairmanship of the party. He had suffered a major defeat, and his party critics—Liu Shao-chi, Peng Chen and others, including Mao's old comrade-at-arms Defense Minister Marshal Peng Te-huai—took charge of day-to-day affairs.

Defeat it may have been, but once more Mao had demonstrated a fundamental fact, one that would later reemerge even more strongly: the call to the people to take matters into their own hands, to break with party rules and regulations, to tap their own resources, to sweep forward like a whirlwind, never mind the chaos, never mind the splits. All of this, Mao had insisted, was healthy, productive, necessary for the strength and well-being of the Communist nation.

On July 11, 1959, a visitor to Ulan Bator, capital of Outer Mongolia, attended a reception in the government palace to celebrate Nadam, the Mongolian national holiday. There were thousands of Russian and Chinese specialists in Mongolia, helping to construct aid projects. The visitor noticed a curious fact. The Russian guests stood on one side of the reception hall, the Chinese on the other. Not one Chinese spoke with a Russian. The Mongols rushed back and forth between their hostile guests, trying to give the impression that it was one happy family. It was not. The Sino-Soviet split, the deepest, most serious confrontation yet to arise in the Communist world, had begun and was manifest in this remote land wedged between China's northern provinces and the long Soviet Siberian frontier.

Moscow and Peking had entered an era of disagreements. In 1957 Moscow pledged China aid in becoming a nuclear power. Mao kept urging the Russians to a more aggressive course internationally. He wanted Soviet backing to take over Taiwan. But Khrushchev was not in a mood to comply. He offered military aid but only if a Soviet general was in charge of the combined forces, and he asked Peking for naval bases on the Chinese coast. He proposed dispositions that Mao later complained would have been tantamount to a Soviet blockade of China. Khrushchev and Mao split completely in their view of the world. China and India went to war over their borders. Khrushchev criticized China, supported India. Khrushchev wanted détente with Eisenhower. Mao held to an anti-American course. Khrushchev said China didn't know what Communism was: You couldn't achieve Communism with "a Great Leap." Mao's Communes were "madness." Mao declared that Russia had abandoned Communism and become a bourgeois country.

The germs of conflict, of course, had been present in the relations between Mao and the Soviet Communists since the mid-twenties. But only now had the confrontation taken critical form. Early in 1960 Khrushchev withdrew from China, on one month's notice, all the 1,390 Soviet experts (and 4,000 family members) stationed there and canceled 343 contracts and 257 projects—from steel mills to farm irrigation systems. The Russians packed up and left, taking their blueprints with them. Soviet Russia and Communist China went their separate ways in deep hostility. Within ten years they would stand at the verge of nuclear war. Twenty years later their hostility seemed likely to endure for the rest of the century.

CHINA

100 Years

of

Revolution

205

The split was a political event of greater profundity than any that China's revolution had yet to confront.

It was no accident that a year later a secretive band of ten or fifteen party officials with a protective escort of security men slipped into the office of the Peking Zoo on the northwestern outskirts of Peking. In this quiet corner where the only excitement was over the mating of the giant pandas, a secret inquiry into the conduct of Mao Tse-tung was launched by his most powerful party opponents. The zoo had been picked for security reasons—who would suspect political intrigue beside the panda cage?

Almost unseen from outside China—and only perceived in partial glimpses within the country—Mao's revolution was heading into stormy waters in which the career and conduct of Mao would play a central role until his death, in 1976.

Those who opposed Mao (they opposed him for many reasons: personal style of leadership, the abortive Hundred Flowers, the failure of the Great Leap, disasters of agriculture and industry) were likely also to oppose him on the question of the Soviet Union, or at least to be charged by Mao with favoring the Soviet course over the Chinese course; thus a political dispute over domestic issues escalated into a question of patriotism.

Almost anything might be used in this struggle, and this was what the search team at the Peking Zoo was looking for—evidence of Mao's "Imperial conduct," high-handed issuance of orders and edicts without bothering to consult his comrades (or even to inform them). In this guerrilla warfare, tactics were often drawn from Chinese tradition. One was the device of analogy: historical articles ostensibly about Emperors long since dead, but actually about the living and particularly about Mao.

The polemics brought to public attention an upright official of the Ming dynasty named Hai Jui. An article published in the *People's Daily* told how the honest Hai Jui upbraided the Emperor Yung Chen, saying, "The last ten years have been chaotic. In earlier times you did a few good things but how about the present? You think you are always right but the country has been dissatisfied with you for a long time."

Later Wu Han, author of this article, produced a play called *Hai Jui Dismissed from Office.* It did not take a very prescient Chinese to understand that "Hai Jui" was Defense Minister Peng Te-huai, who had been dismissed in 1959 after a sharp quarrel with Mao in which Peng criticized the Great Leap and shouted at Mao a classical Chinese oath: "In Yenan you fucked my mother for forty days. Now I have been fucking your mother for twenty days and you're trying to call a halt."

The venerable Chu Teh, who had fought shoulder to shoulder with Mao and Peng, sadly interjected, "To think that we all ate out of the same bowl in the past."

But Peng was blown out of office by Mao's anger, leaving the party even more bitterly split. The shadow of Hai Jui would come back more strongly with the launching of the Cultural Revolution in Shanghai in November 1965.

★

What of the study party at the Peking Zoo? It was headed by Teng To, aide to Peng Chen, mayor of Peking and close associate of Wu Han, who wrote the Hai Jui articles. And it was searching the documents for evidence to be employed by Liu Shao-chi against Mao Tse-tung in a coming showdown. The party was split. Mao was on one side. On the other was arrayed a formidable bloc headed by Liu Shao-chi. Whether, as Mao had said, "a split is healthy" remained to be seen. Despite his success in causing Peng's resignation, Mao, as he later conceded, was more or less put on the shelf. Open propaganda against him, Aesopian in form but understandable by all informed Chinese, accelerated. The *People's Daily* began a series of articles called "Notes from the Three-Family Village" and "Evening Chats in Yen-shan." They were written by Teng To, Wu Han and a man named Liao Mo-sha. A typical article told of an athlete who boasted he had broken the record for the broad jump—a satirical play on Mao's Great Leap.

For a time Mao said little. He watched, read and listened. Later he would make it plain that he never had a doubt about the identity of Hai Jui and the Ming Emperor and he understood all of the satirical shadings of the "Three-Family Village" and the "Evening Chats."

Mao turned back to the old Chinese classics and read them again. He quoted frequently from them to his visitors. And he wrote poetry, a great deal of poetry. Ross Terrill calculated that Mao wrote more poems in 1961 than in any other year of his life. The conduct of government and party was mostly in the hands of Liu Shao-chi and Teng Hsiao-ping. Military matters were being handled by Lin Piao, who had succeeded the ill-fated Peng Te-huai.

Mao waited. In 1963 he wrote a poem that his opponents would have done well to study:

> So many deeds cry out to be done
> And always urgently;
> The world rolls on,
> Time presses.
> Ten thousand years are too long.
> Seize the day, seize the hour!
> The Four Seas are rising, clouds and waters raging.
> The Five Continents are rocking, wind and thunder roaring.
> Our force is irresistible!
> Away with all pests!

What pests did Mao have in mind? Nine years later, when President Nixon came to Peking, he quoted a few lines of this poem back to Mao. The Chairman looked on inscrutably.

CHINA

100 Years

of

Revolution

**207**

NIKITA KHRUSHCHEV ONCE CALLED her "Mao's nice mattress"—she was Chiang Ching, the Shanghai actress whom Mao had married in Yenan. So far as the world knew—and the gossipy Peking cadres shared this estimate—at fifty-one Chiang Ching had never played a political role, either as Mao's bedroom intimate or in a public sense. In fact, it was generally understood that she had abided by the prohibition on political activity imposed when the party gave Mao permission to marry her. Since the proclamation of the People's Republic she had been in eclipse. Her health was poor, she suffered from nervous disorders and between 1949 and the end of 1957 she had spent four long periods in the Soviet Union undergoing treatment, much to her anguish. Her imposed medical exile reminded her too vividly of the fate of Ho Shih-chen, her predecessor who had been packed off to Moscow when the party granted Mao's request for a divorce. During Mao's visits to Russia in 1949 and 1957 he did not see Chiang. (Despite the furious polemics between Moscow and Peking and scurrilous Soviet attacks on Mao's personal conduct, including charges of cruelty and complicity in the death of his family members, the Russians have never revealed a detail concerning the sojourns of Chiang Ching or Ho Shih-chen in the Soviet Union.)

In any event, Chiang Ching found her situation during her years in the Soviet Union anomalous at best and, as she later made plain, not just frustrating but intolerable.

Now, during Mao's semi-rustication, he began to turn toward his family. He had long talks with his niece, Wang Hai-jung, daughter of his brother Tse-min, an English-language student and later a Foreign Office interpreter and official, and with his nephew Yuan-hsin. Mao spent time with his daughter by Chiang Ching, Li Na, and Li Min, Ho Shih-chen's daughter. (Mao had lost his eldest son, An-ying, in the Korean War; his second son, An-ching, was a mental case; two infant children by Ho Shih-chen were left in the care of peasants during the Long March and never found.)

More and more Mao began to talk and consult with Chiang Ching. Chiang Ching later was to say that she had over many years acted as private secretary to her husband, sorting out documents, reading passages to him, bringing important matters to his attention. This was an exaggeration but gradually it began to happen. Mao, during his struggle with Marshal Peng, had written Chiang Ching of his difficulties, and against his orders she rushed from the summer resort of Pei-tai-ho to be at his side. Now, it seemed, she was always there, not merely comforting him in his isolation but (at least as she recounted it) serving as his active aide, his pair of eyes, almost, it began to seem, as his chief of staff.

Mao was seventy-two in 1965, not as robust as he had been, slower in gait, a large, intimidating man. He liked to swim and for some years had swum almost every summer in the Yangtze at Wuhan and in the new Ming Tomb reservoir built by the people during the Great Leap Forward. His health was good, except for the first symptoms of Parkinson's disease.

On the surface, it seemed that he was beginning to accept the position of a benign sage, letting the reins of government fall into the hands of younger comrades while he sat on the mountaintop enunciating moral dicta or composing cryptic Chinese poems, dipping his brush in the crushed carbon ink and displaying his very creditable calligraphy. Not infrequently Mao would remark to visitors on his mortality, the impending end of his life. He would say that soon he would be meeting Marx or that soon he would be meeting God—he didn't seem to make much distinction. His talk was consistent with the image of a philosopher who had put the mundane world behind him.

There was one exception to Mao's "retirement" and it was an important one. Since Lin Piao had replaced Peng Te-huai, Mao had worked closely with Lin. His relationship with the army was intimate and pervasive. Lin had demonstrated his military abilities time and again during the Long March and since. But he was not an outgoing man. He had played no major public political role. In September 1965 Lin published an important article, "Long Live the History of the People's War," in which he outlined China's strategy, comparing China in the world of her enemies (the Soviet Union, United States, India and the rest) to the Chinese Communists in Yenan. Just as Yenan was surrounded but emerged victorious because of the support of the peasants, the poor and the countryside, so China would emerge victorious because of the support of the poor and the peasants of the Third World. It was the West and the Soviet Union that were surrounded, not China. Lin Piao began to publish *Quotations from Chairman Mao* in the army newspaper, *Liberation Daily*. Soon he would collect the quotations in what came to be known as the "little red book." Millions of copies would circulate. Everyone in China would possess a copy and know the Chairman's words by heart. Surgeons engaged in operations would hold the book in one hand, a scalpel in the other. Gold prospectors in the Tien Shan would attribute their nuggets to Mao's words in the "little red book." Millions of Chinese would wave the book high at rallies in Tien an Men Square. It would become sacred writ.

In August 1965 André Malraux came back to China after an absence of nearly forty years. He had been in Shanghai in 1927 and his record of the betrayal of the Chinese Revolution by Russia and Chiang Kai-shek in *Man's Fate* had become a classic. Now he was General De Gaulle's Minister of Culture and he bore an official letter for the chief of the Chinese state, Liu Shao-chi. When Malraux went to the Great Hall of the People to deliver his message he found Mao present. The Chairman took over the conversation. He spoke to Malraux of China's youth, on whom he said the fate of China and the world depended. Soon, he said, they must be put to the test. He did not spell out what test he had in mind. There had been foreign speculation that Mao contemplated "blooding" China's young people by engaging them in war with the United States. Not infrequently he had made plain his belief that a new generation was growing up ignorant of the zeal, hardship and sacrifice of the Long March, the testing ground for the Revolution. The question of war did not arise in his talk with Malraux, but he did say that he did not think the military offered a solution to China's problems. The man who had said "All political power comes from the barrel of a gun" insisted that "We will never allow the gun to rule the party."

As Malraux left, Mao whispered to him, "I am alone with the masses—waiting." Waiting for what? Mao did not say. Malraux could not guess. Shortly after this meeting Mao quietly left Peking with Chiang Ching. He would travel in central China and the south and then he would stay in Shanghai for the winter. More and more often in recent times he had been spending the winters there. The climate was warmer than Peking—no bitter winds off the

Gobi. Chiang Ching liked Shanghai; she felt at home there. She had gotten to know some political leaders in Shanghai very well. So in late October 1965 Mao and Chiang Ching settled down in Mao's residence, a building that had once been the French Club. Outside the tight circle of the top leadership no one knew where Mao had gone. He had not appeared in public since the October 1 holiday and there was not a word in the *People's Daily* about him, about where he was or what he was doing, no outward sign of crisis. Mao busied himself, as he had in recent years, in the rereading of the Chinese classics. Occasionally he went for excursions to West Lake at Hangchow. He had been fond of West Lake since he first saw it with Siao Yu in 1921, at the time of the founding of the Communist Party. Mao sat beside the lake and watched the play of the sun on the waters, or walked a bit in the gardens, which for hundreds of years had existed in jewellike beauty around the lake. It was, it seemed, one more period of relaxation and contemplation for China's sage.

On November 10, the Shanghai newspaper *Wen Hui Pao* ("Literary Gazette") published an article by a sharp-penned young literary critic named Yao Wen-yuan. The subject was Wu Han's play, *Hai Jui Dismissed from Office*, the one about the virtuous official dismissed by the evil Emperor, and, by analogy, about Marshal Peng Te-huai's dismissal by Mao. Only the inner circle knew that in September Mao had demanded that the Politburo launch a campaign against this play; only the inner circle knew that the Politburo had refused; only the inner circle knew that once again Mao had taken matters into his own hands. Not a dozen persons in all China knew that Mao had dictated the contents of Yao Wen-yuan's article. According to one account Mao read eleven drafts before getting the version that was published. Yao's article charged that the play was a concealed attack on Communism, Communes and the ruling party.

The *Wen Hui Pao* article seemed a small stone tossed into a placid pond. It was republished by a few provincial papers in eastern China. That was all. But behind the scenes there was excitement. Peng Chen, mayor of Peking and Wu Han's supporter, telephoned Shanghai demanding, "Why did you not announce that you were going to publish this text? This probably comes from the Boss. But all are equal before the truth."

Later on Mao was to explain that he had to present the piece in Shanghai because he couldn't get it published in Peking, which in a sense was true, since the Politburo had refused to take up the campaign. Even now the Peking press was slow to respond. Mao threatened, he said that he would bring out the article in pamphlet form and spread it all over China. Lin Piao published it in the *Liberation Army Daily* on November 29, and then, after Premier Chou En-lai personally intervened, it appeared in the Peking *People's Daily* on November 30—with a note disclaiming any political significance for the article. It was, said the *People's Daily*, only an academic discussion, a literary exercise. Some exercise!

The difficulties Mao encountered in getting his article published and in launching criticism of his Peking enemies were real. But not quite as overwhelming as Chiang Ching and he were later to contend. The evidence was clear that in any showdown he could and would get his way. But there was plenty of foot-dragging by his party opponents.

Over the years Mao had expressed himself about the therapeutic values of *luan*, the Chinese word for "chaos," "uproar," "disturbance." It was Mao's belief that disturbance for disturbance's sake was a healing phenomenon. He often spoke of this to young people. He encouraged them to revolt, to talk back to their elders, to stir things up. Sometimes he talked like this to young party cadres and even to his fellow leaders of the party. (But never, so far as the record shows, was he inclined to use this argument to the peasant masses.) He talked this way to his niece, whom he thought much too conventional in her attitude to authority.

It would be a mistake to suggest that there was any scent of *luan* in the atmosphere as 1965 turned into 1966. True, there was a feeling that *something* was in the air. But neither inside nor outside China did a crisis seem at hand. There was a good deal of jockeying for position during the winter—Wu Han made a "self-criticism" but couldn't wriggle off Mao's hook; Mao got Lo Jui-ching dismissed as the army chief of staff because Lo didn't accept Mao's increasing tendency to equate the Americans and the Soviets as equally dangerous opponents (Lo jumped or was pushed from a sixth-floor window but was not killed; crippled, broken, ill, he was made to appear before howling thousands at "struggle" sessions); an investigation of Wu Han was undertaken by Peng Chen, his erstwhile supporter. Peng Chen—perhaps by chance, perhaps not—was chairman of a five-man committee that had been named to conduct a "Cultural Revolution." No one had a clear idea of what a "Cultural Revolution" was but it would very soon become evident that Peng Chen's definition differed from that of Mao.

This maneuvering occupied the winter and early spring. Liu Shao-chi left Peking on March 26, 1966, for a diplomatic swing to Pakistan, Afghanistan and Burma. Signs began to appear that events were rapidly engaging the whole of the Communist Party leadership. Politically acute Chinese were beginning to suspect that Liu might be the focus.

Later Mao was to describe the domain of his political enemies in Peking as a "watertight kingdom" which could not be pierced by a needle. Possibly a needle could not prick the kingdom, but the bludgeon blows of Mao were beginning to be felt. Mao had ranged Kang Sheng, chief of the Chinese political police, on his side. He was supported by Premier Chou En-lai and, for a considerable period, by the mercurial Teng Hsiao-ping and, of course, Lin Piao, most of the military, the powerful Shanghai party organization and other influential segments of the party.

With the departure of Liu Shao-chi, Mao began to lay down heavy verbal artillery. In early April he lashed out at the party's propaganda department, controlled by Peng Chen and Liu Shao-chi, as "the palace of the King of Hell." "Down with the King of Hell!" he roared. "Liberate the little ones! I shall call for rebellion in the provinces. Everywhere there must be innumerable wise monkeys. They will rise up and tear down the palace of the King of Hell."

Mao's words set the tone for what was to come. It was not long before Wu Han, Peng Chen, Teng To and other collaborators in the anti-Mao campaign, the articles about *Hai Jui*, the "Three-Family Village" and the "Evening Chats" at Yenshan, began to vanish.

The *Liberation Army Daily* spoke of "a black line," of "an anti-party black gang"—language that made its debut coincident with Chiang Ching's assumption of responsibilities as head of army cultural propaganda in an alliance with Lin Piao. For the first time Chiang Ching's political participation emerged publicly.

Events raced along pell-mell. A new "Cultural Revolution Committee" was set up in which Chiang Ching, Kang Sheng, Chen Po-ta (party secretary and former personal secretary to Mao), Chang Chun-chiao (Shanghai party power) and Yao Wen-yuan, author of the *Hai Jui* articles, played leading roles. There would be changes as time passed, but Chiang Ching and her Shanghai colleagues would continue to the end and, with the addition of Wang Hung-wen, a young Shanghai textile worker, would become the Gang of Four.

★

Ayoung woman philosophy teacher at Peking University named Nieh Yuan-tzu and several of her friends spent most of the night of May 24–25 splashing out a poster in large Chinese characters which they headed "Bombard the Headquarters!" It attacked the "sinister reactionary gang" at Peking University, headed by President Lu Ping, and called on students to "wipe out all ghosts and monsters and all Khrushchev-type revisionists." The words about ghosts and monsters and "Khrushchev types" had been spoken in private party sessions by Mao. "Khrushchev" was a code word for Liu Shao-chi.

Who was Nieh? She had been in contention with Peking University authorities for some time and later there was to be strong evidence that she was, in effect, Mao's chosen instrument. The appearance of her poster on the campus of Peita, as the students called their university, generated electric excitement. At Mao's orders Miss Nieh's poster was broadcast to all of China on June 1, a week after its appearance. Next day it was republished in full in the *People's Daily*.

The effect was like that of uncorking a bottle of champagne. Peking University exploded. So did every other university and institution of higher learning in China.

Later on there were many who said that Nieh was close to or had a connection with Chiang Ching. Whether or not that was true, Chiang Ching paid a visit to the university and Nieh showed her around. They met with students and inspected the posters written in huge Chinese characters, which by this time lined the walls of the campus. Nieh, Chiang Ching later told Roxanne Witke, was a true revolutionary. This evaluation was eventually overruled by Chairman Mao after Nieh and her radical faction had torn the university apart, spread anarchy through Peking and even affected the countryside. Nieh ended up being sent into exile on a distant pig farm and then imprisoned. She was one of the few Cultural Revolutionists specifically charged with crimes against the state.

But there was no sign of that in June 1966. All was ebullience, wild revolutionary slogans, violent physical attacks on anyone perceived by Nieh and the students as reactionary, disloyal to Mao or harboring bourgeois sentiments. Within a week the Chinese educational system was brought to a halt. It would remain closed down and in disarray, for more than a decade.

As a young man Mao once had said, "To rebel is justified." He meant that rebellion for the sake of rebellion was good. Now the young people of China put Mao's aphorism to the test.

In the storm of events a smell of anarchy arose, of wild and mindless violence, of *luan*. This although there was a great deal of behind-the-scenes management by Mao, by Chiang Ching and by the group close to the Chairman. Senseless turbulence there was, and more was to come, a *luan* which Mao himself had set in motion and, in general, favored. As he wrote Chiang Ching on July 6, 1966, from the quiet and reposeful mountains of Pai Yun Huang in Hupeh Province, "Great disorder across the land leads to great order. And so once again, every seven or eight years monsters and demons will jump out themselves." He was bothered a bit about the personal aggrandizement of Lin Piao and Lin Piao's campaign to turn Mao into an icon ("I could never have imagined that my little books could have such magical powers") but felt there was little he could do about it. He worried about the future of Communism in China, worried about its future in the world, feared that he was talking a bit like the "black gang" that wanted to overthrow the party and himself. He seemed to feel that the "black gang" might come to power on his death and then use the doubts about Communism Mao was expressing to support its power. It was an equivocal, meandering letter, much in the vein of Mao's later musings, skeptical of his role and place in history, sounding like a man carried along by the tide of history rather than directing it. He expressed doubts as to the intentions of Lin Piao and reflected almost nostalgically on Liu Shao-chi and his old comrades. The letter was addressed to Chiang Ching. It sounded as though it was written for the record.

Symbols. The "little red book" was a symbol. The big character posters were symbols. Mao had become an icon, the greatest symbol of all. Rumor after rumor had swept China: He was in ill health. He had suffered a stroke. Perhaps he was dead. He was no longer in charge. (That was the worst rumor; in fact, it had been, at least in part, a feeling that he *was* no longer in charge that had led Mao to launch the Great Proletarian Cultural Revolution, as it was now called.)

So, on July 16, 1966, at his favorite watercourse, he walked into the Yangtze River at Wuhan and, before television cameras and in the presence of tens of thousands of spectators, many of whom joined him in the water holding aloft on bamboo poles great banners with slogans, he swam and floated down the river for an hour and five minutes, covering, it was said, a distance of some eight miles. He used an eclectic sidestroke, sometimes turning into a kind of backstroke, his great head bobbing above the water like a pumpkin.

Soon Mao was back in Peking and ready to move the Cultural Revolution onto the fast lane as the country simmered with awe over the man who was now hailed as China's Great Helmsman. A middle school at Tsinghua University formed a detachment of Red Guards on July 20, and Red Guards sprang up everywhere, million upon million upon million of them, with red armbands, boundless energy, total naïveté, prepared to carry out any deed, no matter how difficult, preposterous or revolting, as long as they believed it to further the will of Chairman Mao, a sea of young people that poured onto the railroads and highways and drowned Peking.

On the day after the Tsinghua Red Guards unit was formed, Mao spoke to his closest party comrades:

"I say to you all: youth is the great army of the Great Proletarian Cultural Revolution. It must be mobilized to the full.

"We believe in the masses. To become teachers of the masses we must first be the students of the masses. The present Great Proletarian Cultural Revolution is a heaven-and-earth-shaking event.

"We must be prepared for the Revolution to be turned against us. The party and government leadership and responsible party comrades should be prepared for this. It is up to you to lead the fire toward your own bodies, to fan the flames to make them burn. Do you dare to do this?"

Everywhere Red Guards tore down idols, besieged party headquarters, "dragged out" the most respected, most venerated heroes of the Long March, compelled them to assume the "jet-plane position" (arms close to sides and extending to the rear, body bent forward, a bit like a swimmer awaiting the starting pistol), clapped dunce caps on decent men and women, beat them, stoned them (sometimes paying children a penny a stone to do the chore), tortured them, forced them into suicide, tossed them from windows, let them die slow deaths of gangrene in cells of filth, drove serious scholars out of their minds, broke the fingers of pianists, put out eyes—all this in the *luan*, perhaps the greatest *luan* China has ever suffered, a *luan* that made that of the Taipings and the Boxers seem like mah-jongg.

On August 5, Mao Tse-tung published his own *tatzepao*, his own big character poster. He titled it: "Bombard the Headquarters! My First Big Character Poster." It charged that "some

CHINA

100 Years

of

Revolution

leading comrades from the Central" had set up a bourgeois dictatorship, "struck down" the Cultural Revolution, "stood facts on their heads and juggled black and white." They had launched a "White terror," suppressed revolutionaries and committed right deviations. "How poisonous!"

The bell had tolled for Liu Shao-chi. It would be months before he was finally imprisoned, tortured, subjected to physical degradation and spirited off to a Hainan Island prison, deprived of medical treatment, and fed a starvation diet till he died of pneumonia. His wife was tortured and held in solitary confinement for ten years. One son was beaten to death, all his children jailed, an eight-year-old dragged before a mass "struggle" session to revile her parents.

Peking became a city of nightmare. Millions of Red Guards streamed in from the remotest parts of China. They congregated in Tien an Men Square. On eight occasions Mao appeared before them and received their salute. Their whim was law. Once they besieged Chou En-lai for more than forty-eight hours in the Great Hall of the People. Neither Mao nor Lin Piao intervened. No military personnel came to his aid. Chou talked himself out of encirclement, the greatest diplomatic feat of a life of superlative diplomacy. They poured a bucket of paste over the head of Ma Sitson, president of the Peking Academy of Music, and beat Lao She, author of *Rickshaw Boy*, to death in his home. They broke into the apartment of Madame Soong Ching-ling in Shanghai and threw her furniture into the street. They threatened to cut her hair. "I'll cut their hair!" Madame Soong rejoined grimly. They tossed copies of Edgar Snow's *Red Star over China* into bonfires. They desecrated the memorial to Dr. Sun Yat-sen in Canton. They vandalized the Potala in Lhasa. They turned university campuses into scenes of trench warfare. They tried to storm the Forbidden City. Mao called them "little devils" and egged them on.

*Luan* reigned. Red Guards and anarchists captured the Foreign Office and put an expelled Chinese military attaché from Djakarta in Foreign Minister Chen Yi's place. They published some of China's secret diplomatic papers. They sacked the British embassy and set it afire. They put a British correspondent under solitary house arrest and refused to let him read his own books. They set upon foreigners in the streets. Xenophobia spread like a pox. An old Communist, a friend of China, came to Peking. His comrades of past years would speak to him only in Chinese, which he could not understand. Chinese students rampaged in Moscow and fought Soviet secret police in front of the American embassy. China edged closer and closer to civil war, to dissolution. Ten years of educational work was lost; at least as much in industrial production; the social cost would be paid in the decades of a century.

Yet, as a thoughtful Chinese later recalled, "You cannot imagine how exhilarating it was! The excitement! Every day something different! We couldn't wait to get up in the morning. To see what the new wall posters said." He talked of the thrill of traveling about the country, young people from small towns swarming into Peking, Peking students taking off with their knapsacks and wandering for weeks in the deep interior, transported by the feeling they were "making the Revolution." As to what that Revolution might be, its content, why it was necessary, no questions were asked. It was enough to believe that it was the will of Chairman Mao, that they were "holding high the banner of Mao Tse-tung Thought." It was a spirit that invited comparison to the children's crusades of the Middle Ages or the fanaticism of a religious cult.

★

Mao could not be unaware of what was going on. Much of it he gloried in. This was *luan* after his own heart. But it was too much even for him. He confessed in late October 1966 at a Central Committee meeting that he had been surprised by its vehemence. "Nobody, not even I," he said, "expected that all the provinces and cities would be thrown into confusion. The students made some mistakes but the mistakes were mainly made by us big shots.

"No wonder the comrades did not understand too much. The time was so short and the events so violent. I myself had not foreseen that . . . the whole country would be thrown into turmoil.

"Since it was I who caused the havoc, it is understandable if you have some bitter words for me. . . . You find it difficult to cross the pass and I don't find it easy either. You are anxious and so am I. I cannot blame you, comrades."

He even had some reassuring words for Liu Shao-chi and Teng Hsiao-ping. They had made mistakes. But so had the Center. It would, in fact, become apparent as the secret records became available, first in documents filched and made public by the Red Guards and later, after Mao's death, in the record published by Teng Hsiao-ping and his associates, that there was no coherent explanation for the Cultural Revolution. True, Mao had started it. True, he wanted to get power back. True, he wanted to displace some party leaders, like Liu, who he felt had taken the wrong course. True, he believed in the virtue of stirring up a typhoon; of kicking over the dustbin; of purification, if you will, through chaos. But he was not clear as to his ultimate aims and he had doubts as the process went forward. And, to be certain, there were many others who played their own games. There was much talk at the time about "waving the Red Flag to defeat the Red Flag"—that is, pretending to be radical in order to conceal a reactionary core. There were those who sought to feather their nests and further their careers, among them Lin Piao, the man who had been so modest and retiring a general, and, of course, the group that centered on Chiang Ching, the Shanghai leaders, each using the other for his own purposes, being used by Mao and, in turn, using him.

*Luan* fed upon *luan*. At Tsinghua University a student faction sprang up called the Ching-kang Mountain Regiment (in honor of Mao's exploits at Chingkang). It was led by a chemistry student named Kuai Ta-fu. He joined cause with Nieh Yuan-tzu's faction at Peking University and other student groups to form what came to be called the "Heaven" faction, which opposed an "Earth" faction. Factions split and proliferated like bacteria. These young people developed paranoid theories of what was happening. Each group thought its members the only true believers. Each saw the other groups as traitors to Mao. When one level of treachery was uncovered they believed that it exposed a deeper level, that the world was composed of layer after layer of treachery and that only they stood between Mao and disaster. Each thought only *they* were the bearers of the word.

Soon Kuai had allies all over China. He sent out plenipotentiaries, diplomatic missions. They raided the home of an army marshal, broke into his safe and seized secret military records. They penetrated northeastern China and attacked military headquarters in Mukden. When four prep-school boys were killed, Kuai's faction turned them into martyrs and raised the "Chingkang Regiment" flag over the military headquarters. In Fushun they captured tanks, machine guns and artillery from the army and fought battles in the streets. Casualties numbered in the thousands, including hundreds of innocent bystanders. Battles in Szechwan, particularly in Cheng-tu, took thousands of lives; in Wuhan the casualties mounted to the hundreds, as they also did in Chang-sha. In Inner Mongolia three hundred thousand people were killed and wounded; in Tibet, tens of thousands. Students tunneled under buildings and blew them up with dynamite, poisoned water supplies, cut off food, light and heat to enemy positions, gouged out the eyes of wounded prisoners.

★

Chen Li-ming was a landlord's son in his mid-thirties. Once he had been a revolutionary cadre in the city of Hsiang-tan but for sixteen years he had been confined to an insane asylum in Peking. In the autumn of 1966 a detachment of Tsinghua students went to the asylum to liberate a classmate who they claimed had been confined because of Red Guard activities. There they found and interviewed Chen Li-ming, who told them he had been institutionalized after writing a criticism of Liu Shao-chi. First, he said, he had been driven from his job, then put in the mental hospital. Kuai Ta-fu and the Chingkang Regiment hailed Chen as a martyr of the Revolution. No matter that the Peking security police insisted he was a genuine mental case, that he had written attacks against Chairman Mao as well as Liu Shao-chi, that he had criticized Marx and Lenin.

The attitude of the police so angered the regiment that it launched an assault on the headquarters of the security police, released prisoners, pulled out telephones and seized the dossier of Chen Li-ming. Soon they proclaimed Chen "the madman of the modern age," linking their protégé to Lu Hsun's famous revolutionary work, "Diary of a Madman." They published Chen's critique of Liu Shao-chi as a new "Diary of a Madman." His story was made into a play that was performed all over China, called *The Madman of the Modern Age*. Performances were presented before Peking's foreign colony, paid for by money collected by Sidney Rittenberg, an American supporter of the Peking regime. Chen Li-ming spoke at mass meetings and traveled from one end of the country to another.

But his career lasted only as long as the paranoid period of the Cultural Revolution. In February 1968 the Central Committee sent Chen Li-ming back to the asylum.

★

It would be March 1971 before the career of Kuai reached a climax. The authorities had long since disbanded the Chingkang Regiment, along with the thousands of other Red Guard detachments. Most of the members had been sent down to the countryside, to tend pigs, to help the peasants, to learn what rock-bottom life in China was like. But not Kuai. He had fought and fought and fought. It had taken tens of thousands of Peking workers and the People's Liberation Army to bring to an end the reign of Kuai and his opponents at Tsinghua University (and this dismal history was repeated a hundred times all over China). Five workers had been killed and nearly eight hundred wounded in the final denouement as they sought by peaceable means to persuade Kuai and his opponents to leave their barricaded strongholds. Dozens of students, professors and bystanders had been killed and wounded. When the PLA finally went in to release prisoners, they found steel sheets welded to the doors of the buildings, each door barricaded with sandbags, the rooms with iron bars on the windows and bare floors for the prisoners to sleep on. Food was a bun and a bowl of cold water a day. They found one young woman student wounded in the posterior. She could neither stand nor sit, had no control of her bladder and no longer knew her name. A male student had been deafened by blows to the head and left without teeth—they had been pulled, one by one, in an effort to compel him to "confess."

Finally, on March 25, 1971, a sixteen-year-old girl (as William Hinton tells the story) stood before Kuai in a large meeting hall and said: "It was you, Kuai Ta-fu, who grabbed away my father's life as he stood guard at the edge of the cornfield. This blood debt must be repaid. In my ears I hear my father's voice. Before my eyes I see his face and the tears roll down my cheeks." The girl was the daughter of a worker killed in the final confrontation with the Chingkang Regiment.

Kuai—contrary to Chinese practice—did not admit his crime. He stood silent and was led out to prison. It is still not clear whether Kuai and the network of violent Cultural Revolutionists were the product of the *luan*, whether they were tools of others (Lin Piao? Chiang Ching? the Gang of Four?), whether they had been driven beyond the bounds of reason by plunging into their paranoid world, in which they saw everyone but themselves as enemies of Mao (the personal testimony of some made clear that such delusions lay at the core of the worst fighting, especially university confrontations between factions barricaded from all contact with the outer world). Mao met with Kuai, Nieh Yuan-tzu and others in the Forbidden City in the summer of 1968 and tried to persuade them that the time for fighting was over, that he was *really* Mao, that it *was* Mao who was speaking to them, that he *himself* was the "black hand" whom they had accused of trying to intervene on the campus, that for the first time in his life he was making a tape of what he said so they could not go back to the university and distort his words. Mao's effort was a failure. Kuai told his supporters that Mao wanted them to fight to the end but could not say so publicly.

China had begun to revolve on an orbit so erratic no one could predict its next movement.

Mao had started by warning the Red Guards that three groups were off limits to them—the army, the factories and the peasants in the countryside. Each of these groups, he said, would in effect manage its own Cultural Revolution.

But by November 1966 Chiang Ching, speaking in Peking, announced that this had been changed, new edicts were issued by the Cultural Revolutionary Group, in which she played a leading role with her Shanghai associates, Chang Chun-chiao, Yao Wen-yuan and Wang Hung-wen. First the factory workers, then the army and finally the peasants were to pass into the sphere of Red Guard agitation. Actually, the peasants remained virtually immune to the *Sturm und Drang*. But the army soon became involved and the factories exploded, nowhere more spectacularly than in Shanghai during what was called the "January storm."

Shanghai was the industrial capital of China. It had a population of ten million, now swollen by several million Red Guards streaming in from Peking and other cities and by returning Shanghai workers, released or simply taking off from jobs all over the country in the spreading confusion.

Into this charged situation Chang Chun-chiao and Yao Wen-yuan—encouraged by Chiang Ching and, almost certainly, by Mao Tse-tung, who was at nearby Hangchow—dropped the grenade of Red Guard tactics. They inspired the setting up of a radical agitational organization called the Rebel General Headquarters and aimed it at the Shanghai party organization, which was trying to resist ouster. The Shanghai party recruited a rival outfit called the Red Defense Department. Soon these organizations, hundreds of thousands strong, were battling in the streets, fighting for control of newspapers and radio stations, commandeering railroad trains and paralyzing the city.

By January chaos was absolute. The Shanghai port ceased to function. A general strike halted all transportation. Nothing worked. Streets were filled with chanting millions. The experiences of the Paris Commune of 1870 had long been idealized by the Shanghai radicals (as well as by Mao), and on February 5 the Shanghai People's Commune was proclaimed—all power would now flow from the people themselves organized in a city-wide Commune which took over governmental and economic direction. In reality, literally nothing was going on in Shanghai by this time except wild speeches, rallies, sorties after "enemies" and confrontations with fallen leaders. The city could not feed itself. Power stations closed down. The lights began to go out. Streetcars halted.

Nothing deterred Chang Chun-chiao and Yao Wen-yuan. First Shanghai, next Peking. All China must become a Commune.

Mao took fright. For some time he had been closeting himself with Lin Piao, ordering PLA units into parts of the country stricken with disorder. Now he summoned the Shanghai leaders to Peking. He was so anxious to meet with them he kept asking his secretary whether they had arrived, and he was waiting at the door of his study when Chang and Yao appeared. The moment for the Commune had ended, just nineteen days after it had arisen. You can't have Communes all over China, Mao said. Then you would have to call the country the "People's Commune of China"—maybe foreign countries wouldn't recognize it. Maybe the West would and the Soviet Union wouldn't. The idea represented "extreme anarchism." Mao repudiated a slogan which Shanghai had been using, an old quotation from his May Fourth days, in 1919: "The world is ours, the nation is ours, society is ours." He didn't think he had used that phrase; at least he couldn't remember it and he didn't want it bandied about in Shanghai. The name "Commune" should be dropped. Mao's remarks about "foreign countries" suggested that Premier Chou En-lai had intervened to keep China on the rails. Chang Chun-chiao and Yao Wen-yuan went back to Shanghai. The Commune was quietly turned into the "Revolutionary Committee of the Municipality of Shanghai." No more Communes were set up.

Shanghai was the apogee of the Cultural Revolution. The movement would go on and on and on and cause endless trouble, but nothing as dangerous as Shanghai. Battles would erupt between reluctant military commanders and firebrand agitators, as in Wuhan, where civil war broke out. The contenders were, on the one hand, the Wuhan military commander, a powerful army veteran, allied with a local group called the Million Heroes (it embraced about 1.5 million workers in the Wuhan region) and a smaller Red Guard organization affiliated with the Red Guard radicals in Peking. At the height of combat, two Peking emissaries were beaten up and held prisoner by the Million Heroes, Premier Chou made a secret negotiating trip (narrowly escaping being kidnapped), battle units of the Chinese Navy were moved up the Yangtze, air-force and paratroop units flew in.

Five years after this struggle the Wuhan party organization had still not totally bowed to Peking. It carried out orders from Peking reluctantly or not at all. The Wuhan battle touched off another conflict, this one to "drag out" of the Liberation Army commanders like those at Wuhan who resisted Peking's radicalism.

★

Slowly the temperature of the Cultural Revolution dropped below flash point. The prestige and power of one man steadily rose: Lin Piao. More and more Mao was compelled to turn to Lin and to the army to restore order—to quell the ferocious civil war in Szechwan; to end the massacres in Tibet, Inner Mongolia, Sinkiang and Manchuria. Scapegoats were found for the excesses—Chen Po-ta and other leaders of the Cultural Revolutionary Group. Even Chiang

Ching and her closest colleagues, Chang Chun-chiao, Yao Wen-yuan and Wang Hung-wen, slipped from the intense prominence they had achieved. Mao had designated Lin Piao as his successor. It was so provided in the constitution of the state: in 1968 a special amendment was incorporated to that effect. Steadily, under the great wings of the cult of Mao Tse-tung there began to emerge a cult of Lin Piao.

The *luan* of Chairman Mao had begun to die away. But more dangerous episodes lay ahead. The Revolution in the Revolution had not yet ended.

CHINA

100 Years

of

Revolution

**219**

## THE FALL OF LIN PIAO

SHORTLY BEFORE MIDNIGHT ON September 12, 1971, a smallish man with a thin, twisted face, spectacles with flesh-tinted rims, narrow shoulders and an air of extreme tenseness scurried up the aluminum steps of a British Trident, No. 256 in China's air force, at a small airport near Pei-tai-ho, a seaside resort on the Gulf of Chihli, north of Tientsin. He turned to his wife and said, "Hurry, hurry." When he ducked into the plane his service cap fell off. He didn't bother to retrieve it.

The small man with the twisted face was Lin Piao, China's Minister of Defense, second only to Chairman Mao in the hierarchy. Now sixty-four years old, he was originally born Lin Yu-jong, son of a well-to-do weaver, storekeeper and small entrepreneur in a little town of Hupeh Province at the foot of the Hui-ling Mountains. His wife was Yeh Chun, like himself a member of the Politburo, an attractive, ambitious woman about forty years of age whom he had married in the late 1950s, after the death of his first wife. With them was Lin Li-kuo, twenty-six, Lin's son, deputy commander of the air force, and, it was later said, four very high-ranking Chinese commanders.

The Trident, hurriedly fueled, supplied only with a few maps and some signal codes, lacking navigator or radio operator, took off in a flurry, grazing a fuel truck planted on the runway, and headed for Outer Mongolia's capital of Ulan Bator, 950 miles to the northwest. At about 2:30 A.M. September 13, near Ondor Haan, the plane crashed and burned. It later was claimed that it had run out of fuel and attempted a forced landing, that a wing hit the ground and it caught fire. All aboard burned to death.

Ondor Haan is an important Mongolian regional center, 672 miles northwest of Pei-tai-ho on an arrow course for Ulan Bator, which is 200 miles farther west. Peking said the plane missed the Ulan Bator airport. A glance at the map suggests this is not likely. More likely is that the plane was on a point-to-point compass bearing for Ulan Bator and possibly was attempting to land at Ondor Haan. Or it may have been shot down by the Mongol air defense. For years Mongolia has maintained intensive air surveillance; a plane detected in the Mongol airspace after sundown is automatically considered hostile and subject to attack, though Lin Piao and his entourage could hardly have been ignorant of this. Many people in Peking believe Chinese fighters shot down the plane.

Whatever happened, nine people were found dead aboard the plane. (Some reports said the bodies bore bullet wounds.) The Mongols led a Chinese diplomatic team to the spot on September 15 or 16. The Chinese said they identified Lin Piao, his wife, his son and the others. Six of the nine were members of the Politburo. Much later the Russians let it be known they had identified Lin by his dental work, done in Moscow. A couple of years after that, Teng Ying-chao, Chou En-lai's wife, told Mrs. Robert McNamara that the CIA had learned of Lin's death before the Chinese and that "their information was a hundred percent accurate." How the CIA accomplished this feat no one has explained.

Lin Piao had been a modest man for many years, a tough, dedicated military man. His background was not unlike Mao's. He came from a comparatively well-off family which saw that he got a good education. He joined the student movement at Kung Chu Middle School in Wuchang, one of the cities of the Wuhan complex. When he graduated in 1925 he entered Whampoa Military Academy, changing his name to Lin Piao.

Lin made his mark during the Northern Expedition in 1927, joined Mao Tse-tung in the bloody Nan-chang uprising and was with him from then on, winning command of the First Army Corps in 1931 at the age of twenty-four. He supported Mao on the Long March and at Yenan had charge of the "Resist Japan University." Badly wounded in 1938, he recuperated in the Soviet Union, fought in the Red Army during the early days of the Nazi attack in 1941 and returned to China in 1942. His big chance came when Mao dismissed Peng Te-huai in 1959. By the time the Cultural Revolution began Lin was Mao's strong right arm. As *luan* deepened, Mao's dependence on Lin and his army grew and grew. Lin made an alliance with Chiang Ching, and by the Ninth Party Congress in April 1969 was able to persuade (or compel) Mao to name him his successor.

Hardly had Lin won the title of heir when Mao began to undermine him. It was the story of Liu Shao-chi all over. There were policy conflicts as well as personal antagonisms. One row was over foreign policy. Peking's quarrel with Moscow was escalating. Violent fighting broke out along the Ussuri River just before the Ninth Party Congress, and it went on escalating. Nuclear attack could not be ruled out. The Soviet Union sent round-robin memoranda to affiliated Communist regimes and parties warning that a first strike might become necessary. Chou En-lai had barely managed to pull the country through the Cultural Revolution and now he was telling Mao that China could not face the Russians without allies; it was time to switch signals, to go back to Mao's old objective and seek a rapprochement with the United States. Lin had a different prescription: call off the quarrel with Russia, go back to the alliance, form a common front against the United States. Many of Lin's army associates had a fondness for the old collaboration with the Soviet military.

Slowly but with increasing momentum Mao began to shift his weight to Chou's side. Mao had no intention of returning to the embrace of the Polar Bear. By the winter of 1971 it was clear that Lin was losing all along the line. Mao had given the signal on the United States in an interview with Edgar Snow in December 1970 in which he said that President Nixon would be welcome to come to China. Chou En-lai was busy with the early, complex details of the proposed trip of Henry Kissinger, which would become a reality in July. Even more ominous to Lin, Mao had begun to shift troops around. He had moved the crack Thirty-eighth Army, Lin's household command, out of Peking and fired its commander and political commissar, both allies of Lin. This happened in January 1971. Later Mao would call his action in shifting the Peking command "digging up the cornerstone" of Lin's apparatus. It was an accurate metaphor.

Lin and his wife, Yeh Chun, met in February at Suchow, the lovely Chinese resort. With them was Lin's son, Lin Li-kuo, a bright, brash young man whom Chen Po-ta is said to have called a "genius." The term had a brassy ring: one of Lin's moves had been to brand Mao a "genius," a title Mao rejected because he perceived that Lin intended to remove him from the cockpit of politics and perch him high on a memorial pedestal. Mao, employing his favorite divide-and-conquer tactics, already had split Chen Po-ta off from Lin and was in the process of drumming Chen Po-ta, his former secretary, out of the party. Lin had seen this happen too many times. He understood that his turn came next.

CHINA

100 Years

of

Revolution

221

At the Suchow meeting, Mao later alleged, Lin and his wife decided they must abandon ordinary politics if they were not to lose out entirely. The alternative was to seize power by conspiracy. Lin was convinced that unless he acted swiftly Mao would remove him from office, just as he had removed Chen Po-ta and so many others. Lin's analysis turned out to be 100-percent correct. Some scholars, Ross Terrill among them, have questioned whether Lin was party to plotting a coup d'état, suggesting this could have been the work of his son and his wife. One argument is the adolescent language in which "Project 571" is couched and its aura of cheap opera. This seems a quibble. Enough material has been made public to define the flavor of struggle within the party elite. The plotting and counterplotting, the terminology and the tactics, come straight from those medieval Chinese classics of which Mao was so fond. The intrigues involved not individuals but families and clans—wives and children, nieces and nephews, the wife and children of Liu Shao-chi, the wife and children of Lin Piao, the wife of Mao and their relatives. Lin's moves and countermoves would have been familiar to the Scotland of Mary Stuart or the reader of Alexandre Dumas. If, as Han Su-yin reports, Yeh Chun cried at one point, "What of the succession?", this was a cry that would be echoed soon by Chiang Ching herself.

That Lin Piao left formal drafting of the plans to his son seems not implausible. The language of the document, code-named "Project 571" (a homonym for "armed uprising"), resembles that of a fraternity initiation but it describes a conspiracy to seize control of a nation of nearly one billion people.

In the scenario Mao is called "B-52"; Yeh Chun "the viscountess"; Lin "the chief"; Lin's army forces "the fleet"; the Gang of Four the "Trotskyites"; Mao is described as the "biggest feudal despot" in China's history, similar in character to Chin Shih Huang-ti, first Emperor of the Chin dynasty, a ruler of extraordinary cruelty. Members of the Central Committee were called "main battleships."

A number of variants are discussed: assassination of Mao; capture and elimination of the whole top leadership at a meeting of the Central Committee; use of poison gas, biological weapons, bombs, a secret Chinese weapon designated only as "543," car accidents, kidnapping, guerrilla attacks, and a frontal assault on the Forbidden City. The most important target (next to Mao) is specified as Chang Chun-chiao, the Shanghai leader, closest associate of Chiang Ching and ultimately a member of the Gang of Four. Nowhere is Chiang Ching's name mentioned, an omission that might be read in two ways—either that she had foreknowledge of the adventure or that Lin was confident of winning her over when need arose.

Project 571 offered a detailed analysis of military units and commanders who were loyal to Lin or might be brought to his side, as well as those counted upon to support Mao.

What, in fact, was done under Project 571? Premier Chou En-lai once reprimanded an American correspondent who suggested there was a "riddle" about it. None at all, Chou said, not nearly as mysterious as the Kennedy assassination. Nonetheless, great gaps remain in the story and there are signs that the text of Project 571 may have been doctored a bit before it was released to the Chinese people and, after eighteen months, made available to the world.

What seems certain is that in the days just before September 12 the affair began to come to a head. Both sides got the wind up. Neither knew exactly what the other knew or intended, but there were enough clues to indicate the climax was near. Mao and Chou knew a plot was afoot; Lin realized that Mao and Chou had become suspicious.

The theory of some specialists that there was no Project 571—that the document and supporting materials were cooked up by Mao—does not hold water. Too many curious things were going on.

Chiang Ching later told Roxanne Witke that she and the Chairman no longer felt secure in their quarters at Chungnanhai in the Forbidden City. The palace had been "infiltrated." There were efforts to poison their food. As early as 1969, she said, toxic substances were put in their meals and they became ill. Once there had been a plot by Lin to kidnap her daughter, Li Na, but it had gone awry. And Lin had a plan to kill all the members of the Politburo. These remarks do not sound coherent and they may not be true, but they reflect the fears that lay behind the walls of the Forbidden City.

The melodrama came to a peak at a moment when Mao was on the road, meeting with military commanders, sounding them out on Lin and, as it is clear in retrospect, lining them up on his side and ferreting out those who might be on Lin's side. Many anti-Lin measures were already in train, such as removal of his posters and slogans, and shifts in the party line away from his positions. Lin had not been seen in public for several months. None of this was accidental, and politically wise Chinese understood it. Mao made it plainer in his tour of military commands. He criticized Lin for power-seeking but acted as though there was still hope Lin would get back to the correct line. He, Mao, would help him.

Mao made a remark in these talks that later took on a curious ring. "I've never approved," he said, "of one's wife heading the administrative office of one's work unit" (as did Yeh Chun with Lin). He, said Mao, sorted all his own documents, read them himself, annotated them himself "to avoid mistakes." These were the functions Chiang Ching was to tell Roxanne Witke she had performed for Mao since the 1950s.

It was Chou En-lai who gave the alarm to Mao as he was returning to Shanghai from Hangchow on September 12. En route, two bombing attacks on Mao's train had been planned, or so it was said. A canister of poison gas and a time bomb were placed in Mao's car. Chou was alerted that something was afoot and he rushed a convoy of limousines down the line. Mao transferred to an automobile and arrived safely in Shanghai.

Later Chou was to say that he did not immediately connect the attempt with Lin, but by this time Lin was alarmed. He had his son, Lin Li-kuo, order Trident 256 to the Pei-tai-ho airport and made plans for a quick getaway with his closest cohorts. It is probable that Lin hoped to go to Canton and set up a rival revolutionary center and Politburo in that traditional seat of revolt. Lin Li-kuo was said to have established a "revolutionary base" in Canton. It is probable that Lin had his son order the Trident in order to keep his own profile low. And it is probable that the plane was ordered to Pei-tai-ho rather than to a Peking military airport for the same reason.

In the midst of this excitement Lin Li-kuo rushed home to collect some papers about the plot. There he encountered his twenty-nine-year-old sister, Lin Toto (Little Bean). The brother and sister were children of Liu Hsi-ming, Lin's first wife, one of the beautiful, upwardly mobile young women who had been attracted to Yenan in the 1930s. Lin was regarded as the "catch" of Yenan, slim, handsome, a confirmed bachelor. Liu Hsi-ming set her cap for Lin and they were married about 1937. Lin Toto had no love for Yeh Chun, a relentless, scheming woman, twenty-two years younger than Lin. When Lin Li-kuo urged Toto to join him she refused, and after he left she telephoned Chou En-lai. Exactly what she told him is not known, but later she was given special mention for "foiling her father's monstrous conspiracy."

Chou was still not clear what was happening. He tried to telephone Lin Piao but couldn't reach him. Finally he talked to Yeh Chun at Pei-tai-ho. She said she knew nothing about any plane, they had no plans for going anywhere and Lin was attending a concert. The story seemed fishy and, as Chou was to tell a group of Americans in 1972, he decided as a precaution (an extraordinary one) to order every plane in China grounded and all airports closed. The order was relayed instantly to Pei-tai-ho.

Yeh Chun immediately got in touch with Lin. They concluded that Peking had uncovered the plot. Lin gathered his associates (perhaps they were all together for emergency consultation) and dashed to the airport. There may have been resistance by the ground crews: the plane seems to have taken off with less than a full quota of fuel.

A second group of conspirators of lower rank took off by helicopter, headed for the Soviet frontier. The two copters were shot down and all were killed.

Such is the official version. Not much has been added over the years except that when the indictment of the Gang of Four was made public it put Lin Piao and his gang and Chiang Ching and her gang in one big plot. They had, it was now said, worked together during the Cultural Revolution and afterward. True, there had been a split, which led to Lin's abortive coup, but this was a falling out among thieves. They had all essentially been in it together until Lin Piao tried to strike out on his own. No attention was paid to Chiang Ching's contention that Lin had been an extravagant man, an "embezzler" who lived on a lavish scale, building himself huge mansions in various parts of the country and bestowing valuable gifts on friends and relatives. By this time the identical charge was being made against Chiang Ching.

There was one small footnote. A year or so later, Lin Toto was relaxing at the famous Tsunghua hot springs not far from Canton. An army barracks was adjacent. One day a volley of shots rang out and Lin Toto fell dead. No one thought it was an accident, but what hand pulled the trigger was never discovered.

★

If the disgrace and death of Liu Shao-chi marked phase one of the Cultural Revolution, so the disgrace and death of Lin Piao closed phase two. To those with a sense of history the Cultural Revolution seemed to have turned into China's Thermidor, the cannibalistic paroxysm into which revolutions so often fall. Thus ended the Bolshevik Revolution, when Stalin devoured his comrades, Trotsky, Bukharin, Zinoviev, Kamenev, Rykov and all the Old Bolsheviks. So the French Revolution devoured its own when on the Tenth Day of Thermidor, Robespierre, Saint-Just and Couthon went to the same guillotine that had taken the head of Louis XVI.

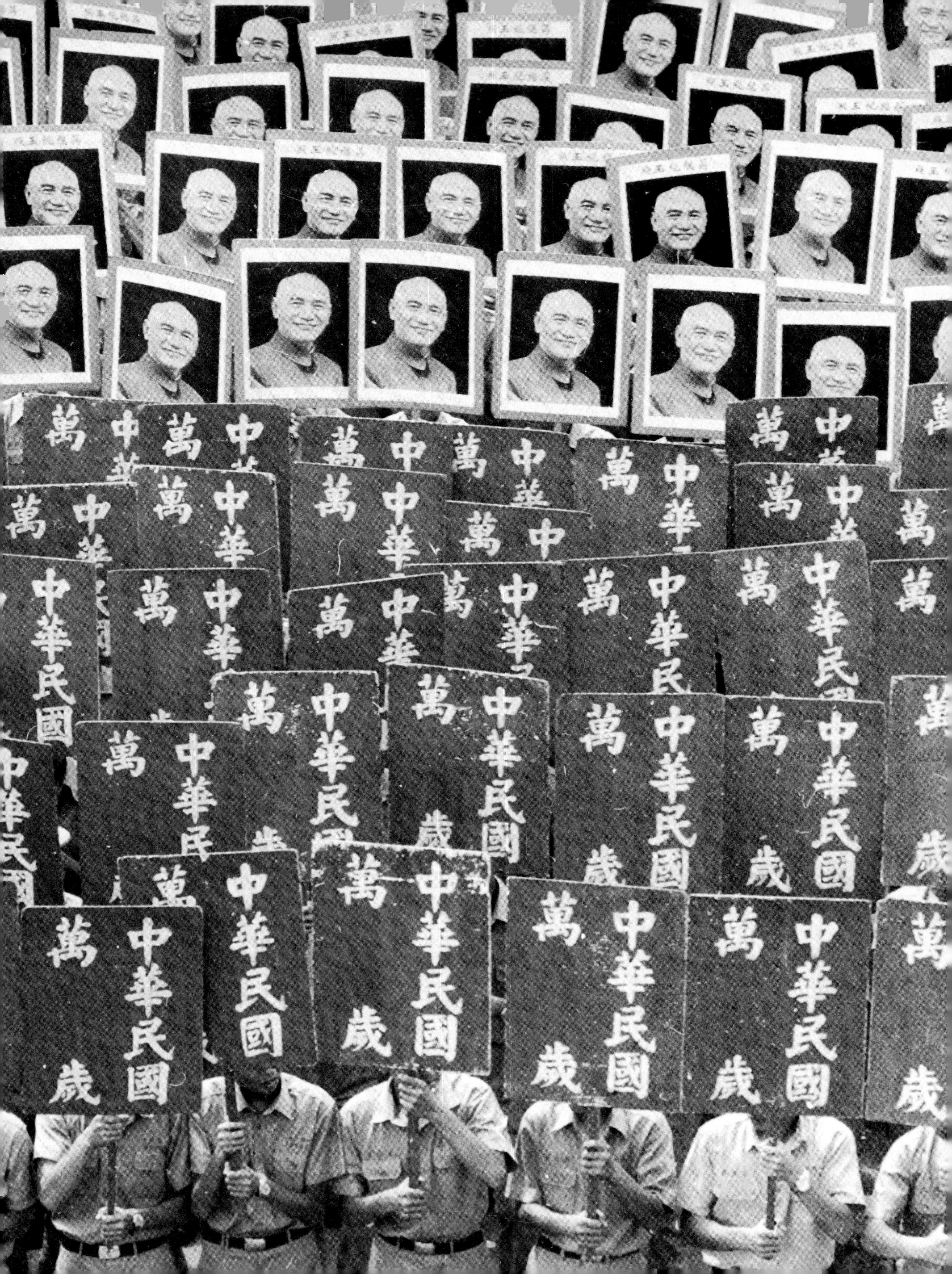
中華民國萬歲

Mao Tse-tung relaxing in his favorite Lushan mountain resort in 1961. CPS

*Opposite:*
People's Liberation Army soldiers parade in Peking streets as an old scholar looks on. CB/M

*Overleaf:*
Banners honoring Generalissimo Chiang Kai-shek at the "Double Ten" anniversary of the founding of the Chinese Republic, celebrated on October 10, 1974, in Taiwan. UPI

*Following pages:*
During the Great Leap Forward campaign of 1958, peasants mass to build flood works along the Yellow River. PIC

Edgar Snow (left), author of *Red Star over China*, meets with Mao Tse-tung, November 20, 1962. In the center is George Hatem, the American doctor who joined the Chinese Communists in Yenan in 1936. WW

Mao reading in the *Peking People's Daily* of the Communist liberation of Nanking in 1949. CPS

The People's Liberation Army enters Lhasa in 1951, driving Dalai Lama from the Potala (shown in background). MRV

Chairman Mao reviews Red
Guards in one of the million-
strong rallies held in Tien an
men Square in the summer and
autumn of 1966. CPS

*Opposite:*
Mao swims the Yangtze at
Wuhan, July 1966, thus providing a national demonstration of his health and fitness
as the Cultural Revolution
moves into high gear. UPI

Wreckage of the Trident 256 in which Lin Piao and his wife, son and close associates were killed while fleeing Peking, September 13, 1971. Their plane crashed in Mongolia. Lin had been plotting the overthrow of Mao. CPS

*Opposite:*
Demonstrators wave their "Little Red Books" as they read big character wall posters during Cultural Revolution in 1967. PIC

Wang Hung-wen, the youngest
member of the Gang of Four.
CPS

Chiang Ching on trial, with
other members of the Gang of
Four, in November 1980. CPS

Yao Wen-yuan, the publicist whose writings sparked the Cultural Revolution, on trial as a member of the Gang of Four. CPS

Chang Chun-chiao, Shanghai party leader, on trial as a member of the Gang of Four. CPS

President Liu Shao-chi, one of the chief victims of Mao's Cultural Revolution. Shown here practicing Chinese shadow-boxing. CPS

Wang Kuang-mei, widow of Liu Shao-chi (who died in imprisonment during the Cultural Revolution), sits among the spectators at the trial of Chiang Ching and the Gang of Four. CPS

# ★ 14 ★

## THE GANG OF FOUR

**A**FTER THE DEATH OF LIN PIAO, China's revolution seemed to reach its apogee. While the party had been informed (more or less) what had happened, while the absence of Lin and his coterie stirred endless rumors, no public word was spoken to mar the roseate triumph that brought President Nixon to Peking. Never mind that to Nixon this was *his* triumph ("The week that changed the world"); to the Chinese the spectacle of the American President flying from Washington to Peking, going directly to Chungnanhai, to Mao's classic Ming dwelling within the Forbidden City, the house beside Middle and South Lakes, to meet the Chairman was symbolism from the ages of Empire: the foreigner come to pay tribute.

It was pure triumph for China, for Mao and not least for Chou En-lai, the man who had foiled Lin's plot, the man who had, after Mao gave the signal by welcoming Edgar Snow and the American Ping-Pong players, concocted the scenario for Nixon's visit with the aid of that other great courtier, Henry Kissinger.

It had been a long, long march from Shao Shan, from Chingkang Mountain, from the peasant struggles of Hunan, over the Snow Mountains, across the turbulent Tatu River, and through the Great Marshes and finally the deserts of Yenan. But China—and Mao—had triumphed.

The surface of China was calm, the people seemed relaxed. True, they were still poor, but any old China hand, be he John Fairbank or Joseph Alsop, could see the enormous gains. China had stood up. For one thing, the flies had been conquered. Never mind how it had been done, never mind the canisters of DDT burning on Shanghai street corners on Saturday nights. True, there had been human cost. Deaths. Painful details of the Cultural Revolution seeped out. True, the workers didn't seem very vigorous; sometimes they even looked sullen. True, there was not much machinery in the peasant fields. But no one was starving. In fact, no one *had* starved, or so it was said. True, the country did seem backward beyond belief, but as Premier Chou was fond of saying, "We are a very poor country. We are not a great power. We are a developing country." And the Chinese were extraordinarily modest. They asked—nay, begged—for criticism. They wanted to know what they had done wrong; how they could do it better; they did not brag; they apologized.

It was a relaxed time. The Chinese were enjoying the new sight of the Americans and of foreign visitors. Everywhere there were colossal statues of Chairman Mao but they were beginning to come down. Visitors often saw them in the process of removal—a heritage of the "cult" which was no longer needed. Premier Chou was gracious. He told visitors, "Everything we have learned we have learned from the Chairman. He is our teacher and we are his pupils." He wore a modest enamel pin that said "Serve the People." Mao buttons were out of fashion. The "little red book" had vanished—or almost vanished—with the disappearance (still unexplained) of its compiler, Lin Piao. Give us a couple more years, Chou told some visitors, and we will have things in place. Knowing visitors understood. In a couple of years the debris of the Cultural Revolution would be cleared away, the tawdry tragedy that had plagued China for the past ten years would be put behind. It would be full speed ahead. Chou had, or so it seemed, a free hand from Mao to get the country going again. Scores of American journalists and China-watchers came to Peking, wandered over the country. They were impressed. After the madness of the Cultural Revolution and the decades of sacrifice there was light ahead. So it seemed.

★

That summer of 1972, among the throngs of visitors was an American woman, a scholar, a student of China, an activist in the women's movement, named Roxanne Witke. She had come to Peking on an academic project. She wanted to meet with China's generation of revolutionary women, to talk of their role in the Revolution and in the society that China was building. The list of women whom she wished to see was headed by the names of Teng Ying-chao, wife of Premier Chou; Kang Ko-ching, wife of Chu Teh; and Chiang Ching, wife of Chairman Mao.

Professor Witke, as she later was to confess, had no real hope of meeting the top ladies of China and was quite prepared to settle for the second echelon or whomever the Chinese might make available. To her astonishment—and awe—after a quick tour of China she spent the morning of August 12, 1972, with Teng Ying-chao and Kang Ko-ching and the evening with Chiang Ching. On August 25 Witke flew to Canton, and there, in the luxurious setting of Chiang Ching's private villa with its fastidious orchid and lotus gardens, Chiang spent six days with Witke, hour after flowing hour of conversation, sometimes trailing fingers in the lotus pools, sometimes inhaling the fragrance of their petals to revive flagging spirits during hours of talk that went on long after midnight. It was a fairy tale, Chiang Ching living out the fantasy of her life to an eager, almost breathless American witness. Edgar Snow's *Red Star over China* had made Mao Tse-tung a world political leader overnight. Chiang had this example in her mind, spoke of it and believed that *Conversations with Chiang Ching* (Witke actually called it simply *Comrade Chiang Ch'ing*) would do the same for her. The talks were a weapon—almost an atom bomb—that Chiang believed would transform her from Mao's consort into the role for which she yearned and strove, the role of Mao's successor—Empress, if you will—of the world's largest Communist state.

Nothing like this had happened before; neither the Communist world nor the rich dynastic history of China provided a clear precedent, not even the case of the Empress Lu or of the Empress Wu Tse-tien, female rulers highly publicized in Chiang's last years.

There was, in fact, no precedent, but Chiang Ching would create one. Alas, before Witke's book could be published Chiang Ching had fallen. And if she had not, the words and images, the boudoir-equipped special plane, the languid life beside the Canton gardens, the preciosity of her interests (photographing flowers; holding private showings of Greta Garbo films), the open neuroticism of her personality, her preoccupation with plots, what Witke called her "relish" for her enemies, the shallowness of her ideological pretensions, the vanity, the narcissistic moods, the crudity with which she applied gilt to her origins in the alleys of the 1930s Shanghai film world—the theatrical portrait of a power-lusting woman who was clawing and plotting her way to the pinnacle constituted a self-indictment so damning she could not have escaped it. As she told Witke at one point: sex when you are young; power when you are older. Her story and her conduct told something of the moral corruption that had eaten into the heart of the party.

Premier Chou himself facilitated Chiang Ching's interview. She spoke of him with palpable sincerity as her "protector." What did that skilled and sophisticated statesman think he was doing when he made possible Chiang's self-exposure? (He was later quoted as saying, "Six hours would have been all right—but sixty!") Did he, in fact, expect Chiang to self-destruct? Quite possibly. It is also possible that he was prepared to woo and win her erratic friendship as one thread in the complex end game of Mao's regime.

Whatever the game Chou thought he was playing it did not work. Within the year his physicians diagnosed cancer. Now began a deadly race—would Chou or Mao first meet Marx and God? Chou was not to have the peaceful interlude in which to restore the damage done by the Cultural Revolution and establish a firm structure to carry on when he and Mao were gone. Already telltale signs of the new struggles were visible. The official announcement of Lin Piao's treachery had been followed by a propaganda campaign: against Lin and Confucius. But now the campaign was tilting more and more against Confucius. Lin was being forgotten. Soon the target would emerge as "the Confucius in our ranks"—Chou, without a doubt.

**W**ithin the interplay of intrigue that dominated the Forbidden City and its lovely Chung-nanhai, where in luxuriant old Imperial villas lived Mao and Chou and Chiang Ching and the rest, it was sometimes difficult to catch the dominant chord of a political fugue, and so it was with Teng Hsiao-ping. Suddenly this doughty five-foot man whose political career seemed to be made of India rubber bounced back onto the scene. The man who had been denounced as the "number-two capitalist roader," second in wickedness only to Liu Shao-chi, casually reemerged as deputy premier in April 1973. He was introduced to foreign correspondents by Mao's niece Wang Hai-jung at an official reception for Prince Sihanouk of Cambodia. Promptly Teng became a stand-in and, it would seem, an ally of Premier Chou. It was assumed that Chou brought in Teng, and that may well be true. But there is a "contrary current," as the Chinese might say, which insists that the initiative was Mao's or possibly Chiang Ching's and that Teng was returned to the political stage in order to nudge Chou into the wings. The motivation did not make much difference. Once back in office, Teng quickly showed that he had come down on Chou's side. Not for nothing had Mao complained that Teng insisted on sitting in the back row and turning his deaf ear (deaf since a battle in the Long March) whenever Mao was talking.

Working against time, Chou and Teng sought to bind up the wounds inflicted on China's state structure, economy, agriculture, science, education and defense by the Cultural Revolution.

But as they toiled, the drums of Chiang Ching's thrust for power beat more and more strongly. She had not lost her allies Chang Chun-chiao, Yao Wen-yuan and Wang Hung-wen, the trio who not only ruled Shanghai but also held firm grip on national propaganda, both print and electronic. One of them was constantly at her side, particularly the handsome young Wang, only a year old at the time of the Long March. More and more Wang was being described as something of a playboy, and even as Chiang's paramour. Peking rumor, never verified, suggested that Yao was married to Li Na, Chiang's daughter (in 1976 Yao was fifty-four years old, Li Na thirty-six).

Chiang Ching had several close allies among the Mao family. Li Na was trained, her mother told Witke, as a historian. She was an intellectual, about the same age as Witke, and had during the Cultural Revolution, when only twenty-six, acted as administrator of the *Liberation*

*Army Daily*, the leading organ in laying down the radical Cultural Revolutionary line. Li Min, Mao's daughter by Ho Shih-chen, was a year or two older than Li Na. Chiang Ching had brought her up almost as her own child. Li Min had studied natural science in college, and she, too, played a political role, particularly during the Cultural Revolution, when she served on the Science-Technology Committee, which oversaw, it was believed, nuclear research. Perhaps Chiang's staunchest family ally was Mao Yuan-hsin, Mao's nephew, son of his martyred brother Mao Tse-min. The nephew was said to call Chiang Ching "Mama" and held a vice-regal position in Manchuria. Earlier Chiang's closest relationship among the Mao children had been with Mao's oldest son, An-ying, son of Yang Kai-hui, a man about Chiang's age. An-ying was killed in Korea.

Tragedy haunted Mao's children. An-ying and his brother, An-ching, had been smuggled to Shanghai after the Kuomintang murdered their mother in Chang-sha in 1930. According to a wall poster put up during the Cultural Revolution, the children were abandoned and took to the streets as beggars, placing a sign on the wall of a deserted temple: "We tell stories— one penny." Eventually the underground Communist Party located the boys and they were sent to the Soviet Union, but An-ching became a mental case—a fact used by Soviet propagandists against Mao. They claimed he had driven his son mad.

There was one flaw in Chiang's alliance system. As long as she and Lin Piao worked together they had strong army backing. Now this pillar was gone. After Lin Piao's death the weakness was never repaired. In Shanghai Chiang's allies created a popular militia, one million strong, with its own arms, independent of the Shanghai garrison. And in Manchuria, northeastern China, where young Mao Yuan-hsin was second in command, Chiang had military backing, as she did in Peking. But the army as a whole was beyond her grasp—and hostile.

So matters stood when, in June 1974, Mao left Peking for the south, not to return for eight months. Before he left, as Ross Terrill has pointed out, relations between Chiang and Mao had become strained. They no longer lived together in the Chungnanhai mansion. Chiang had her own house nearby and had lost her automatic access to Mao. He had sent her a series of curt notes, such as: "It is better not to see each other. You haven't carried out many of the things I talked to you about over the years. What's the use of more meetings with you?" In July 1974 Mao warned Chiang and her associates, "You'd better be careful, don't let yourselves become a small faction of four." In December he repeated the warning: "Don't become a faction. Those who do so will fail!" And he observed of Chiang, "She is poking her nose into everything. Is she ambitious? I believe she is." He told the Politburo, "Chiang Ching speaks only for herself; she cannot speak for me." In 1975 Mao is supposed to have written Chiang, "I am too old, already 81, and in poor health and you don't even show any consideration for me." All of these quotations were published after Mao's death and Chiang Ching's arrest.

Despite his private complaints Mao gave Chiang and her associates a fairly free hand. He stopped short of inserting either Chang Chun-chiao or Wang Hung-wen as Premier or Minister of Defense, but he wavered back and forth, back and forth, between the constructive policies of Chou and Teng and the radical views of Chiang Ching. Three times there were proposals, it later would be said, from Chiang Ching to launch a full-scale campaign against Chou, now in the hospital, emerging only at rare intervals. Mao refused permission but he let the sniping go on. Soon the question of a replacement for Chou would arise. The prickly Teng was doing the daily chores but, as it turned out, Mao had his eyes on Hua Kuo-feng, a moon-faced man whom he had first met on an inspection trip to Hunan in 1959 and had brought into the Central

Committee in 1969. Hua was from Shansi Province, an agriculture specialist now holding the post of Minister of Security, very low-profile.

On January 8, 1976, Chou En-lai died at the age of seventy-eight, and his death cleared the stage for the final acts of the Mao epoch. The nerves of the Chinese people drew taut, in grief and apprehension. They watched every move like hungry hawks—Mao did not stand honor guard beside Chou's coffin, and all the other leaders, even ninety-year-old Chu Teh, did. (Mao had visited Chou in his last days at the hospital but this was not made known.) Chiang Ching did not remove her military cap when she viewed Chou lying in state; only two members of the Politburo accompanied Chou's funeral cortège; the official mourning period was short; the press did not mention the millions who turned out to view the cortège and to pay tribute to Chou in Tien an Men Square.

There were other portents. Teng Hsiao-ping gave the funeral oration, then disappeared from public view and public mention. His appointment as Premier should have been announced almost automatically. Instead the press began a criticism of Chou which quickly broadened into an offensive against Teng. On February 7 it was revealed that Hua Kuo-feng, the man nobody knew, had become acting Premier. The Politburo decision was said to have been unanimous, which meant only that Mao had voted for Hua after explaining that he was "not a stupid man." Chiang Ching had wanted Chang Chun-chiao to have the post. He didn't get it, but Mao gave Teng a kick in the slats, quoting a famous saying of Teng's that it didn't matter whether a cat was black or white as long as it caught the mice. That, Mao said, showed that Teng was no Marxist.

Ching Ming is the Chinese term for Spring Festival, a special occasion at the beginning of April to mark the end of winter, the beginning of new life, a time for honoring the dead, for putting wreaths and flowers on graves, for spending a moment in reflection, perhaps for writing a poem to the one who is gone.

The first wreath to honor Chou En-lai was placed at the Monument to the People's Heroes in Tien an Men Square on March 30. Within three days people were thronging into the square by the thousands. Actually, the movement to honor Chou had begun a few days earlier in Nanking, where great numbers of wreaths were brought to Yuhuatai, the memorial to the revolutionary dead. The wreaths were placed to an accompaniment of speeches against those who had criticized Chou (notably the Shanghai paper *Wen Hui Pao*) and tributes to Mao's second wife, the martyred Yang Kai-hui, designed as oblique criticism of Chiang Ching. There were attacks on Chang Chun-chiao, some of which were plastered on railroad trains to spread the message throughout China.

In Peking, Ching Ming flowered into the first great popular manifesto of the Communist era. Thousands of poems were written, declaimed, plastered on walls, dedicated to Chou or attacking the regime. One copied down by Roger Garside read:

> *Devils howl as we pour out our grief*
> *We weep but the wolves laugh.*
> *We shed our blood in memory of the hero*
> *Raising our heads, we unsheathe our swords.*

The mood was one of grief mixed with anger that rose to the verge of rebellion. On Saturday and Sunday, April 3 and 4, there were hundreds of thousands in Tien an Men Square. A young man attacked the "new Empress Dowager." Others sang laments for Chou.

Everything changed on Monday, April 5. A convoy of trucks roared into the square before daylight and swept it clean of the tens of thousands of wreaths. The poems and laments were washed from the Monument to the People's Heroes. When crowds shouted, "Give us back our wreaths," police vans appeared. The mood turned ugly. A Tsinghua University student who shouted out against Chou, "He was the biggest capitalist roader of all," was seized by the crowd and badly beaten. Later it was claimed that he and other young leftists had been infiltrated into the crowd by Wang Hung-wen to provoke a riot. The angry crowd set upon a militia station, set fire to it and began to overturn cars and jeeps. Half a dozen were destroyed. There were thirty or forty thousand people in the square. In this tension Chiao Kuan-hua appeared. Chiao, long deputy to Chou, was now Foreign Minister. After the death of his first wife, he had married Chang Han-chih, a close friend and English teacher of Chiang Ching. He had been sent by Chiang Ching or possibly Wang Hung-wen to try to get the crowds to disperse. He made an angry speech that had little effect on the crowd but, later, a considerable effect on his career. Finally, at mid-evening, after many demonstrators had left, floodlights were turned on the square and thousands of police and workers' militiamen appeared. They blocked all exits and slowly, carefully, methodically beat the people with cudgels and staves, arresting men and women as they moved across the square. How many were arrested was never known precisely but there were estimates of three or four thousand. There were also estimates of a hundred killed.

New squads of clean-up men and women appeared. The square was cleared. Every vestige of tribute to Chou or criticism of Mao or Chiang Ching was washed away. The Politburo met in an emergency session (Mao was too ill to attend himself but stage-managed the meeting). It dismissed Teng Hsiao-ping and appointed slow-moving, slow-speaking Hua Kuo-feng as Premier and first vice-chairman of the party, a post that had never before existed. Teng was charged with instigating the demonstrations.

Ching Ming was over.

★

The year 1976 rumbled ahead, with portents of trouble everywhere. Mao's health declined by the day. After Ching Ming he was so weak he could hardly make himself understood. His niece Wang Hai-jung, now in charge of American affairs in the Foreign Office, and her close friend Nancy Tang, the brilliant Radcliffe-educated interpreter, hovered at Mao's side, trying to understand what he said. Often he scrawled ideographs on a scrap of paper because he could no longer articulate. His last more or less coherent conversation was with Richard Nixon. It was Nixon's first important public appearance since his resignation. Earlier Mao had met Julie and David Eisenhower and said, "You're part of our family."

The curtain had begun to fall, and darkness descended on China. In July, Marshal Chu Teh, Mao's oldest surviving comrade-at-arms, died. They were all shuffling off the stage. In that month there was a terrible earthquake, the most disastrous of modern times, 250,000 killed and 164,000 injured at the coal-and-steel complex of Tang-shan not far from Peking. Peking was shaken as a dog shakes a rabbit. Many hutung houses fell down. For three years hundreds of thousands of Peking residents would live in huts and tents lining the city's broad boulevards. There was trouble in the army, but news of this was carefully kept secret. Peasants rioted in remote districts. What Mao knew or could understand no one could tell. But tensions at the apex grew. Chou's widow, Teng Ying-chao, feared that at any moment she might be arrested. She warned her secretary not to resist if they came for her—but to telephone the Central Committee immediately. It was a hot summer, and in Chungnanhai everyone watched everyone else like a cat; most of all they watched the comings and goings at Mao's residence, where Chiang Ching appeared more and more as the Chairman grew more and more feeble. Mao Yuan-hsin, Mao's thirty-year-old nephew, was spending more time at his uncle's bedside, less in Manchuria. He seemed almost like Mao's chief of staff.

Amid the whispers, the hurried corridor consultations, the figures of three men began to emerge in strong profile. One was that of Hua Kuo-feng. Mao had put his blessing on Hua. "With you in charge I am at peace," he was quoted as saying. Second was the staunch, stern old Long March veteran, Marshal Yeh Chien-ying. In his youth Yeh had been a piano player. In the Yenan days his favorite song was "I've Been Working on the Railroad." He had not played that tune for many years, particularly not since his son, also a pianist, had been nearly killed by the Red Guards, his fingers crushed so that his musical career was ended. Yeh made no secret of his distaste for Chiang Ching and her friends. He had stalked out of the Politburo meeting when Mao fired Teng Hsiao-ping. Now Yeh was much with his old army comrades. It was hardly a secret that many shared his views. The third man in this behind-the-scenes world was Wang Tung-hsing. Wang had been Mao's bodyguard for years, going back to Yenan days. The party had always taken the guarding of its leaders with intense seriousness. Even in Yenan, when Mao moved about he trailed a bodyguard of ten to twenty men, sometimes more. After he began to see Chiang Ching, *she* acquired a bodyguard. All the leaders had bodyguards and, it was insisted, with good reason. Each had a price on his head. Chiang Kai-shek sought to infiltrate gunmen into the party ranks, hoping to pick off the Red leaders. (In her years in Shanghai, Madame Soong Ching-ling had been openly guarded by bodyguards provided by her brother T. V. Soong, to protect her from assassins who might be sent after her by her brother-in-law Chiang Kai-shek.)

So it was that Wang, once a simple, tough, hardbitten bodyguard, now commanded the elite Special Unit 8341. He had at his disposal two guards divisions of PLA troops, an armored regiment, anti-aircraft units, air force, engineers, a large body of secret agents, possibly forty thousand men or more. His functions had broadened. He now acted, in effect, as Mao's *chef de cabinet*; his men manned Mao's office, carried out every function from emptying bedpans to providing escorts for distinguished visitors. They washed the dishes, ironed the clothes, fitted Mao with a new suit when he needed one and kept his calligraphy tools in order.

These were the men into whose hands power would flow once Mao died. There was one other—an enigma for the moment—Teng Hsiao-ping. He was in Kwangtung Province and had been since his fall from the inner circle, living there quietly at the same hot-springs spa of Tsunghua where Lin Toto had been shot to death. Teng was under the protection of General Hsu Shih-yu, the powerful commander of the Kwangtung region, a man of dedicated opposition to Chiang Ching and her group, an iron-fisted military leader who had firm alliances with many military men who shared his viewpoint. Marshal Yeh spent some time in Canton and, it would later be said, met very privately with Teng.

In his last days Mao, like it or not, was closer to Chiang than he had been for years. She hovered over his bedside with her ally Mao Yuan-hsin. To judge from the propaganda organs, the policies of the Cultural Revolution were rapidly overtaking those of Chou's last days. Then, on September 9, Mao died, at eighty-two years of age. His long career, synonymous with China's revolution, came to an end and the fight for power was on. It was waged over Mao's body as it lay in state. Word was that Chiang Ching had not been with the Chairman in his last moments. She was playing bridge at her comfortable palace at the Temple of the White Pagoda in the Western Hills not far from the Ming Tombs. Warned that Mao was sinking, she went on playing for two hours. When she arrived at the bedside he was dead. She had, it was said, made his last days miserable. She had insisted on having him moved from place to place, she had wheedled six thousand dollars from him for some personal purpose, possibly for an addition to her collection of hundreds of gowns, including old court gowns worn by Empresses of China, which she apparently delighted in trying on, or possibly for the acquisition of new foreign films from Hong Kong. With such films she idled away her evenings with a group of young friends that included several handsome young men, a champion Ping-Pong player, a Minister of Physical Culture.

Now Mao was dead and the moment of which she had long dreamed was at hand.

She sent a wreath with the inscription "To my esteemed teacher Mao Tse-tung—from your student and comrade, Chiang Ching." Before the public ceremony, the mighty of the party gathered behind the scenes. The Chairman's niece Wang Hai-jung was inspecting the wreaths. When she saw Chiang's message she turned in fury upon the widow. "How dare you write that inscription?" she shouted. The two women—Chiang Ching, tall, sinewy, wearing a long black scarf theatrically flung across her shoulder, and Wang, small, compact, plainly dressed—flew at each other. Before anyone could intervene they were scratching and clutching. Wang grasped Chiang by her black bobbed hair and nearly fell backward as the hair came off in her hands— a wig! Somehow the combatants were pulled apart and their clothing readjusted, and the party made its way into public. Later it would be said that Wang and her friend Nancy Tang had moved away from association with Chiang Ching in the last year of Mao's life, but this was not enough in the end to save them from political reprisals. Wang lost her job in the Foreign Office, as did Tang, who also was dropped from the party's Central Committee.

The skirmish over Chiang Ching's wig was private. But the fight for the party was public. Mao, it was said, had uttered a deathbed injunction: "Act according to the principles laid down." Exactly what this meant—if indeed Mao had uttered the words—was not clear. But it was used as a banner by Chiang to demonstrate that Mao wished to follow "her" policies, the radical policies derived from the Cultural Revolution. The words were proclaimed in the *People's Daily*. They were shouted from television and radio. But when Hua Kuo-feng addressed a memorial meeting for Mao on September 18, he did not use them. On the same day, but, because of the time difference, *after* Hua Kuo-feng omitted the Delphic words, Foreign Minister Chiao Kuan-hua, speaking in the United Nations General Assembly in New York, uttered the fateful phrase. Only later did it become known that in so doing he had violated specific instructions cabled by Hua. For this act of defiance—plus his earlier associations with Chiang—Chiao paid dearly. He was in due course "set aside," confined to his home, compelled to study and compose a self-criticism. Five years after the death of Mao, a broken man, he had still not been returned to useful occupation.

The struggle over Chiang's wig was not the only unseemly behind-the-scenes quarrel. The most protracted concerned the disposal of Mao's body. Chou's had been cremated and the ashes scattered to the winds of China, by his personal wish. Many in the inner circle wished to do the same with Mao, particularly those looking to a future in which his image would be more human. Around and around the argument went. Finally it was decided that the symbol of Mao was needed for the unity of party and country and that a crystal sarcophagus would be built in Tien an Men Square to contain his mummified corpse, like Lenin's in Moscow and Choibalsan's in Ulan Bator. But, as Peking gossips were to say maliciously, "The argument went on so long that *he* decided." Because of the delay, it was alleged, the embalming was imperfect, and each night the sarcophagus had to be lowered into a deep-freeze compartment to prevent decay.

The tale of Mao's corpse is tittle-tattle. The battle over it was not. Sometime between September 9 and October 6 a firm alliance was forged—Hua Kuo-feng, Marshal Yeh, the military men, Teng and his backers and, perhaps most important, Wang, the bodyguard, now a member of the Politburo, master of the forty thousand security troops, the household troops—the Praetorian Guard, as they would have been called in another incarnation.

Of these men Wang was the key. He was the boss of 8341. Within 8341, however, there were personal security detachments. Chiang Ching had hers, Chang Chun-chiao had his, Hua had his. Each personal detachment was presumed to have a loyalty to the object of its protection. Wang could give orders to 8341 but an individual detachment might elect to defend Chiang Ching regardless. The possibility of last-ditch resistance had to be taken into account.

Thus, it was felt, trickery must be used. First, Chang Chun-chiao and Wang Hung-wen were lured to what they thought was a meeting of the Standing Committee of the Politburo. When they arrived they were arrested by Unit 8341 men as, according to Roger Garside, Yeh Chien-ying and Hua Kuo-feng watched on closed-circuit television.

Then squads arrested Yao Wen-yuan at his home, with the connivance of his personal bodyguards. What happened in the case of Chiang Ching is not clear. She was at her home in the Western Hills. It was well guarded. There were concrete bunkers, machine-gun emplacements and an underground nuclear shelter. One version describes a vicious firefight between Chiang's guards and the arresting detachment, which included tanks. There were a number of casualties before the attackers stormed in and found Chiang crouched in the bunker. Another version contends that her personal guards were taken by surprise, that she was quietly reading in her boudoir and when she heard a slight commotion looked up to see the commander of Unit 8341, who told her she was under arrest. She shouted, "Guards! Guards!" But no one came. There was a serious fracas over the arrest of Mao Yuan-hsin, who was seized as he tried to get away to Manchuria by plane. Several guards were killed and Yuan-hsin was wounded.

That settled the key forces in the capital. But Shanghai remained, Shanghai and its militia of one million which was supposed to ensure the security of what quickly came to be called the Gang of Four.

In Shanghai trickery was also used. The top leaders in the city, firm adherents of Chiang Ching, were lured to Peking for "an important meeting." They were suspicious because they could not get in touch with their allies, but they had no alternative but to go. Those left in Shanghai became increasingly upset at the lack of information and rumors of something amiss.

The top leader left in Shanghai was a brilliant young lieutenant named Chu Yung-chia. Chu was a bold, intelligent, energetic man who once had talked for seven hours without cessation, giving a foreign guest a play-by-play report of what had happened during the "January storm" of 1967 in Shanghai. He would have been quite willing and able to talk another seven hours if the interpreters had not been dropping from exhaustion. This iron-nerved lieutenant of the Gang tried to steer a course that would give Shanghai an opportunity to come to the defense of its leaders. He mobilized a striking force of the armed militia. But it was no use. The Shanghai military commander had thrown in his lot with Hua and Yeh and the other military. By October 13 Shanghai had been neutralized and, for practical purposes, the political power of Chiang and her associates wiped out. All important members and allies of the group had been arrested or had joined the succession regime of Hua Kuo-feng. Teng Hsiao-ping was still in the shadows. But soon he would be back in Peking, preparing for the third time to take command of China's revolution. The era of Mao had ended. The Revolution, it seemed clear, would go ahead. But it would have a new form, a new content, and, of course, new leadership.

Teng would return and take power; the verdicts of Mao's last years would be reversed, as the Chinese say; Chiang Ching and her colleagues, the Gang of Four, would stand trial and be sentenced to death but the death sentence would be remitted and changed to life imprisonment in January 1983 ("We will keep them in jail and feed them," one Chinese said); Liu Shao-chi would be rehabilitated, a memorial hall erected in his memory, his books published again, his widow given high office; the victims of the Cultural Revolution and the Gang would be rehabilitated, their names and reputations made whole, but millions were dead (it was estimated that a hundred million had been "repressed" in the *luan*). But in a sense all of this was a new epoch, the founding years of China's postrevolutionary time. The hundred years that had begun in the mid-nineteenth century had run their course. *China had stood up*. Where she would go was the question that would determine not just the fate of a great people—but of the world.